THE
School-Smart
PARENT

THE
School-Smart
PARENT

GENE I. MAEROFF

For Janine, Adam, and Rachel

Copyright ©1989 by Gene I. Maeroff

All rights reserved under International and Pan-American Copyright Conventions. Published in the United States by Times Books, a division of Random House, Inc., New York, and simultaneously in Canada by Random House of Canada Limited, Toronto.

All acknowledgments for permission to reprint material are found on pages vii and viii.

Library of Congress Cataloging-in-Publication Data
Maeroff, Gene I.
The school-smart parent/Gene I. Maeroff.
Includes index.
ISBN 0-8129-1631-X
1. Home and school—United States.
2. Education—United States—Parent participation.
3. Academic achievement.
I. Title.
LC225.3.M34   1989
370.19′312′0973—dc19   88-29506

Manufactured in the United States of America
9 8 7 6 5 4 3 2
First Edition
Book design by The Sarabande Press

ACKNOWLEDGMENTS

Grateful acknowledgment is made to the following for permission to reprint previously published material:

American Library Association: Excerpt from *Notable Children's Books 1987*. Reprinted with permission of the American Library Association.

Association of American Geographers: Excerpt from *Guidelines for Geographic Education: Elementary and Secondary Schools*.

Susan Becker: Excerpt from "Helping Parents Choose Wisely," from *Instructor*, 1986.

CTB/McGraw-Hill: Excerpt from *California Achievement Tests, Forms E and F, Class Management Guide*. Copyright © 1986 by McGraw-Hill. Reprinted with permission of CTB/McGraw-Hill.

Reo Christenson: "List of Values and Attitudes."

The College Board: Excerpt from *Degrees of Reading Power—Test Booklet Form PX-1*.

Edgell Communications: Excerpt from "What Is Hands-On Science?" from *Instructor*. Reprinted with permission of Edgell Communications.

Evanston Educators: Excerpt from *Family Software Catalogue*.

The Executive Educator: Excerpt from "The Essentials for Reading Programs" by Nicholas P. Criscuolo. Reprinted with permission of *The Executive Educator*, March. Copyright © 1986. All rights reserved.

International Business Machines Corporation: Excerpt from *Child Care Handbook*. Copyright © 1984 by International Business Machines Corporation. Reprinted with permission of International Business Machines Corporation.

Missouri Department of Elementary and Secondary Education: Excerpt from *How Does Your Child Grow and Learn? A Guide for Parents of Young Children*, revised edition, 1982.

ACKNOWLEDGMENTS

H. L. Mountzoures: "At the Tutor's" from *The New Yorker*, June 16, 1986. Reprinted by permission of the author.

National Association for the Education of Young Children: Excerpts from *Toys: Tools for Learning* and "Helping Children Learn About Reading" by Judith A. Schickedanz.

National Association of Secondary School Principals: Excerpt from "Teaching Thinking" from *Curriculum Report*, 1986.

National Committee for Citizens in Education: Excerpt from "Your School: How Well Is It Working?" 1982.

National Council of Teachers of Mathematics: Excerpt from *Curriculum and Evaluation Standards for School Mathematics, Working Draft*.

Nebraska Department of Education: Excerpt from *The Position Paper on Kindergarten*.

Mike Olenick: Excerpt from "What Is Quality Child Care?," a speech to Los Angeles County League of Women Voters, June 7, 1986.

Phi Delta Kappan: Excerpts from "Computers in Education Today —And Some Possible Futures" by Alfred Bork; "Evaluating Educational Software . . ." by Gail Caissy; "Junior First Grade" by M. R. Solem.

Reading Is Fundamental, Inc.: Excerpt from "When We Were Young." Copyright © 1987 by Reading Is Fundamental, Inc. Used by permission.

Allan Shedlin, Jr.: Excerpt from "New Lenses for Viewing Elementary Schools."

Totowa (N.J.) Board of Education: Adapted excerpt from *New Jersey Test of Reasoning Skill*.

World Book, Inc.: Excerpt adapted from *Getting Ready for School*. Copyright © 1987 by World Book, Inc.

PREFACE

Until the late 1970s it was assumed in America that children would always exceed the accomplishments of their
parents. Upward mobility was an article of faith held
with every bit as much assurance as the belief that the
sun would rise each morning. And, for the most part,
children did exceed their parents. Then something happened. People began to realize they were dancing to a
tune that had stopped playing.

Inflation struck, and homes that had always cost about
the same relatively low price skyrocketed in value.
Cokes and candy bars that had sold for a nickel started
pushing toward the dollar mark. The prices of items that
had been cheap and abundant—gasoline and heating
oil, for example—zoomed as scarcities developed. Jobs
that had always awaited college graduates became subject to intense competition. Teenagers in affluent sub-
urbs realized they might not be able to afford to live as

adults in the communities in which they were growing up.

Pressures were intensified by a climate in which American workers found their companies dying in the face of foreign competition. An industrial stalwart like General Motors saw its share of the automobile market forced to a low point in the mid-1980s. Three of the four companies that made Akron, Ohio, the tire capital of the world virtually gave up the business. An entire new industry based on the videocassette recorder came into full bloom, with all 12 million sets that were sold each year in the United States manufactured abroad.

More than ever, the need has been underscored for a sound education that equips one to cope with a changing world. Success depends on a lot more than doing well in elementary school, but surely elementary school is the foundation for all that follows in formal education. Students who do poorly in elementary school enter secondary school at risk and there is a good chance that they will take that disadvantage with them when they reach college—if they get that far.

The school-reform movement that swept through America's classrooms during the 1980s blew away some cobwebs and improved some practices. Elementary education, though, remained essentially unchanged during the 1980s; there are still few provisions to ensure that the system provides a safety net for children whose parents don't look out for them.

This is not to say that teachers and principals and school board members and lawmakers are uncaring. They often do what they can to protect the interests of schoolchildren. But with 45 million kids in school there is just so much that even the most responsive and humane system can do for each child.

Thus, parents who step into the breach and try to learn enough about elementary education to become helpers and advocates for their children can make a marvelous contribution. This book is useful for any parent serious about taking this step, whether the child attends public or private school. It is no less valuable for someone who simply wants to be better informed about the workings of elementary schools.

After about a quarter of a century as a specialist writing about education throughout the country, I have found that this book has allowed me to tap into a wealth of observations. I am indebted to the many experts whom I have interviewed over the years and, in particular, to those who have made time available specifically to discuss aspects of the topics covered in this book. I offer my appreciation in this regard to Richard Anderson, John Chaffee, Jeanne Chall, Bob Davies, Roger Farr, Shirley Brice Heath, Barbara Nuding, Catherine Snow, Bill Ward, Mel Wasserman, and Burton White.

My research for this book included visits and interviews in school districts around the country, from New York City to Seattle, from Palo Alto to Brookline. I am grateful to the teachers, principals, and central administrators in those districts for sharing their ideas and curriculum materials with me. I also appreciate the cooperation of numerous textbook and test publishers. Special gratitude is owed to the National Assessment of Educational Progress (NAEP) and the two agencies that have operated it, first the Education Commission of the States and then the Educational Testing Service. The NAEP reports have been invaluable to my work on this book.

In addition, I want to thank Ernest Boyer, president of the Carnegie Foundation for the Advancement of

PREFACE

Teaching in Princeton, New Jersey, for his colleague-
ship and for the supportive atmosphere in which I am
able to pursue works of educational interest.

Finally, I am grateful for the encouragement I have
received in all ways from my wife, Sarah, who has been
there for me always, even when I thought I lost some
manuscript pages and she found them.

CONTENTS

CONTENTS

THE
School-Smart
PARENT

1

WHY YOU MUST
BE AN ADVOCATE IN
YOUR CHILD'S SCHOOLING

Parents can no longer take for granted anything about the future of their children, including the quality and outcome of their
schooling. There are, to be sure, still advantages conferred upon offspring by benefit of
the education, wealth, and social class of their parents,
but even those who are college graduates cannot make
assumptions about what is in store for their children.
How much can be passed along to children is no longer
as certain.

"For millions of breadwinners, the American dream is
becoming the impossible dream," commented Steven
Greenhouse in *The New York Times*. "The prospect of
owning the proverbial split-level with a two-car garage
is receding. The cheerful expectation of being better off
than one's parents has died among many baby boomers.
Even the most basic tenet of the dream—that a young
family will be more prosperous in its middle age—has
grown more elusive."

What every family needs today is a plan for the success of its children. Like generals preparing for battle, parents must weigh the consequences of their actions and map out strategies. They must bear in mind that the struggle starts early. There is more than humor involved when a parent dresses a toddler in a sweatshirt that reads: HARVARD, CLASS OF 2008. That parent is wishing as much as joking. In a city like New York, parents start vying to find places for their children in the most desirable nursery schools by the age of two. Interviews and even tests—yes, tests—are the order of the day. The toddlers with the highest IQs have the best chance of being accepted.

By the time the children are completing nursery school, they are engaged in a fierce competition for the most prestigious private schools. Again, the race is to the brightest. The right school more often than not leads to the right college. The statistics from the colleges tell the rest of the educational story. At the most selective of them, Harvard, only 16 percent of the applicants for the freshman class are accepted. The chances of getting into other top Ivy League schools are not much better, with only 17 percent accepted at Princeton, 18 percent at Yale, 19 percent at Brown, and 20 percent at Dartmouth. Students with scores as high as 1,200 on the Scholastic Aptitude Test, which has a maximum score of 1,600, often find themselves denied admission to top colleges.

To make matters worse, young people who on the surface appear to be educated properly are often shaky in their academic achievement. Most students who participated in a test administered nationally by the federal government in 1986 had difficulty organizing their thoughts and presenting them coherently in response to more difficult assignments.

The same federal school-monitoring program, the National Assessment of Educational Progress, released a separate report in 1986 showing that while 95 percent of adults twenty-one to twenty-five—the most recent products of the high schools—could read and understand the printed word, only a very small percentage could understand complex material. Yet another study by the National Assessment, this one on knowledge of mathematics, showed that while declines had leveled off by 1983 and students were improving in simple one-step skills, many had great difficulty in solving problems that went beyond the routine.

And so it is clear that the more parents can do to help their children reach full potential in school, the more likely the children are to find fulfillment in the competitive era ahead.

This is a book meant to help parents achieve that goal; it is a blueprint for success. Parents must start early to groom their children for school. By the time a child is three years old, a substantial portion of his or her intelligence has already developed. And by the age of six, according to some experts, the child's whole future is determined.

Books, books, books. Everything possible must be done to surround a child with the printed word and to make books a part of the natural environment. Parents can never read too much to their children. Kindergarten teacher after kindergarten teacher says she can tell which children have had the benefit of being read to extensively. Often, but not necessarily, they are the ones who learn to read the soonest.

The home is the first and foremost classroom. Parents are the primary teachers, whether or not they want to be. The responsibility is awesome. And teachers are not satisfied with the job that parents are doing on behalf of their children. Six out of ten teachers give unfavorable marks to parents, according to a poll done for Metropolitan Life by Louis Harris. This does not mean, however, that the task of getting children ready for school and helping them once they are enrolled is so formidable that it is impossible. It just takes care and thought.

While children are still barely toddling, it is possible to begin planting within them the right attitudes about school and learning. This is the time when language takes root. A normal child is going to learn to talk without being directly taught. Like walking, talking is something that comes in the natural course of development. But there is learning language and there is learning language. The building blocks of vocabulary are stacked in place during this stage. Parents can help determine how high the stack will rise. Inquisitiveness can be stimulated or turned off at this point, and the children who are encouraged to probe and think will sprout intellectual wings and soar to the heights.

The pattern grows clearer and clearer as school approaches. By the time a child is three, a parent has the choice of whether or not to send the child to a school-like preschool setting. No family has to apologize for keeping a child home if the environment there is rich and nourishing and a loving family member or an equally acceptable substitute is available to provide full-time attention. More and more, though, parents are not at home during the day and the challenge is to identify the best substitute for the home.

What is more important than finding a place to send a preschool child is finding the right place. These years in a child's life are much too precious to be squandered, and parents must carefully weigh the options.

Parents must know how to evaluate nursery schools and child care facilities. They must know what to expect from the increasing number of preschools being run by public school systems. Four-year-olds are not smaller versions of kindergarteners, and they should have a separate, distinct curriculum that meets their special needs. Don't forget: a kindergartener's extra year of age represents 25 percent of the lifetime of a four-year-old. What is appropriate in kindergarten is not necessarily proper for a four-year-old.

Kindergarten can be a wonderful place where the tone of schooling is set for children. Parents cannot be too careful about what happens to children at this point in their education. They must be alert for the signs of adequate progress that will lead to a happy and successful career in elementary school. Readiness for learning is supposed to be cultivated at this age, and parents who are knowledgeable about what to expect can use the home to augment and complement what happens in kindergarten.

Some children will learn to read by the end of kindergarten; most will not. Parents need perspective and context, which this book provides, so that they can be assured that their children are developing at a reasonable pace. It is also important to bear in mind that there is more than a child's intellectual development at stake in kindergarten. Children must also gain the social and emotional maturity that will enable them to cope with gradually increasing amounts of independence and, at the same time, learn to work with classmates in constructive ways.

The centerpiece of instruction in the first grade is reading. Nothing that happens in all of school is more important than learning to read, and parents who are not satisfied with the way their children are being taught to read should assert themselves. Reading is the basis for studying all other subjects, and children who do not gain a sure footing in reading are likely to slip and slide as they struggle for a toehold through the rest of their education.

Similarly, the introduction to mathematics represents the foundation for much of schooling, and because it is sequential, children who are allowed to move along without gaining a firm understanding of previous lessons are soon at risk in mathematics.

In general, the first three years of school are the ones that count most. It is the period when parents should most closely monitor the education of their children. What makes it so difficult for conscientious parents at this point is the unevenness of child development. Children who are trailing in the first or second grade are not necessarily less smart and may not be the victims of bad teaching; they simply may not be as ready to handle the work usually presented at this age. It is not easy for a parent to be patient when this happens, and if the gap isn't closing by the time a child is eight years old, there is reason for concern, though it does not necessarily mean there is anything wrong with the child.

Children will get a taste of social studies and science during their first two or three years in school, but the focus will be on reading and mathematics. The student ought to attain enough reading competence during the first three grades in school to take on books by the fourth grade that truly delve into subject mattter. What distinguishes reading in the upper elementary grades is that it becomes a tool for exploring the subjects and is no longer simply a subject in its own right.

It is in the upper elementary grades that parents must

be especially vigilant to be sure that their children are gaining the higher-order thinking skills that are the basis for the advanced learning to follow. William Bennett, the U.S. Secretary of Education in the Reagan administration, said, "Something seems to happen between the first few grades of elementary school and its conclusion. In general, as our elementary students get older, their performance begins to decline."

The teacher is a parent's most valuable resource in assessing the progress of a child in the classroom. A wise parent gets to know his or her child's teacher and establishes a dialogue with the teacher that lasts the entire school year. The teacher is the expert and a parent should be prepared to defer to the teacher on many judgments. But the parent can learn to ask the right questions so that the interaction between teacher and parent can be most productive. And a parent who is not satisfied with a teacher's response should be prepared to take the question up with the principal.

Life is more complicated for the parents of a child who is handicapped or gifted. One pauses in mentioning these two kinds of children in the same sentence, but their plight is similar in that each needs special attention to reach full potential. The schools find it easier to meet the needs of the handicapped than they do those of the gifted, so schools end up serving the handicapped better than they do the gifted. Also, families with handicapped children have a weapon more potent than that possessed by parents of other youngsters: a law enacted by Congress that prescribes a whole series of procedures to which the handicapped are entitled in the public schools. The children of parents who become familiar with the regulations enjoy an educational advantage unavailable to others.

No such federal requirements undergird the gifted; they must depend largely on the largesse of the school system. This is one very good reason why parents of the gifted who expect to send their children to public school should thoroughly explore a district's commitment to the gifted before moving there.

Whether or not a student—any student—is making adequate progress is more difficult to judge in the upper elementary grades than in the lower ones. Achievement is more subtle, since it is no longer the raw basics that are at stake. Children begin delving into more intricate mathematics; the rudiments of language arts yield more extensively to the demands for critical thinking and inferential reasoning. Parents are probably more dependent on the judgment of the teacher at this stage than at any other time in the education cycle. Surely, when students move into secondary schools and each subject is more clearly defined it will be easier to gauge whether a youngster's progress is adequate.

This book does not limit its purview to the lessons of the classroom, because much of what occurs outside the school determines success in school. There are chapters on homework, computers, and television. Yes, television, which commands more of a child's time than any teacher. In fact, television is one of the prime teachers of the young. Parents who fail to take into account its impact may find that the lessons learned at the foot of the tube have far more influence than those taught by the teacher. Few parents are going to be able to banish television altogether from the lives of their children— nor is it wise to try to do so—but there are ways to harness the force of television so that its influence may be more benign and, believe it or not, perhaps even somewhat beneficial.

Chapters describing the duties of the staff of a typical elementary school and the policies of the school are meant to help parents better understand the people in whose trust their children will be spending much of the day. Also, this information can provide insights into how to convert school professionals into advocates for your child. Human nature is such that parents who are savvy can in fact often get more out of the school for their children than less sophisticated or less concerned parents. This is probably not as it should be, but it is the reality and parents ought to work with it.

However, parents should not limit themselves to the school when it comes to finding professionals who can help their children. Tutoring out of school sometimes makes a great deal of sense and, for parents using public schools, the cost is a pittance compared with the expense of sending children to nonpublic schools. So valuable is tutoring that even parents who use private and parochial schools sometimes resort to it because of the advantages it can afford their children.

The boost provided by out-of-school activities goes beyond tutoring and involves the sorts of activities in which children participate in the afternoons, on weekends, and during the summers. A chapter discusses the choices parents can make that will allow their children to find intellectual enrichment along with fun during out-of-school hours. Children certainly do not have to spend all their waking hours in pursuits that advance their academic aspirations. But at a time when there are science institutes on Saturdays, after-school lessons in oil painting, and summer camps devoted to computers, there are some significant educational decisions for parents to make beyond choosing the schools that their children attend during the regular school day.

The inclusion of a chapter on values may be somewhat surprising. So often parents say they expect the schools to be value-neutral. But such a stance is amost impossible for a school or a teacher to take. Schools teach values whether or not parents approve and whether or not it is the intent of the teacher. So it is better to understand just what is occurring in this realm and to try to make it work in your child's interest than to pretend values are not an issue. Many parents who select nonpublic schools are consciously or unconsciously influenced by the values that they perceive as being attached to those schools. It is time that public school parents, too, see the schools in terms of the values they represent—or do not represent.

Finally, and in this case not surprisingly, the book concludes with a chapter that looks toward junior high school and beyond. Elementary school, after all, is merely the rehearsal stage for the rest of formal education. Parents who are knowledgeable about what is to follow can do more to help the long-range education of their children during the elementary years.

In many ways it was much easier to grow up a generation ago than it is now. There were fewer pitfalls into which children could stumble and the world was in some ways a gentler, simpler, less harsh place. But the changes cannot be rubbed away no matter who wields the eraser. The challenge is to live with the new circumstances in ways that mitigate the dangers and gain maximum advantage. This book will teach you how to do that in the education of your children.

2

CHOOSING A SCHOOL

Selecting a school for a child is one of the most important decisions a family will ever make. Since 90 percent of the nation's elementary and secondary school students attend public schools, the decision is usually closely linked to the choice of a place to live. There is of course more leeway for families that use private and parochial schools, since enrollment is contingent on paying the tuition and not on residency in a particular school district. In either case, there are factors to weigh.

For those who buy houses with the idea of using the local public schools, the location of the home will usually determine where the children must attend school and a bad choice is not easily rectified. Making a change could well mean selling a house and buying another if the goal is to relocate the child in a better public school system or even within a different attendance zone in the same school district.

The quality of the public schools is an important consideration to all homeowners—whether or not they have children in public schools—because real estate values are almost always affected by the perception of school quality. A home in a less desirable district is less costly than the same home elsewhere, but it is also likely to be more difficult to sell. Montgomery County, the affluent suburb of Washington, D.C., took advantage of a technicality in the law for the first time in 1986 when it turned down construction proposals by several builders of housing subdivisions. County officials argued that allowing further residential construction in the affected neighborhoods was undesirable because of the potential for adding too many extra pupils to the public school system. Those who already owned homes in the affected neighborhoods applauded the decision.

Thus, for those planning to use the public schools it is important to assess both the entire school system and, if possible, the particular schools that their children will attend. "If possible," because the neighborhood school is no longer always the school to which a child will be assigned. School closings, periodic redrawing of attendance zones, and—in some places—desegregation plans have made it less certain that moving into a particular house or apartment means that a child will attend a certain school. Furthermore, some districts now give parents an opportunity to choose from among several schools—sometimes called "magnet" schools—rather than directing them to use a certain school, as was once almost always the case.

The way a family should go about evaluating the schools is rather similar whether it is considering a public school or a nonpublic school. As far as public schools are concerned, the assessment should begin with the school district itself, regardless of which school within the district a child will attend. Here are some of the topics you should examine:

• *Expenditures.* Figures are available in every school district to show how much is being spent, on average, per child. This amount is determined by totaling the expenditures and dividing the sum by the enrollment of the district. Per pupil expenditures, as they are called, tend to differ widely among districts, and parents should be wary of a school system that spends considerably less per pupil than most neighboring districts. There is not anything particularly wrong per se with thriftiness in education, but it could come at the expense of your child's education. Comparisons among states are not as meaningful as comparison of districts within the same state, given the differences in the cost of living from state to state, but they do provide a baseline. Here are the statewide average per pupil expenditures, based on average daily attendance, against which to judge the district you are considering:

Alabama, $2,610	Illinois, $3,980
Alaska, $8,842	Indiana, $3,310
Arizona, $2,784	Iowa, $3,740
Arkansas, $2,772	Kansas, $4,150
California, $3,887	Kentucky, $3,107
Colorado, $4,107	Louisiana, $3,008
Connecticut, $5,552	Maine, $3,650
Delaware, $4,776	Maryland, $4,660
District of Columbia, $5,349	Massachusetts, $4,856
Florida, $4,056	Michigan, $3,967
Georgia, $3,167	Minnesota, $4,239
Hawaii, $4,372	Mississippi, $2,534,
Idaho, $2,555	Missouri, $3,345

Montana, $4,070

Nebraska, $3,437

Nevada, $3,548

New Hampshire, $3,682

New Jersey, $6,177

New Mexico, $3,537

New York, $6,224

North Carolina, $3,473

North Dakota, $3,174

Ohio, $3,764

Oklahoma, $3,082

Oregon, $4,383

Pennsylvania, $4,691

Rhode Island, $4,574

South Carolina, $3,096

South Dakota, $3,190

Tennessee, $2,842

Texas, $3,551

Utah, $2,455

Vermont, $4,459

Virginia, $3,809

Washington, $3,808

West Virginia, $3,619

Wisconsin, $4,607

Wyoming, $6,253

• *Taxes.* The key statistic here is assessed valuation per child, which is figured by adding up all of the assessed property wealth in the school district and dividing by the enrollment. The higher this figure is, the better. A higher figure means that the district can use lower taxes to produce the same amount of revenues that would take higher taxes in a district with less property wealth. The related statistic to watch is the amount of actual tax per $1,000 of assessed valuation. If it is unduly high compared with neighboring districts, it could put a strain on homeowners.

• *High school outcomes.* The ultimate measure of a school district is what becomes of its high school students. If the dropout figure is high, it is not a desirable school system. There are big city school districts, for example, in which as many as 40 to 50 percent of the students do not complete high school; in contrast, there are suburban school systems in which fewer than 2 percent of the students are not graduated. Sometimes the dropout percentage is reported for a single year and other times it represents four years. If the figure is for a single year, multiply it by four to see what happens to a class of ninth-graders from the time they enter high school until the end of the senior year.

What percentage of the seniors enroll in such courses as physics and calculus? How many courses are offered in connection with the College Board's Advanced Placement program? Are the courses for C-level students challenging and interesting or are they watered-down? How many semifinalists did the school district have in National Merit Scholarship competition? What percentage of the high school graduates in June went on to four-year colleges and universities? Almost every high school has a list of the colleges its most recent senior class is attending; the list can be obtained from the school's guidance department.

• *Facilities.* The school building itself should be considered. Is it adequate for the demands placed on it? Sometimes a fine structure can be made inadequate by squeezing in more children than the building was intended to accommodate. Is there a real library in the elementary school where the children can get introduced to the research techniques and procedures that will be so valuable to them in secondary school? Is there a gymnasium? What are the science facilities like? And most of all, is the school properly maintained, inside and out? If a building, regardless of its age, is not kept clean and in good repair, this may say a good deal in a quiet way about how the children are regarded and about the system's commitment to excellence.

• *School climate.* A good school is orderly. There cannot be teaching and learning where there are discipline problems. This does not mean that children are never heard or that they sit like statues. Children are sometimes going to be louder than adults. The difficulty is when they disrupt classes or turn the building into a zoo. That is not a setting in which any parent should want a child, and certainly it is a place where the principal is not doing his or her job.

The best way to assess the climate of a school is to spend some time there. Walk the halls and sit in the classrooms. Talk to the teachers, the administrators, and the students. Yes, the students. Be insistent about your right to visit and observe. What you see and hear might be more revealing than any other information available. The principal may say that visitors are disruptive and that it would not be possible for the parents of every prospective student to go into the classrooms and observe. Remind the principal that you are just one parent and only you are asking for permission to visit classes.

• *Class size.* The smaller the classes the better. While it is true that research is inconclusive on the effect of class size on learning, common sense dictates that smaller classes, in general, are desirable. This is especially true in kindergarten, first, second, and third grades. A school that has more than thirty children in a class at this level is a school to be avoided. What is ideal? Realistically, it is best to see no more than twenty to twenty-five children in a class below fourth grade, and it is even better if there are fewer than twenty students. From the fourth through the sixth grade, class size may rise to the high twenties, but again, the smaller the better. The more children a teacher has, the less individual attention each one will get.

• *Student/teacher interaction.* Closely watch the teaching style of the teacher. Is the teacher patient? Is the teacher supportive of children and are compliments readily made? Don't let your child be in the class of a teacher who ridicules children, and be wary of a teacher who does not use praise, where appropriate, to reinforce children. Teachers should not spend too much time lecturing to children. Questioning is an art in the hands of a good teacher. Children are encouraged to think and to dig deeper into their minds. You may get bored at a lecture that lasts an hour; a child sits in a classroom for about six hours, and if what the teacher does mostly is lecture imagine how bored the child will be.

There should be group activities, individual activities, and other ways of learning that are not centered around the teacher. Also, there should be activities initiated by the students and in which the students do much of the talking, sometimes conferring with each other. Some teachers are traditional and some are loose and relaxed, letting the children roam the room. What counts is that the children are happy and excited by learning. Many students unfortunately are jaded by the time they reach high school, but this certainly should not be true in elementary school. Something is wrong if children in the lower grades are not full of enthusiasm about school.

• *Expectations.* Children are not of equal ability and some enjoy greater success than others, but a teacher should still maintain high expectations for each child. Studies have demonstrated that teachers who expect less than the best from a child often get sub-par performances from that youngster. Thus, the teacher for your child should be the one who believes in the ability of all children to reach goals and fulfill their potential.

A parent considering a school should try to learn about the curriculum. Reading and language development should form the core of the program in elementary school. This means that writing, speaking, and listening are taught in alliance with reading, each complementing the others. Math should be the next most important subject in the curriculum after reading.

Science and social studies are offered in the lower elementary grades, but usually more sparingly because children are not yet proficient enough to use reading to delve into such topics. More likely these subjects are taught in a hands-on approach. There are, for example, science demonstrations and visits to the fire station and other places allowing for learning experiences not based on reading. Books with science and social studies content are used increasingly in the upper elementary grades.

An important gauge of an elementary school is the amount of individual attention that children get from the teacher. Of course, class size has something to do with this, but the teacher's own style is another factor. The kind of teacher to seek is one who finds the time to roam the classroom, working with individual children. This sort of teacher also invites discussion with the class and is responsive to questions.

The great danger if a teacher is not in touch with individual needs is that the lesson will move along without each child understanding what has been taught. The deficits that develop are cumulative. Teachers should monitor the progress of their students to know whether they are keeping up. In elementary school, lots of individual contact is the main way in which good teachers keep track of their students.

Some schools substitute elaborate testing programs for individual attention. Testing serves a purpose in schools and it can provide information on each child's progress, but it has serious limitations. Be wary of overtesting. Supposedly, testing is used to check on progress, but personal attention is more valuable to the child. Tests may help monitor the progress of students, and students who do not have experience in taking tests will be at a disadvantage, but testing must be kept in perspective and not come to dominate the program.

The best curriculum in education can fail in the hands of an inept teacher. One of the difficulties is that poor teachers may go on and on in their jobs, spending an entire career in a school and spoiling the education of countless children. A nonpublic school can more easily rid itself of such a person because the school does not face the same legal constraints in hiring and firing.

Look for some continuity in the teaching staff. There should be a mix of younger teachers and experienced ones; they can gain from each other. It could be a sign of trouble at a school if too many of the teachers leave each year. So inquire not only into the number of years that teachers have been teaching, but also how long they have been working at the particular school.

Furthermore, it is not sufficient that there are good teachers in a school. What counts most is that your child is taught by one of them, particularly in the lower elementary grades, where a weak teacher can leave a pupil with deficits that may take years to ameliorate, not to mention the possibility that the teacher might turn off the child to school.

As was already mentioned, watching a teacher in action tells a lot. There is just so much camouflage that the teacher can present to an observer. The very appearance of a classroom, especially in the lower grades, gives clues as to what is likely to happen in that room when no parent is watching. A good classroom in elementary school tends to be one in which the children's work is prominently displayed, fortifying their tender egos. The walls and bulletin boards are covered with learning aids. Lots of books and helpful teaching materials— many of which the youngsters are free to use on their own—are readily available on tables and shelves and tucked into crannies.

And there is the principal, the person who should take ultimate responsibility for the school. A school without a capable principal is like a ship without a helmsman. More than one school has lost direction and drifted aimlessly when there was not proper leadership.

One thing to watch during a visit to an elementary school is whether the principal is in evidence in the halls. An elementary school principal who mostly sits in an office may be an ineffective principal. Children and teachers should see the principal roaming the building, conversing with them, popping in and out of classrooms, and just generally "showing the flag." Many of the best principals are at the front door to greet arriving students in the morning and again in the afternoon to bid them farewell. This is more than show; it helps bring order to what could be a troubled procedure and adds to the sense of community. To watch a good elementary school principal at work is to observe a person in perpetual motion. When in the office, a good principal tries to make time for children or teachers who arrive with questions or comments.

A principal ought to be familiar with how the teachers are doing and should get into their classrooms frequently to sit and observe. Also, the relationship that the teachers have with the principal is telling. Ask the teachers for candid evaluations of the principal. Find out whether the principal is open to their overtures. It isn't as important that they like the principal as that they respect him or her. Try to get a sense of the morale of the teachers, because a school where morale is bad is not the best place for a child to be.

Good principals come in all ages and both genders. Their common denominator is leadership. They inspire children and adults and help them feel good about themselves. A school usually benefits from having the same principal for at least three to five years. It takes time to get a climate established and to get a program operating efficiently. Schools where principals change as frequently as the seasons suffer from lack of continuity.

Principals report to administrators in the central headquarters of the school system, and it probably would not be easy for a parent of a prospective student to get an appointment with the superintendent or one of the superintendent's top aides. Nor is such a visit likely to be of use, since these officials are far removed from the day-to-day activities in the classroom.

Instead of trying to visit with central administrators, parents can get another perspective on the school district by attending a meeting of the board of education. In even a small suburban district the chances are that the school board meets at least once a month. The law generally requires that these meetings be open to the public. Above all, what an observer might glean is whether or not there is acrimony in the school district—between the superintendent and the board or among the board members. If there is conflict on a board of education that need not mean a school system should be avoided, but it is useful to know about the problems because sometimes the trouble affects individual schools.

Not only staff, but parents as well are an important resource for anyone trying to learn about the operations of a school. The names and phone numbers of the parents who are officers in the PTA should be made available for the asking, and it is wise to contact several of them. If there is no parents' organization, that in itself should raise questions about the principal's openness and about whether parents can have input.

Ask other parents about the school. Find out what they like most and least about the school. What opinions do they have of the teachers and the principal? How much influence do the parents have through their organization and as individuals? Parents should regard themselves as advocates for their children and evaluate the school in terms of how easy or how difficult it will be to look out for their children's learning and developmental needs at the school.

Other parents who have children in the school can tell you, for instance, how difficult it is to get a child transferred to another class if you are not satisfied with the teacher. You may never have to press this button, but if it is not available when you need it your child may suffer through an entire school year.

Schools have policies that run the gamut in this regard, ranging from the handful that let parents pick the teachers for their children to those that allow no transfers whatsoever. The general practice is for the school to assign the child to a teacher and to permit transfers on an informal basis for parents who protest loudly enough. Schools do not like to let it be widely known that parents can get class assignments changed. One problem with a very small elementary school is that there is only one class at each grade level and nowhere to transfer a child except to a different school in the district. Such a transfer is more difficult to obtain than getting a teacher change within a school.

Thus, choosing a school, if done conscientiously, is a lengthy process to which parents must be prepared to devote many hours over several days. Where there are two parents, each can take a portion of the task and they can combine their findings to paint a composite portrait. The alternative is to rely on skimpy impressions and gossip, which may be adequate, but is less than ideal. All too many adults, it seems, end up spending more time going to automobile showrooms and reading brochures before buying a new car than they do visiting schools and studying reports before selecting a school. A child's education is certainly worth at least as much time as a new car. And, unlike purchases of automobiles, there is little leeway for trade-ins if a bad choice has been made.

3

GETTING READY FOR PRESCHOOL

The early years, the twos and threes and even sooner, ought to be viewed as a dress rehearsal for school. A child is like an actor getting ready to try out for a part. This is the time to learn and practice the lines. The parent is a combination drama coach, director, and producer, having overall responsibility for the ultimate performance. The aim is to help the child win an Oscar. This does not mean parents should be heavy-handed or single-minded. Children should not be pressured and certainly nothing should be done to squeeze the joy out of childhood. The way to strike the proper balance is to ensure that the experiences that occur in the normal course of growing up will help prepare a child for school. This should be done informally, though.

Delivering lectures or forcing memorization upon children is as ill-advised as ignoring them. The formal instruction that characterizes a schoolroom has no place at a very early age, according to most experts. But—and this is the key—a good parent should not hesitate to be nature's assistant, providing settings that support the kind of intellectual, social, and emotional growth that will ensure success once a child reaches school.

The importance of using this period wisely cannot be overemphasized. An enormous amount of mental development occurs during the first three crucial years. "My own studies, as well as the work of many others, have clearly indicated that the experiences of those first years are far more important than we had previously thought," Burton L. White concluded in his book *The First Three Years of Life.* "In their simple everyday activities, infants and toddlers form the foundations of all later development."

Does this mean that a child who shows less development than others during the preschool years is doomed to failure, destined never to close the gap? Not necessarily, but such a child can be placed at risk in terms of the expectations of most schools. It is within the power of parents to take steps that will reduce the possibility of this happening to their children. Acquisition of the kind of knowledge that IQ tests define as intelligence can be affected by parents. After all, the child who has been more widely exposed and more extensively stimulated mentally is apt to score higher on an intelligence test.

In a sense, a parent can "manipulate" the environment to raise the IQ of a child. IQ scores of children, as well as their scores on standardized achievement tests, tend to parallel the social, economic, and educational backgrounds of parents. Children from the families of greatest advantage usually attain the highest scores. This is because such families are most likely to provide their children with experiences that enable them to do well on tests. However, less advantaged families can devise strategies to aid their children in similar ways. They can try, in effect, to mimic the behavior of more affluent families with an eye toward promoting the scholastic success of their children.

"Parents with relatively low levels of education or occupational status can provide very stimulating home environments for educational achievement," said Benjamin Bloom, education professor at the University of Chicago. Bloom drew on the findings of two doctoral students to illustrate how parents influence their children during the earliest years in ways that later lead to higher achievement when the youngsters reach the schoolroom. This is what such parents do:

- Hold high aspirations and reward achievement.

- Use good language and expect their children to do the same.

- Provide academic guidance.

- Initiate the kind of activities at home that stimulate a child in settings outside the home.

- Develop routines for their children to follow so that the children can be organized in their approach to everyday life.

In other words, chances are that a child's work in school will be better—even while he or she is very young and not yet in school—if the parents already have lofty goals for the child. Most people have a way of fulfilling the role that others prescribe for them, for good or for worse. Parents, of course, do most of their teaching by example even though they sometimes would like to believe otherwise. Thus, parents whose grammar is faulty and whose language lacks richness should not be surprised if their children speak in the same way.

Parents are the first teachers and the home is the first school. When preschool children are encouraged to play games with numbers and words and to solve problems, they will be more likely to be receptive to the learning tasks that await them in school. Youngsters who already have a sense of order in their lives and follow routines will probably adjust more easily to the routines they must follow to be successful in school.

Chances are that the same children who are better prepared for school are going to score higher on IQ tests and other kinds of standardized tests than children who are less ready. The argument over nature versus nurture —that is, whether IQ is shaped more by heredity or environment—rages without resolution, and it is not the aim of this book to resolve that controversy. More important, there is ample evidence, regardless of how much genetics has to do with intelligence, that parents have an opportunity to raise a child's IQ.

Some authorities contend that parents should pay no attention to IQ and that they surely should not dignify it by trying to increase their children's IQ scores. These critics are against IQ testing and are especially appalled by the use of IQ tests to sort out children at very young ages. In response to this sort of concern, the New York City public schools and some other districts have banned IQ tests.

There is no question that some teachers have, upon learning the IQ scores of their students, stereotyped them and set low expectations for those with low scores. As it is, there is a serious question as to whether Alfred Binet, the French psychologist who is the father of IQ testing, ever intended it to be used in the way that it is.

"Binet was commissioned by the French Ministry of Instruction to develop a test to identify children in need of remedial instruction," observed James Fallows. "Binet never viewed 'normal' children as appropriate subjects for his test, which, like the white-blood-cell count, was designed to indicate the presence of disease, not to rank degrees of health."

Unfortunately, the use of IQ testing of small children persists, and some elite nursery schools around the country insist on testing applicants. This makes parents anxious, and often they transmit their lack of ease to their children, the classic case being that of the tot whose parents have filled him with so much dread that he refuses to speak to the interviewer.

Not speaking to an interviewer who is trying to administer an IQ test at a nursery school can be fatal to the child's hopes of gaining entrance. An IQ test for a three-year-old, after all, is administered verbally. The goal is not to find out how many facts the child knows. There are no questions, for example, calling for the name of the president of the United States or for identifying the planets by their positions from the sun. What the interviewer will want to do is gauge the youngster's exposure to the world and to see how much common sense the child has. These are the areas covered on an intelligence test for a preschool child:

- Vocabulary

- Coordination

- Memory

- Common sense

Vocabulary may be tested by showing the child pictures of common objects that should be familiar and asking him or her to identify them—a coat, a chair, a spoon. Parents who have made it their practice from their child's infanthood to refer to objects by name have already aided their children and bolstered their vocabulary. Parents who speak of "this thing" and "that thing" have begun setting up the obstacles that their children will have to overcome.

The kind of coordination expected for a preschooler is that which comes during normal development. No one is going to request that the child thread a needle or walk a high wire. But the child may well be asked on the test to copy a circle or a straight line that is shown by the examiner. Or there may be a request to stack some blocks.

One way that memory might be tested is for the examiner to pronounce a few numbers and to ask the youngster to recite them back in the same order. Or the child may be shown two pictures, one a star and the other a plus sign. The two are turned upside down as the child watches, and then the child is asked to remember which, say, is the star. There are all sorts of informal activities in which parents can engage children to cultivate their memories, and youngsters who have the benefit of such experiences are likely to give their memories more exercise.

Common sense is, well, common sense. What should you do when you are hungry? Why do we have cars? Such are the questions that might be asked on this portion of an intelligence test. There is latitude for answers and the test-giver's own common sense is used to decide whether the child has answered acceptably. "Go in the kitchen," or "eat" would probably be proper answers to the first question. "To see Grandma" or "to go" would likely be acceptable for the second question.

Of all the areas to which a parent can give attention during the preschool years, language development is most important. More than any other attribute, language will give a child a running start in school. Like a mason putting a foundation in place, a parent who attends to this area of development will assure a child of the best possible foundation for success.

Spoken language is the beginning because it is the precursor to reading and writing. And, of course, children learn to speak in the normal flow of events. Very few children under the age of three or four can read or write, nor is it necessary that they be able to do so. However, when the day comes that they start reading and writing, the heights to which they can climb will be greatly determined by how well spoken language has developed during the preschool years. No parent can talk too much with a child in the preschool years; nor can a parent listen too much to what a child has to say during this crucial period.

In all but the most utterly unnatural settings, children will acquire the ability to speak no matter how little attention is accorded them. Just as they will crawl and then walk, they will gurgle and then talk. Nature takes its inexorable course. What is at stake, though, is the quality and richness of language, not simply the acquisition of the ability to communicate. People who lived in caves could communicate by grunts and, similarly, a child exposed to the most rudimentary vocabulary could, in all likelihood, make himself understood. But there is a big difference between simply "communicating" and truly using language. Language is the basis for higher thinking and for the reading that is needed to unlock the mysteries of all the subjects that are studied in school. This is what the U.S. Department of Education said about language development:

When children learn to read, they are making a transition from spoken to written language. Reading instruction builds on conversational skills; the better children are at using spoken language, the more successfully they will learn to read written language. . . . Research shows a strong connection between reading and listening. A child who is listening well shows it by being able to retell stories and repeat instructions. Children who are good listeners in kindergarten and first grade are likely to become successful readers by the third grade.

The less a young child hears by way of good language, the less the child will build a vocabulary and begin the process that leads to reading and higher-order thinking. To get a sense of the deprivation suffered by a child whose opportunity to hear spoken language is limited, think of the deaf child—the most extreme example on the progression.

"The prelingually deaf, unable to hear their parents, risk being severely retarded, if not permanently defective, in their grasp of language, unless early and effective measures are taken," said Oliver Sacks, the neurologist and writer. "And to be defective in language, for a human being, is one of the most desperate of calamities, for it is only through language that we enter fully into our human estate and culture, communicate freely with our fellows, acquire and share information. If we cannot do this, we will be bizarrely disabled and cut off—whatever our desires, or endeavors, or native capacities."

Fortunately, few children are so severely afflicted. But the problem serves to illustrate how the absence of rich spoken language penalizes a child in acquiring what is needed for success in school. One cannot say too much about the need to build vocabulary. Words, words, words. Surrounding a child with the fullness of spoken language should be the goal of every parent. Eventually, this spoken language will translate into reading and writing. There is no need to hurry the process. It will come in due time and will occur magnificently in a child whose spoken language has been fully stimulated.

Since spoken language is so vital to their development, conversation helps children develop a readiness for school. During the first few years of life children are like computers that are being programmed. A computer, no matter how well constructed, cannot perform if it has not been filled with instructions and information. A child needs the same sort of input and the parent is the one most likely to be in the position to provide it.

The role that conversation plays in language acquisition cannot be too strongly emphasized. Did you ever notice the young mother wheeling a tiny infant down the street and talking to the baby even though the child is obviously incapable of responding? No matter how young the child, the practice can inculcate the right habits so far as conversation is concerned. Parents are not going to be the only ones to provide oral stimulation to their children during the preschool years, but their role —in almost all cases—is pivotal. In an interview, Catherine Snow, a professor at the Harvard Graduate School of Education, reminded parents who have more than one child how important it is to find some time to spend alone with the youngest. This child might otherwise get very little individual experience in conversing with a parent on a one-to-one basis.

Conversation implies a flow that goes back and forth, not just in one direction. Listening to what children have to say is every bit as important as talking to them. Consider how boring it is when someone dominates a conversation and does not let you get in a word. A child suffers the same frustration when a parent does all the talking. Experts stress the importance of responding to the points raised by children and resisting the temptation to give back more information than the child sought. "If a child brings up the subject of a particular dog," Snow said, "it is appropriate to give information about dogs in general, but don't go on and talk about mammals, carnivores, and other subjects the child hasn't opened." In other words, a parent should piggyback on what the child says in building a conversation.

A parent plays another role, as well, in responding to the questions of children. The parent becomes a resource to the child, a kind of research tool. After all, where are three-year-olds to turn for answers to their questions? They don't know how to read, so they can't use encyclopedias and dictionaries. Snow said that a child who learns how to use a parent well as a source of information is likely to have a greater sense of the importance of research to learning. "It is the beginning of research for them and ultimately it will generate a self-motivated learner in school," she said. So, even if there is so much questioning that it is annoying, the questions should usually be welcomed.

In effect, a child of preschool age is learning how to learn. Human beings cannot grow unless they devise ways of gathering, sorting, and making sense out of their experiences. Often, the highest praise for a liberal arts education in college is that it teaches a person how to learn, imparting the critical thinking that allows someone encountering a new, unfamiliar situation to weigh the circumstances, draw conclusions, and make judgments.

On a less sophisticated level, a child must learn to make sense of each new experience—and there are many such experiences when you are still of preschool age and have not been in this world for all that long. The process starts in the crib as soon as the infant's eyes start following anyone in the room who is moving. It continues as the child becomes a young, crib-bound Columbus, visually exploring and making great discoveries, such as noticing his or her own hand and the fingers that are attached to it. Helping a child learn how to learn is one of the most valuable contributions a parent can make to a child's eventual success in school. Questioning plays a vital role in all this. The questions asked by a child and the questions asked by parents are equally important. Socrates educated his students by asking them questions that challenged them and provoked their thinking. It is a mode of teaching, used in an informal style, that serves parents well in dealing with their developing children.

Careful use of questions and comments can enable an adult to help a child develop the kinds of observational skills basic to school. "What color is that mailbox?" the parent may ask as he or she drives down the street with a youngster. "What shape is this pie plate?" is a natural question to ask a child who is watching a parent prepare to bake. "How many people are waiting in line with us?" the child might be asked in the supermarket. Snow said that questioning has an added value beyond building a reservoir of information about counting, shapes, and common objects. Questioning is the form of instruction often employed in the classroom. Teachers pose questions and want students to answer them. Children accustomed to this style of discourse are prepared to participate more completely in the life of the classroom.

Parents often wonder whether their children are progressing adequately, whether their skill development is appropriate for their age. Children mature at such uneven rates that no one can say for certain exactly where a child should be in achievement at a given age. But there are some benchmarks worth keeping in mind. One effort to provide parents with yardsticks of this sort comes from the Missouri Department of Elementary and Secondary Education, which sponsored a project to help parents aid the intellectual development of their children. Trainers went into homes to work with parents in small groups. The program, Parents as Teachers, suggests, for example, that a child normally does the following sometime between the ages of two and three:

- Joins in songs and nursery rhymes.

- Repeats names for hair, mouth, nose, shoes, and other parts of the body and personal objects.

- Constantly asks names of objects.

- Uses a vocabulary of 50 to 500 words.

- Begins to use such pronouns as *mine, me, you,* and *I.*

- Comprehends the meaning of "another," as, for instance, in the sentence "We will go to Grandma's on 'another' day."

- Understands such prepositions as *on, under,* and *in.*

- Rolls, pounds, squeezes, and pulls clay.

- Likes to use paint, but is not necessarily interested in the picture.

- Asks questions in sentence form.

These tend to be behaviors that a child exhibits between the ages of three and four, according to the Missouri program.

- Uses a vocabulary of 900 to 1,500 words.

- Acts out simple stories.

- Tells a story from a picture.

- Repeats 6-word sentences.

- Names hidden objects from memory.

- Understands such concepts as bigger and smaller.

- Assembles simple puzzles.

- Builds a bridge of blocks when shown how.

- Shows some awareness of past and present.

- Uses names of objects and action words.

Then, between the ages of four and five, the child becomes even more sophisticated in the thinking skills needed for school and shows an inclination to do the following:

- Repeats sentences that contain 8 to 10 words.

- Uses 5- to 6-word sentences without coaching.

- "Reads" through a story by figuring out the pictures.

- Can count four objects.

- Has a vocabulary of 1,500 to 2,000 words.

- Identifies four to eight colors.

- Speaks distinctly enough to be understood by a stranger.

- Asks for meanings of words.

- Asks "Why?," "When?," and "How?" frequently.

- Relates events in nature, such as falling leaves, to the seasons.

- Understands the concepts of weight, size, and temperature.

In many cases the learning that occurs during these preschool years is an outgrowth of play, a fact that adults —oriented as they are toward the notion that learning is supposed to be tedious and unpleasant—sometimes find difficult to accept. Bruno Bettelheim provided one of the best explanations of the role that play fulfills for a child. Said Bettelheim:

Play is the child's most useful tool for preparing himself for the future and its tasks. Play's function in developing cognitive and motor abilities has been explored by Karl Groos (the first investigator to study it systematically), Jean Piaget (to whom we owe our best understanding of what the child learns intellectually from play), and many others. Play teaches the child, without his being aware of it, the habits most needed for intellectual growth, such as stick-to-itiveness, which is so important in all of learning. Perseverance is easily acquired around enjoyable activities such as chosen play. But if it has not become a habit through what is enjoyable, it is not likely to become one through an endeavor like schoolwork. That we rarely succeed at a thing as easily or promptly as we might wish is best learned at an early age, when habits are formed and when the lesson can be assimilated fairly painlessly.

An excellent example of how play can promote learning is seen when preschool children use blocks for building. Though small children seem to have short attention spans, this is an activity in which they can remain rapt for long periods. And when they play, especially with unit blocks (sets in which smaller blocks make up the multiles of a unit), they gain a sense of how fractional parts equal a whole unit. One expert, Sally Cartwright, maintains that building with unit blocks aids the development of preschoolers in five ways. According to Cartwright, physical development gains from the muscular control and dexterity required, social development comes as the children work together, emotional development is contained in the satisfaction of mastering building tasks, intellectual development is the result of working with the units and their components to design and build the structure, and intuitional development is promoted by the initiative and discovery of such tasks.

Play may simply be the result of a couple of children being together and interacting, but very often, perhaps too often, play depends on the presence of toys. There is nothing wrong with children using toys as objects that help stretch their imagination, but frequently today toys are supposed to entertain in the way that television does, stealing away opportunities for creative play. Furthermore, the prevalence of so-called high-tech toys can lead to isolation, because having such toys to occupy themselves may mean that children feel less need for the companionship that eventually leads to socialization.

This is not the way it always was, we are reminded by Brian Sutton-Smith, a professor of education and folklore at the University of Pennsylvania. "Babies had no toys," Sutton-Smith said, looking back not too many generations. "The nature of play throughout history has been predominantly play with others, not play with toys. Today, even though children often prefer playing with other children to playing on their own, they spend the greater part of their time playing alone. This is even more true of suburban children than of city children. The wealthier the children, the more likely they are to be confined to their houses and a bedroom usually stuffed with all kinds of toys."

The dominance of toys in the lives of children is, in part, an outgrowth of the life-styles of families that sought easy ways to keep children busy, a role also fulfilled with devastating effect by television. In addition, toys are prevalent because toy manufacturers seek to build a market for their products. Toys are certainly here to stay and the best thing parents can do about them is shop carefully and exercise supervision over the toys—especially guns and others that are militaristic—made available to their children.

Some aid is available from the National Association for the Education of Young Children, which has produced the pamphlet *Toys: Tools for Learning.* Single copies of the pamphlet cost 50¢ from the organization at 1834 Connecticut Avenue N.W., Washington, D.C.,

20009. An important part of the brochure is the following checklist of questions that parents should ask themselves when shopping for a toy:

- Is this toy safe for my child's age?

- Will my child be interested enough to play with it over and over again? For several minutes or even an hour at a time?

- Is it constructed well? Will it hold up to lots of use?

- Does my child provide the power and imagination to operate the toy?

- Will my child feel successful when using this toy? Does it challenge my child's abilities just enough?

- Can the toy grow with my child? Will it still be appealing in a year? For several years?

- Can my child use the toy in different ways? Can it be used creatively?

- Will it help my child learn about other people, nature, or how things work?

As already mentioned, the contribution that play—with or without toys—makes to socialization is important and should not be underrated. Academic success often depends on mastery of social skills. A child who cannot get along with other students or with teachers is, in effect, handicapped in a classroom. In the frantic effort to enhance the intellectual side of development, parents sometimes overlook the importance of rounding out the child's personality.

Ideally, good teachers will discourage competition

and encourage students to pursue cooperative learning ventures. Early socialization helps prepare youngsters for this. The behavior of a child who is withdrawn or one who is overly hostile may well interfere with his or her learning. Getting along in a group is important in school, and children who are selfish and do not know how to share may find such traits are obstacles in their schooling.

Burton White reminds parents that they must start early to go about making certain that their children gain the ability to share:

It is important for a six-year-old to be socially comfortable and socially adept. Parents can do things to avoid having a child who is spoiled rotten. A child has to learn to share and to take "no" for an answer. You can't teach very small children to share, so you have to teach them the things that precede sharing, like respecting the rights of others.

One time to do this is when the child makes a request for help or attention. If it is an awkward time for the parent, then the parent need not drop everything. After all, a child will approach a parent with such requests about 10 times an hour. There should be quick response by the parent, but it may only be to say, "I'm in the middle of something I don't want to drop right now." A parent has to occasionally tell a child who is 13 or 14 months old, "I hear you, but you will have to wait." A parent who doesn't do this will end up with a child who thinks he or she is the most important person in the world, a child that no one else enjoys.

Some may find it surprising that a chapter on the pre-school years in a book for parents who want to enhance their children's opportunities in elementary school ends by emphasizing the social dimension rather than the intellectual. This approach is taken because it is important with all the stress these days on priming children for academic success to remember that the whole child should not be neglected.

Too many parents concerned about grooming their children for a future of achievement tend to be indulgent with their children in matters of socialization, viewing this as an area of minor significance. These parents forget about the importance of helping their offspring to be not only bright, but also leading them to become caring, humane, and giving. A prominent figure in education, John Dewey, addressed this matter almost a century ago. "The social life of the child," Dewey said, "is the basis of concentration or correlation in all his training or growth. The social life gives the unconscious unity and the background of all his efforts and attainments."

4

BUILDING A READING
FOUNDATION

A primary mission during the early years should be to instill a love of language, both oral and written, in a child. Yes, written. Children can be led to believe that something wonderful and miraculous lurks between the covers of books, something that they will want to explore for themselves just as soon as they are able.

Setting an example is obviously an aim that a parent ought to have. Some of the most powerful messages are tacit, as for instance the absence of books, magazines, and newspapers in a household. What is a child to think when there are few printed materials to be seen?

Sad to say, there are children who encounter books for the first time when they arrive in school. No wonder they conclude that books, and the printed word generally, are not particularly valued. "Children who become good readers are those who have had many experiences with print during their early years," said

Judith A. Schickedanz. "They probably have seen their parents reading for pleasure or to obtain information. Reading becomes a part of their lives long before elementary school."

On the other hand, not every child raised in a home without books is doomed nor is every child in a home fecund with books destined to succeed. Interestingly, Bernard Malamud, the novelist who died in 1986, said that he grew up in a home with few books. In an interview reminiscing on his childhood, Malamud recalled that he had little cultural nourishment as a child. He is one of those who overcame this disadvantage and ended up not only reveling in the printed word, but producing words of his own that hundreds of thousands of readers cherished.

Children are not frozen into predestined achievement patterns, but it is clear that some have advantages. Anyone who doubts that a child's social class and upbringing affect school performance need only read the findings of the research of Shirley Brice Heath of Stanford University. She compared the patterns of language use in three neighboring communities in North Carolina—mainstream middle-class blacks and whites in the same geographic area, a community of white mill workers of Appalachian origin, and a black mill community made up of people of rural origin. Heath carefully identified the ways in which the cultivation of literacy among the mainstream middle-class blacks and whites set their children apart from those in the other two communities, contributing to the school success of the middle-class children.

• As early as six months of age, children paid attention to books and information derived from books. Their rooms contained books and were decorated with murals, bedspreads, mobiles, and stuffed animals that represented characters found in books.

• Children, from the age of six months, acknowledged questions about books. Adults expanded nonverbal responses and vocalizations from infants into fully formed grammatical sentences.

• From the time they started to talk, children responded to conversational allusions to the content of books; they acted as question-answerers who had the knowledge of books. Adults strived to maintain with children a running commentary on any event or object that could be book-related, thus modeling for them the extension of familiar items and events from books to new situational contexts.

• Beyond two years of age, children used their knowledge of what books do to legitimate their departures from "truth," that is to make up tales of their own. Children were allowed to suspend reality, to tell stories that were not true, to ascribe fictionlike features to everyday objects. In other words, they could let their imaginations run free.

• Preschool children accepted book and book-related activities as entertainment. If there were no books present, adults talked about other objects as though they were pictures in books. Adults often asked children to state their likes or dislikes, their views of events, and so forth, at the end of a book-related activity.

• Preschoolers announced their own factual and fictive narratives and they used formulaic openings borrowed from stories in books as their own openings to stories.

• When children were about three years old, the approach to reading stories to them changed. Children listened and waited, more as an audience, and no longer did adult or child repeatedly break into the story with questions and comments. Instead, children listened, stored up what they heard and, on cue from an adult, answered questions.

Heath found that children from such families were helped to develop in this mainstream pattern by parents who frequently engaged in running narratives or ongoing commentaries about what was taking place. This "event casting," as Heath calls it, occurs in all sorts of situations around the home—as, for example, when a parent helps a child get dressed and talks about each article of clothing as it is put on, or relates each step of the procedure in the kitchen as a salad is being prepared. This informal teaching of sequence and order eventually leads to children, once they are in school, being able to organize and mobilize themselves to tackle assignments and solve problems, as well as to being able to follow the sequence of events in a story.

Every child has the potential to become a reader and perhaps even a writer, whether or not there are books in the home in which the child is reared. But clearly, a parent who wants to increase such a likelihood should strive to create a setting in which words hold an honored place. These are some of the ways that parents can promote that objective:

• Don't stash books in a closet or hide them in an attic. Put books out where a child can see them and accept them as being as normal a part of the home as a television set or a refrigerator.
• There are going to be some precious or fragile books that parents don't want handled by children and they should be placed as far out of reach as possible. But if a

child shows persistent interest in holding such a book and opening it, the child might sometimes be permitted to do so under parental supervision, so that the child does not conclude that books are inappropriate for children.

• Parents who have not been active readers might consider trying to acquire the habit for the sake of their children. It is important for children to see their parents reading and to know that reading is an activity pursued beyond the classroom and not limited to children.

• Borrowing children's books from the library is fine, but this should not be the only source of children's books that come into the home. Library books, after all, must be returned. Children should have some books they can keep and consider their own. Therefore, some books should be bought for the child's permanent library.

These suggestions are aimed at making books a natural and familiar part of a child's environment. This is just one more step in making it likely that children will enjoy books and eagerly read them. "The children able to profit most from instruction in reading are those who come to school already interested in books," Glenna Davis Sloan of the City University of New York wrote in a brochure for the International Reading Association. "The mechanics of reading instructon may be left to the schools, but school reading lessons can be futile unless the young child is convinced that reading is worth the time and effort. Early, enjoyable experience with books offers powerful persuasion that reading is worthwhile. Taking delight in the exploits of Horton the Elephant and Curious George comes before taking an interest in the vagaries of long and short vowel sounds."

Children can also learn to appreciate books at a tender age by gaining the pride of authorship, even if they are unable as yet to write. Parents can let their children dictate stories that the parent copies down on paper in the child's own words. It is a practice that teachers are likely to use with children in preschool and in kindergarten. A parent might want to set aside a large notebook for this purpose—a notebook that the child comes to know as "his" or "her" own book. The stories that have been dictated can be read back to the child, who then might be encouraged to draw pictures to illustrate the stories on a page that has been left blank for that purpose.

Imagine what it means for children two or three years old to feel the thrill of having their own words read back to them. It is a wonderful prod to creativity. What power. What achievement. And it is just one more way to cement the attachment of the child to the written word. After all, this is not just any book; it is the one that the child "wrote." Such an exercise can also help children understand where books "come from." They will realize that books are not simply items manufactured in plants. They will see that books are the product of authorship, springing from the minds of people.

It is also easier for a child who does not yet read to understand upon having work read back to him or her that the marks on paper are letters and words with meaning, representations of speech, and that the alphabet is a code for putting speech on paper. Curiosity about the letters and the way they are pronounced might add to interest in written language and heighten the desire to read, as well as to be able to write one's own words.

No reasonable list of tasks to be expected of preschool children says that they ought to be able to read. Some will learn to do so; most won't. And parents who try to force their children to learn to read run the risk of extinguishing the natural enthusiasm that children have for learning. Each task comes in its time and the adage about crawling before walking is simply an indication of the continuum along which children develop if left on their own. Experts say that children must progress through levels. They use the phrase "developmentally appropriate" to describe the activities that are reasonable at each stage. For a thorough understanding of these stages, you might read the works of Jean Piaget, but be warned that he is not easy to follow, and reading a commentary on his work may be the best way to get into it.

Some educators insist—and some parents have been more than happy to go along with the urgings—that it is to the advantage of the child to speed up development. This approach calls for treating toddlers like tomatoes, putting them in educational "hothouses" where they will grow into intellectual superbabies. It is probably not worth the risk. The weight of responsible opinion is that parents should be chary of exposing their children to such high-charged settings.

While it is clear that many children, perhaps most, could blossom to a greater degree than they do, the main task is to find that uncharted outer boundary beyond which it may not be healthy to push them. Enriching their environment and exposing children to greater opportunities for learning is desirable. Opportunities are one thing; compulsion is another.

"It's true that a three-year-old can be taught to read," said Burton White, "but the ultimate question is whether a three-year-old *should* be taught to read. Probably not. My guess is that the best thing parents can do for a three-year-old is rig up a world that lets the child experiment. Self-initiation on the part of the child is better than using flash cards for an hour a day."

Perhaps parents can proceed best in this uncertain territory by doing all they can to surround children with the books, toys, companionship, and experiences that promote development, while keeping vigilant for signals indicating that what ought to be joyful has become stressful. That is the time to cut back. Pressure is trouble enough for thirty-five-year-olds; it ought never to be applied to three-year-olds.

What is reasonable at any age is reading aloud to a child. Jim Trelease, author of *The Read-Aloud Handbook*, recommends that parents may start reading to infants almost as soon as they are brought home from the hospital. The choice of books changes, obviously, as children get older, but what is most important is that parents try to read to their children every single day.

While reading aloud is an informal activity, without the kinds of rules that govern a classroom, there are a few points that parents can bear in mind to aid them. These are some of those tips, culled from several sources:

- Read to the child at about the same time every day, perhaps at bedtime. Whatever time is chosen, the place for reading should be comfortable and with as few distractions as possible.

- Don't be afraid to interrupt the story for discussions or to answer questions or discuss whatever comes into the child's mind.

- If the story is truly boring or just isn't right, drop it and try something more appealing. There is no virtue, for you or your child, in staying with a story that doesn't work.

- When children are still very young, a parent can edit the text while reading it to eliminate long stretches that might cause interest to wane.

- The child should be able to see and watch the pictures as the story unfolds. The younger the child, the more the illustrations help maintain interest.

- Read slowly and add expression.

- A reasonable time limit for reading is wise, but don't stop at a cliff-hanger—unless your audience has fallen asleep. Otherwise, provide a sense of completion, stopping at the end of a chapter if the book itself cannot be completed.

Trelease says the most common mistake in reading aloud is reading too fast. "Read slowly enough for the child to build mental pictures of what he just heard you read," he suggests. The purpose of reading to children is more than just entertaining them. On the most outward level, it is to build an appreciation of books. But reading aloud also gives them a feeling of sequence, something mentioned previously in connection with "event casting." To become successful readers, children must learn that there is a logical order to a story: a beginning, a middle, and an end. This will help them immeasurably in writing, as well, when the time comes for them to create their own stories.

Small children like to be told stories, and they seem to enjoy them most when they are accompanied by pictures. Parents searching for the finest illustrated books to read to their children should include the Caldecott

Medal winners. These are the books honored by the American Library Association, which each year selects the most distinguished picture book for children. The lovely artwork adds a special dimension to the books at a time when young children are starting to acquire a love for stories and the books in which they are contained. Caldecott Medal winners are so popular that they tend to be carried in libraries for many years after they are published. The most recent winners, going back to 1980, are the following:

Ox-Cart Man by Donald Hall with pictures by Barbara Cooney. Viking and Puffin, 1979.

Fables by Arnold Lobel. Harper, 1980.

Jumanji by Chris Van Allsburg. Houghton Mifflin, 1981.

Shadow by Blaise Cendrars. Translated and illustrated by Marcia Brown. Scribners and Aladdin, 1982.

The Glorious Flight: Across the Channel with Louis Blériot by Alice and Martin Provensen. Viking and Puffin, 1983.

Saint George and the Dragon retold by Margaret Hodges and illustrated by Trina Schart Hyman. Little, Brown, 1984.

The Polar Express by Chris Van Allsburg. Houghton Mifflin, 1985.

Hey, Al by Arthur Yorinks and illustrated by Richard Egielski. Farrar, Straus, 1986.

Owl Moon by Jane Yolen and illustrated by John Schoenherr. Philomel, 1987.

Some parents tend to think of reading aloud as an activity to be limited to the preschool years or perhaps lasting for only a few years in elementary school. This is shortsighted, according to experts, who urge that reading aloud continue at least into junior high school and perhaps even into high school. When older children are involved, parents and children should, of course, take turns reading.

Margaret Kimmel, a professor at the University of Pittsburgh, is one authority who thinks reading aloud can continue indefinitely. "Reading needs to be encouraged," she said. "It is like playing the piano—once you learn the notes, you still have to practice." Kimmel even reads Dickens aloud to her college students, asserting that his convoluted sentence structure was meant to be read aloud.

Kimmel tried to spread the gospel of reading aloud. She worked with a pilot program in Pittsburgh—the Read Aloud Revival—through which workshops on how to read aloud to children were developed by parent groups. State and local funds were spent on paperback books so that packets of four books each could be distributed to parents of preschool children at workshops. Also, volunteers were sent to read aloud in women's shelters, playgrounds, and in the waiting rooms of juvenile courts.

Once they get involved in reading to their children, parents should understand that sometimes the youngsters will want to hear the same story over and over again. There is nothing wrong with this. It is a normal request and not terribly dissimilar from an adult who borrows or buys a favorite old movie to watch time and again on the videocassette recorder. Just as adults say that they are repeatedly fascinated by the same film or that they discover fresh nuances each time, a child can grow with each exposure to the same story or book. Children also enjoy being able to anticipate what awaits them on the next page. So it is important that parents be responsive when their children want to hear a book read to them again. Do not say: "Oh, no, we already read that story."

The question for a parent frequently becomes one of which book to read. Hundreds upon hundreds of books for children are published each year, and one of the difficulties is selecting those that are most appropriate. You should not be afraid to trust your judgment. Look for books that seem interesting and are well illustrated.

Librarians and booksellers who specialize in children's literature are excellent sources of advice. Of course, a book appropriate for a nine-month-old may not be the best one for a two-year-old. Here is a list compiled for the National Association for the Education of Young Children by Judith A. Schickedanz. It is not intended to be exhaustive or all-inclusive, but it gives parents a starting point:

For children two to six months old

Baby's First Golden Book Series: Little Animal Friends, What Does Baby See?, Play with Me, Winnie the Pooh's Rhymes. Western, 1977. A set of four books including the work of A. A. Milne, with content related to the baby's life: animals, toys, games, and rhymes. Plastic-coated paper that can be mouthed.

The Baby's Lap Book by Kay Chorao. Dutton, 1977. Rhymes and verses.

Looking at Animals. Price/Stern/Sloan, 1981. Stiff cardboard and colorful.

My Toys by Dick Bruna. Methuen, 1980. Good for propping up and naming pictures.

For children six to twelve months

Baby's First Book. Platt & Munk, 1960. Stiff cardboard with many familiar objects to name.

B Is for Bear by Dick Bruna. Methuen, 1967. A colorful alphabet book.

The Cow Says Moo by John P. Miller. Random, 1979. A cloth book with farm animals and their sounds.

Ernie and Bert Can . . . Can You? Random, 1982. A little chubby book with cardboard pages that spring up to ease page turning.

The First Words Picture Book by Bill Gillham. Coward, McCann & Geoghegan, 1982. Color photographs of familiar objects.

My House. Golden Books, 1978. Stiff cardboard with colorful pictures of everyday objects. Rounded corners on the pages.

For children one to two years old

Baby Animals by Gyo Fujikawa. Grosset & Dunlap, 1975. Simple text and charming pictures.

Best Word Book Ever by Richard Scarry. Golden Books, 1980. Filled with pictures to name and talk about.

The Blanket by John Burningham. Crowell, 1975. A little boy can't find his blanket, so everyone looks for it.

Corduroy by Don Freeman. Penguin, 1968. Toddlers may not yet have the patience for the story, but they love to find the bear on each page.

Goodnight Moon by Margaret Wise Brown. Harper, 1947. Simple story in which many things are told goodnight.

For children two to three years old

Gobble, Growl, Grunt by Peter Spier. Doubleday, 1971. Pictures of dozens of animals and their sounds.

The Snowy Day by Ezra Jack Keats. Penguin, 1962. Children will identify with Peter, who has fun in the snow.

The Very Hungry Caterpillar by Eric Carle. Philomel, 1972. A caterpillar grows fat from eating, and the repetitive verse and illustrations appeal to children.

For children three to five years old

Blueberries for Sal by Robert McCloskey. Viking, 1948; Picture Puffins, 1982. A little bear and a little girl mix up their mothers while gathering berries.

Brian Wildsmith's ABC by Brian Wildsmith. Franklin Watts, 1962. Beautifully illustrated.

Chickens Aren't the Only Ones by Ruth Heller. Grosset

& Dunlap, 1981. A beautiful book about animals who lay eggs.

One Dancing Drum by Gail Kedenser and Stanley Mack. S. G. Phillips, 1971. A counting book with wonderful alliteration.

5

FINDING THE BEST
CHILD CARE

The prototypical American family of the 1950s —working father, homemaking mother, and two and a half bouncing kids—is as much a relic of that generation as is the Edsel. The fact is that women, including those with children, are less and less likely to remain homebound. They hold jobs regardless of how young their children are. Fifty-three percent of all children under the age of six have working mothers.

Where once it was regarded as scandalous if a mother gave over her child to the care of someone outside the family except for an occasional baby-sitter, there is no longer much compunction about doing this. The result is a broad new program of child care for youngsters younger than the traditional school-starting age of five. So widespread is this practice that such cities as San Francisco and Los Angeles require child care facilities in new office buildings. "San Francisco has offered child care in order to remain competitive with outlying areas where businesses in more spacious suburban environments were planning child care facilities of their own," said Erik Schapiro, an aide to the San Francisco supervisor who sponsored the legislation.

There is much room for growth, however, *Fortune* magazine having estimated that only a few hundred companies in the entire country have on-site child care centers. Some other companies give employees financial assistance to pay for child care or offer referral services to help them find centers. In 1988, the 100th Congress considered several major proposals of national support for child care, including one costing $2.5 billion annually, before a compromise measure finally fell ten votes short of passage.

The issue of how best to serve the developmental needs of preschool children has become a major topic of discussion across the country. What heightens the importance of the issue is that the level of preparedness that children bring with them to school will be affected by the ways in which the debate is resolved.

There are still experts who assert that mothers—or at least one of the two parents—ought to stay home and care for their children. This position has been buttressed by research showing that child care had adverse effects on infants, undermining their sense of trust and their feelings of security, leading them to become more anxious, aggressive, and hyperactive. But the validity of such findings has been challenged by other authorities. In any event, there is little chance that the trend of mothers seeking employment out of the home will reverse itself, and not very many fathers are apt to remain out of the work force to care for children.

American women have been liberated from the mores that limited their aspirations and kept them confined to the home. The prejudices of the workplace, where mainly "female" jobs were available to them and "male" occupations were verboten, have yielded to a new generation of women impatient to enjoy the successes previously available largely to men. Thus, the question now is what is to become of the children born in this new age, when their mothers may not be available to tend to their needs during the day? How are families to reconcile parenthood with the new reality of a father and mother who both work or with situations in which there is only a single parent whose job makes full-time child care in the home impossible?

While there are still extended families in which relatives care for preschool children, the option increasingly is for child care, a virtually new institution that has arisen to cope with society's shifting realities. Where once there were only nursery schools for the children of a relatively few affluent families, institutions that operated only a few hours a week for children at least four years old, there is now a network of care-givers that cuts across all social and economic lines to begin accommodating children almost as soon as they are born.

Some toddlers attend child care centers for as many as twelve to fifteen hours a day, five days a week. Then, by the time they are four years old, a growing number of these children get the opportunity to attend prekindergartens, often run by school systems, that have many features formerly not available until kindergarten.

Thus, parents face the difficulty of making decisions about their children that once could be deferred or did not have to be made at all. Child care was not considered because it did not exist. Now that it is here, though, the question of finding the best kind of child care is paramount. Parents must ensure that the setting is clean and safe. Scandals over child abuse in a few places have sent shivers through parents everywhere, and now parents must also keep their eyes open for this problem. Also, they must find child care centers that offer proper educational, social, emotional, and physical development for their children.

Unfortunately, the monitoring of child care by local and state governments is terribly deficient. *Caveat emptor,* Let the buyer beware. Almost any group or individual can open and operate a child care facility. And it is easy to get around the minimal regulations for those who run small operations out of their homes. Licensing, where it exists, frequently means little in terms of quality assurance.

Thus, parents who are going to use child care or nursery school facilities should be prepared to do some "licensing" of their own, inspecting potential sites, rating them, and ferreting out the ones that are potentially best for their children. Word-of-mouth opinions of people who are respected are, of course, helpful. But for any parent who takes this responsibility seriously, as certainly it ought to be taken, there is some work involved in finding an acceptable site.

The only national accreditation of child care centers is voluntary, and it began in 1985. So far, only 641 of the nation's 50,000 child care facilities have been accredited through the process carried out by the National Academy of Early Childhood Programs (1834 Connecticut Avenue N.W., Washington, D.C. 20009). Another 1,844 centers are undergoing the self-studies as the first step to accreditation. Obviously it is not yet possible for more than a small number of families to use child care centers that have national accreditation, but it is surely worth checking with the academy to see if there is one in your city.

Many states license child care centers, just as they do barber shops and liquor stores, but few states accredit child care facilities in the way that schools and colleges are accredited. It is worth an inquiry to the appropriate state agency to find out if a child care center is licensed. At least that is a starting point, even though it does not mean as much as accreditation, which involves an evaluation of the educational program. A hint at the magnitude of the problem is seen in New York City, where there were 250,000 children under the age of five in need of out-of-home child care, according to Child Care Inc., and only 44,000 licensed spots available.

The criteria for licensing vary widely from locale to locale and seldom afford more than minimal protection for a child. Instead of addressing matters of educational quality, licensing usually deals with such items as square footage, fire exits, and ventilation. Often, smaller centers that operate out of private homes evade the licensing process altogether. Ultimately, what is most important in evaluating a child care center are the impressions that parents form upon visiting the site. No parent should ever use a child care center without first seeing it.

Michael Olenick, a child care expert in Los Angeles, wrote his doctoral dissertation on conditions in the field. He came up with some suggestions that parents might use in comparing child care facilities. These are the qualities Olenick found in the very best child care centers:

- Children had a wide choice of activities.

- The environment was rich and interesting.

- There was much interaction between the children and the adults who worked at the center, one indication of this being at least a daily conversation between child and teacher.

- Adults spoke about emotions with the children.

- Allowances were made for individual differences among the children.

- There was a variety of creative activities, including painting, building with blocks, playing with sand and water, and performing carpentry.

- Little dramas were performed by the children with the use of props to promote learning on specific topics.

- Puzzles and games were readily available.

- Activities were available for both small groups and large groups.

- Adults read stories to children.

- Adults copied down stories that children dictated and then the stories were discussed.

- Children had time to converse with other children.

- Outdoor facilities were utilized part of the time and the equipment was pleasant and challenging, allowing a wide variety of activities.

If you think this list sounds like what exists at every child care center, you have an idealized notion of child care. The fact is that far too many facilities fail to measure up to what Olenick found at the best centers. At the opposite end of the spectrum, Olenick pinpointed this set of common characteristics in the worst child care centers. He called the negative approach to child care in such places "Sit Down, Shut Up, and Count to 100."

- Children were expected to sit still in one place for long periods of time.

- There was little time spent out of doors and very little for the children to do in the playground.

- Children, penned up all day, were aggressive and it was usual to see many of them crying because they often hit each other.

- There was no interaction between children and adults, either inside or outside the facility.

- The main reason for adults speaking to children was to tell them they were doing something wrong.

- Adults often used negative and harsh language with the children.

What a parent should seek is a setting where a child will both be well cared for and his or her ability to learn will be heightened. Everything should be structured so that the child gains positive personal feelings. That means no one shouts at or belittles the child. The child is not made to feel inadequate because of an inability to perform some task, and in fact, the child retains and builds the confidence necessary to take risks. Listening and speaking skills, the foundation for reading and writing, are cultivated in a good child care center, and there are lots of games and facilities to develop muscle control. Children do not run wild. They are taught to respect each other, starting to learn to cooperate with each other to achieve common goals.

Getting children ready for school should, after all, be a main function of child care. Since so much of the child's time is spent at a center, it would be a shame if it were nothing more than a baby-sitting service. A child care center should be a place that stimulates the intellect and curiosity of a child. Youngsters should be read to and have a chance to tell stories and ask questions. There should be lots of picture books. On a rudimentary level, it is desirable that children be introduced to mathematics and science. If there is a chance for them to hear music and make music, that is great. Whatever is done, there should be great sensitivity to the developmental needs of the children and to the fact that they are of varying ages.

Because standards are so uneven for child care centers it is in the interest of families to seek facilities where the personnel have sound educational credentials. This may sound like a reasonable proposal, but in reality it is controversial. Many child care centers are staffed by people of limited education, and any suggestion that such men and women may not be fully competent is sure to arouse someone's ire. So be it. Let someone else send their children to child care centers that are supervised by people with no formal education beyond high school. Better to be a snob and expect that the people to whom you entrust your precious children have some college training for the task they are trying to perform.

Does this mean that you should categorically refuse to use a child care center that does not require that its personnel attended college? No, but parents must be careful in an industry in which there are so many practitioners who have no business minding children. If there is good supervision, it is entirely possible that child care workers without extensive formal credentials can make a fine contribution.

Thus, the first place to look in deciding whether to use a center is in the supervisor's office. Do not be afraid to ask the supervisor about his or her formal training. If the supervisor has less than a college degree, then be especially careful about the center. Next, inquire about the education of the staff. Try to find a place where the staff members, too, have at least attended college.

The pay of the supervisor and the staff are very much related to their educational credentials. More often than not, the places that pay the worst salaries have the least educated personnel. In general, people who work in child care are notoriously low-paid, getting salaries well below those of public school teachers. Don't be bashful about asking about pay scales, and then compare the salaries of the personnel at the centers being considered. The final choice should not simply be the center with the highest salaries, but that should be a consideration. Of course, it is almost certainly going to cost a family more to send its child to a center that pays higher salaries. But then you know when you buy a Mercedes that you are going to get more out of it than you would out of a Plymouth.

Olenick found in his study that the child care workers in the programs he determined to be best generally received higher pay and better benefits—more sick days, more vacation days, and more medical coverage. "This was all possible because the higher quality programs spent more money on personnel and generally had more money to spend," he said. In turn, according to Olenick, supervisors and staff members in the higher-paying programs had higher levels of formal training in child development. They also were involved in more ongoing training.

Child care providers who are properly prepared for their jobs know how to set examples for the children by their own behavior and attitudes. After all, the children are at an age when learning by example is everything. Such teachers provide a healthy balance between assisting the children and letting them achieve independence. They also are skillful in helping children cope with their emotions and getting them to understand anger and fear.

IBM Corporation is one company that tried to make it easier for its employees to find high quality child care for their children. IBM did not set up the centers itself, but sought to help employees in making placements in existing centers through its Child Care Referral Service. These were some of the attributes of child care centers that IBM suggested in its *Child Care Handbook* that parents seek:

- A staff-child ratio of at least one staff member for every four children at the level of infants.

- Programs in which parents participate, not only by feeling free to drop in and visit classes, but also by having parents among the members of the board of directors.

- Care providers who are patient and skilled in helping children learn self-control and self-discipline and who provide discipline in ways that are neither harsh nor humiliating to children.

- A director who is open, friendly, and interested.

- An environment that besides being safe, provides children with opportunities to test new skills and explore new things. The setting should be organized so that children know where to find materials they are seeking and there should be small places where children can withdraw from the group when they feel a need for privacy.

Even in a small child care setting such as a private home rather than a full-scale center, there are tip-offs to parents about the quality of the care. The handbook prepared by IBM suggests several questions that parents should have about the child care provider, wherever the service is provided:

- Does the care provider seem happy and energetic?

- Does the provider listen carefully when the children speak? Are the responses individualized to the children's needs?

- Can the provider state clearly the rules that children must follow? Do those rules sound reasonable?

- What methods does the provider use to promote toilet training and other self-help skills such as dressing and eating?

- What attitude does the provider have toward discipline? How does the provider handle misbehavior and treat children who are upset?

- Is the provider open or defensive when asked questions about the program?

Parent involvement, which was cited by IBM, is paramount. The best child care centers provide booklets and materials to assist parents. The teachers and administrators are also available to discuss special problems with parents and to suggest ways that experiences in the home can be integrated with those in the child care center to maximize the child's learning.

One of the country's better child care centers, the Children's Village in Cambridge, Massachusetts, is a cheerful, carefully designed place where children are treated with love and dignity. An appealingly disheveled place, it has a large outdoor recreation area where youngsters are able to romp and enjoy the facilities in all but the worst weather. It is also a place where half the board members are the parents of the students. Children's Village is divided into five age groups, by no means the only way to organize child care but an approach that is instructive to parents as they evaluate the center they are considering for their children.

At Children's Village, the infant group serves babies from three months to fifteen months, with an adult for every three infants. The babies are given ample time to creep and explore, both inside the building and outside, with lots of physical and verbal contact with the child care providers. The toddler group has children from the ages of fifteen months to thirty months. At this point the children are able to do a little more on their own, but there is still continual contact with a reassuring adult. The staff-child ratio at this level is one adult for every four children.

The "sprout" group serves two- and three-year-olds, overlapping with the toddler group. There is a great variety of learning experiences and the ratio is larger, with five children for each adult. The staff facilitates the transition from diaper to toilet, from nonverbal to verbal communication. Three- and four-year-olds are in the preschool group, where there are six children per staff member. Youngsters this age have access to learning stations for experiences in science, arts and crafts, language development, water play, and blocks. Social interaction among the children is promoted by the staff, and the children go on some trips to visit sites that would interest them around Cambridge.

Finally, the oldest group at the village is in the prekindergarten for four- and five-year-olds. The ratio is one staff member for each eight children. An individual approach to learning is contained in a curriculum that includes math, science, reading readiness, and language arts. A certified reading teacher is available. "What's most important is that the kids are somewhere they can trust, feel loved, and know they are safe," said Ellen Snowden, an administrator at Children's Village.

A feature of good child care repeatedly mentioned by experts is that it be nurturing and supportive of children. Lots of hugs and the chance to sit on the lap of adults help fulfill this requirement. A few years ago, parents would have readily welcomed such a setting and would not have thought twice about the idea of a care provider showing affection to their children. Needless to say, this is a new era. The disgusting revelations of the middle 1980s, when it became known that some child care people had abused their sacred trust, have left every parent uneasy.

There is, unfortunately, no surefire advice on how parents selecting a child care facility can be certain that their children will be free of such dangers. A parent must observe very carefully and take mental note of the behavior of the care providers. A good child care center should be willing to let the parents of a prospective student have a thorough look at the facilities, and no rooms should be off-limits. The supervisor should monitor everything occurring in the center and should have a good idea of what is happening in every room. Employees should have lists of good references that are carefully checked.

Parents also should talk to other parents who have used the center and ask them how their children reacted to the personnel. Then, reasonably sure that they have chosen one of the vast majority of child care centers where staff members are responsible in their behavior toward children, parents must be willing to go with their intuition, as they do in most decisions regarding their children.

If the center meets the child's needs, according to Snowden, it is self-evident. "Children who are satisfied are happy and they want to be there," she said. "Lots of them don't even want to leave when their parents come to pick them up. On the other hand, there are many clues if children are unhappy. They may not talk about it, but watch out for sleeplessness and irritability. Kids aren't sophisticated enough to hide their feelings."

The safety and health of children in child care transcends most other concerns. A growing problem involves the spread of diseases. In Marietta, Georgia, in 1986, the spread of hepatitis was attributed to conditions in a group of child care centers. Because very young children are so prone to infection, some observers have started referring to child care centers as "incubators" for disease.

"We are in a new era of infectious diseases," said Dr. Stanley H. Schuman, an infectious disease expert at the medical center of the University of South Carolina. "Day care centers have become breeding grounds for a number of communicable diseases." Hygiene is difficult because many of the children still put almost anything in their mouths. Furthermore, infants in child care centers are still being toilet trained and there is the danger of illness and disease being transmitted through feces.

Parents should restrict their search to child care centers where there are hygienic standards and concern about cleanliness. It is important that the center maintain health and immunization records on the children. The meals and snacks should be nutritious, and the food areas should be properly maintained. Overall safety should be promoted by adequate ventilation and lighting. Furniture should be as child-proof as possible, with few sharp corners or dangerous protuberances. Soft material should be on the ground or on the floor below equipment on which children are likely to climb or jump.

In the final analysis, a good child care center is an acceptable substitute for home and the care providers are surrogates for parents. A child care facility is not the same as a school, nor should it be. But it should be, just as a good home should be, a place that promotes the healthy development of children, giving them enriching experiences.

6

MAKING THE MOST OF
THE YEAR BEFORE
KINDERGARTEN

Increasingly, parents of preschoolers must decide how much formal education they want for their children. The trend today is to push down into the preschool years more and more of the teaching that did not formerly occur until kindergarten and even first grade. More than a dozen states provide money for prekindergarten programs in the public schools, and many individual school districts have already moved in this direction. At least 10 percent of the school districts in the country have some of their four-year-olds in classes, though the total numbers are still small.

By 1986, according to federal figures, 49 percent of all four-year-olds were enrolled in some kind of preprimary program, mostly in child care and nursery schools. The figure in 1965 was only 16 percent. "The pressures are building for public schools to step in where only child care centers have dared to tread. And if the four-year-olds are coming into the classrooms, can the three-year-olds be far behind?" asked an editorial in *Principal,* the journal of the National Association of Elementary School Principals.

There are several reasons why this is happening now. Competition in all walks of life is probably more keen than it used to be and the schools feel the pressure just as much as any other sector. Parents want their children to have more education and want it to begin sooner. Closely tied to this trend is the push to accelerate learning. "What is being taught to kindergarten children today is what was expected for the first-grader fifteen years ago," said Anne K. Soderman of the department of family and child ecology at Michigan State University. As the curriculum has gotten crammed with more and more material, the tendency has been to push as much as possible down to the lower grades. By the time they reach the upper elementary years children are starting to be taught lessons that they used to have to wait until junior high school to receive.

Public school systems and private schools are responding with programs for four-year-olds. Typical is the move in the nation's largest school system, New York City, to make regular prekindergarten classes available for all four-year-olds whose parents want to send them—taking the voluntary approach that is usually used by school districts for children this age. Approval is widespread, as was seen by the editorial in *The New York Times* proclaiming: "The mayor's initiative deserves the widest support. If society wants to save the next generation, there is no more sensible place to intervene."

For parents in New York and elsewhere, such initiatives will mean having to make choices. Circumstances are such that millions of children simply are not going to be cared for in the home. The tide cannot be turned back, so the way to proceed is in a manner that best serves the needs of the children involved. Ideally, each family will find the optimum setting, the middle ground, where the child—though not pushed to succeed—gets all that is required to reach full potential during this crucial age period. Parents must evaluate the programs offered for their three- and four-year-olds with this thought in mind.

If a child is going to be cared for out of the home it is reasonable for a parent to expect a strong educational component in the program. Emotional, social, and physical development are all important and should not be ignored, but the cognitive side of the child should not be downplayed either. The benefits of early intervention have been abundantly demonstrated in preschool programs that social scientists have studied. Helen Featherstone, writing in *The Harvard Education Letter*, said: "The difference is to be found, most often, not in standardized test scores but in children's ability to meet their teachers' expectations and to avoid being labeled failures. In study after study, children who have attended preschool repeat fewer grades and land in special education classes less often than their peers. . . . It is possible that preschool attendance influences children's attitudes and behavior in school more than it influences their test scores."

There is the accumulated evidence of more than twenty years of preschool education for the disadvantaged, findings that indicate that children who get early academic attention end up doing better in school. One of the most thorough reviews of a large number of the preschool programs for the disadvantaged came to the following conclusion: "Children from both one- and two-parent families benefited; only children, oldest, middle and youngest children benefited; children whose mothers worked outside the home did as well as those whose mothers stayed home all day. Briefly, regardless of their backgrounds, low-income children enrolled in these programs more often met school expectations than did the children who were not." The study, entitled *As the Twig Is Bent: Lasting Effects of Preschool Programs,* was done by the Consortium for Longitudinal Studies.

A widely publicized long-term study of the effects of preschool education on disadvantaged children was done by the High/Scope Educational Research Foundation of Ypsilanti, Michigan. These are some of the positive results, continuing throughout the high school years, for the children who attended preschool:

- Improved intellectual performance.

- A better attitude toward school and higher college aspirations.

- Higher marks in school.

- Fewer absences in school.

The validity of these results is now widely accepted, but whether the findings justify the push to educate three- and four-year-olds is another matter. Cynics say that farming out children in the name of better education is a rationalization by some parents who don't want to admit that they merely need a place to park the kids during the day. "If some parents feel residual pangs of guilt about leaving their young offspring in out-of-home care, they can place their youngster in a high-pressure academic program," David Elkind observed. "If the child were not in such a program, the parents tell themselves, he or she would fall behind peers and would not be able to complete academically when it is time to enter kindergarten."

This charge may be harsh, but the fact is that it is still unclear just how much there is to gain for a more affluent child in a preschool class. Because much of the evidence for early schooling comes from programs for the disadvantaged such as High/Scope and the federal government's Head Start, there is some question as to the relevancy of the findings for children who are not economically deprived. Do they get the same benefits from their home environment in the natural course of development that the disadvantaged need special programs to obtain?

One skeptic, Edward Zigler, notes: "Preschool intervention may be particularly effective for the most economically disadvantaged children. . . . A large body of evidence indicates that there is little, if anything, to be gained by exposing middle-class children to preschool education." While there is wide agreement with Zigler about the favorable impact of preschool on the disadvantaged, there is less concurrence with his reading of the record so far as the middle class is concerned.

Some parents, not willing to have their children wait around while scholars hold their debates, have taken matters into their own hands. They have decided that what is good enough for the disadvantaged ought to be good enough for the children of the middle class. In Lawrence, New York, for example, affluent parents demanded that a prekindergarten program limited to ninety disadvantaged children be thrown open to the whole community.

What is a parent to do? Should families that are not disadvantaged seek prekindergartens for their children? Is it in the best interests of all children, regardless of economic circumstances, to be in prekindergarten programs?

Parents should do what they judge to be best for their children, and that means giving them every advantage possible. In most circumstances, it is not going to serve a child's academic needs to stay home at an age when peers are in school starting to be equipped with the skills and information that will help them in elementary school. Socialization alone may be a sufficient reason for sending a child off to such a program.

Gordon M. Ambach, a former state education commissioner in New York, thought the issue was clear-cut. He wanted prekindergarten for everyone, and to bolster his case, he cited the effects on children who participated in a five-year pilot project in several New York districts. "They showed higher general reasoning ability and better verbal skills, and they had healthier relations with other children," Ambach said.

This is not to say that children who remain at home until kindergarten are going to end up at the bottom of the class. But there is no reason to make it more difficult for a child than it has to be, and most children will not be harmed—and may even be aided—by participating in a solid preschool program that is supportive and nurturing without placing academic demands on them. So important is a meaningful early start in school that John Goodlad, in his highly acclaimed book, *A Place Called School,* proposed that children begin school on their fourth birthday, rather than running the risk of missing a deadline and losing a year. "It is difficult to make up the time lost, even for youngsters who take readily to the school environment," Goodlad said.

Yet even if one accepts the notion that the programs are desirable for children from all backgrounds, there remains disagreement about what sort of approach is best. Much of the concern centers on whether programs that are overly academic are perhaps harmful in the long run. As mentioned earlier, it is well established that small children pass through stages of development, and that hurrying or altogether bypassing a stage can be devastating.

"Young children do not learn in the same ways as older children and adults," said Elkind. He added:

Because the world of things, people and language is so new to infants and young children, they learn best through direct encounters with their world rather than through formal education involving the inculcation of symbolic rules. The fact of this difference is rooted in the observations of such giants of child study as Froebel, Montessori and Piaget, and it is consistently supported by the findings of research in child development.

What is happening in the U.S. today is truly astonishing. In a society that prides itself on its openness to research and on its respect of "expert" opinion, parents, educators, administrators and legislators are blatantly ignoring the facts, the research, and the consensus of experts about how young children learn and how best to teach them. All across the country, educational programs devised for school-age children are being applied to the education of young children as well.

In selecting the right preschool program for your child you must bear in mind several points that can be gleaned from the various studies and from conversations with experts. They are these:

- *Academic style.* Sitting little kids down at desks and teaching lessons to them as though they were teenagers is simply wrong. They do not learn that way and some of the worst fears of critics about permanent harm might be realized. The teaching should be of a more informal variety.
- *Academic content.* These preschool children certainly can—and probably ought to—be introduced to letters and numbers. But that is a far cry from teaching them to read and add.
- *Academic expectations.* Modest expectations are best for this group. If a child ends up leaving such a program and entering kindergarten with the ability to read, that achievement should be regarded strictly as an inadvertent bonus, not a goal. On the other hand, it is not unreasonable to expect a child who has been through preschool to be able to identify some letters and numbers.
- *Nonacademic expectations.* Maturity ought to be enhanced by preschool, and a child should be more able to function on his or her own and have less anxiety about going off to kindergarten.

The High/Scope study reinforced the notion that a highly formal, doctrinaire approach to teaching preschoolers is probably not beneficial. While confirming that participants in such programs showed higher intellectual performance than nonparticipants, the study disclosed some unsettling information about those taught in a highly structured way, as opposed to the participants whose program had been more informal. By the age of fifteen, youngsters from the highly structured program had engaged in twice as many delinquent acts, including five times as many acts of property violence and twice as many acts of drug abuse and such offenses as running away from home. Researchers caution that any conclusions drawn from these findings can at best be tentative. But there is something here for parents to think about if they are comparing a curriculum for four-year-olds that is authoritarian and highly prescribed with one that is looser and more open to individual needs.

This consideration is reinforced by the work of researchers who looked at the long-term effects of four other preschool programs on children in the upper elementary grades and junior high school. They found that where the curriculum had stressed drill and lots of practice students did well initially on tests but did not retain the gains. In contrast, those who had attended preschool programs that emphasized strengthening attitudes toward learning, fostering curiosity and creativity, and providing time for exploration and experimentation had less impressive short-term gains but greater gains over time.

Floral Park—Bellerose, a small suburban school district on Long Island, just over the line from New York City, has been a national leader in providing classes for four-year-olds. The district, solidly middle class, offers the classes to children of all families, not just those who are from disadvantaged backgrounds, which is the more usual approach by public school systems that accommodate four-year-olds. Thus, 99 percent of the four-year-olds residing in the district attend the half-day classes, though some ultimately enter parochial schools when they are five or six.

The school system strives to get parents involved in the program and schedules them to assist the teachers on a regular basis. The idea is not only to get parents more oriented toward being allies of the school, but also to let them see lots of four-year-olds beside their own, so that they will have a better idea of what sort of behavior four-year-olds exhibit. There is a room in each of the school system's elementary schools where parents can read and obtain educational materials. Basically, the Floral Park–Bellerose preschool program shuns specific goals, instead enunciating six main objectives for the children:

1. To develop a positive self-image.
2. To develop independent thinking.
3. To develop language skills.
4. To express their ideas and feelings in different ways.
5. To learn about their bodies.
6. To feel comfortable about school.

"We like to be vague," said Margaret Merle, program director. "A lot of what we teach comes from the objectives. There are curriculum goals, but no curriculum per se. If a child spends a weekend at the shore and brings in a bag of shells we'll use that to teach a lesson." The vagueness of the approach is indicated by the fact that the objective of developing language skills can mean most anything, depending on how much the school wants to push the children. At Floral Park–Bellerose, Merle said there is no pushing. There is attention to helping each child become more proficient in language, but how far each pupil goes will be entirely up to him or her.

"Broadly," Merle said, "it means getting them to

speak clearly, use sentences correctly, increase vocabulary, follow directions, listen to stories and tell back those stories, and express feelings." There is no passing or failing for the four-year-olds in Floral Park–Bellerose and, ultimately, the program means something entirely different for each child. Within the broad parameters, Floral Park–Bellerose does have objectives for the four-year-olds, as exemplified by the kinds of problem-solving skills with which teachers try to imbue them: discovery, sorting, ordering, classifying, matching, questioning, observing, recording, charting, generalizing, recognizing likenesses and differences, using trial and error, using mistakes to learn, and understanding cause and effect.

Whether a four-year-old is enrolled in a prekindergarten program under the auspices of the public school system or a private nursery school or a child care center the goals should be about the same. The teacher, knowing what is contained in the usual kindergarten curriculum, should concentrate on helping the child prepare for the upcoming year. Most important, the youngster should be helped to feel confident and to be willing to take mental risks without worrying about whether he or she will be correct.

Since the development of four-year-olds is so uneven, it is difficult—and unreasonable—to have uniform standards for all of them. Perhaps it is best to look at children in this age group in terms of what sort of traits many gain during the year between the ages of four and five. It is during this period that they finally acquire enough patience to sit and listen to an entire story without squirming. They develop sufficient coordination to dress themselves. Their social skills reach the point that they can work on projects with other children and resolve conflicts through talking instead of pushing. They take more responsibility around the house.

The more personal resources they have for coping with kindergarten, the better off children will be. World Book, the encyclopedia publisher, asked 3,000 kindergarten teachers in the United States and Canada what skills and knowledge they thought a child needed to get off to a good start in kindergarten. World Book's program for preschoolers, Early World of Learning,™ is based on the results. The school-readiness skills listed by the teachers were these:

Size

Understands big and little.
Understands long and short.
Matches shapes or objects based on size.

Colors and Shapes

Recognizes and names primary colors.
Recognizes circles and rectangles.
Matches shapes or objects based on shape.
Copies shapes.

Numbers

Counts orally through 10.
Counts objects in one-to-one correspondence.
Understands empty and full.
Understands more and less.

Reading Readiness

Remembers objects from a given picture.
Knows what a letter is.

Has been read to frequently.
Looks at books or magazines.
Recognizes some nursery rhymes.
Identifies parts of the body.
Identifies objects that have a functional use.
Knows common farm and zoo animals.
Pronounces own first name.
Pronounces own last name.
Expresses self verbally.
Identifies other children by name.
Tells the meaning of simple words.
Repeats a sentence of six to eight words.
Completes incomplete sentence with proper word.
Has own books.
Understands that print carries a message.
Pretends to read.
Uses left-to-right progression.
Answers questions about a short story.
Tells the meaning of words heard in a story.
Looks at pictures and tells a story.
Identifies own first name in manuscript.
Prints own first name.

Position and Direction

Understands up and down, in and out, front and back, over and under, top and bottom, beside and next to, hot and cold, fast and slow.

Time

Understands day and night.
Knows age and birthday.

Listening and Sequencing

Follows simple directions.
Listens to a short story.
Listens carefully.
Recognizes common sounds.
Repeats a sequence of sounds.
Repeats a sequence of orally given numbers.
Retells simple stories in sequence.

Motor Skills

Is able to run, walk a straight line, jump, hop, alternate feet walking down stairs, march, stand on one foot five to ten seconds, walk backward for five feet, throw a ball.

Pastes objects.

Claps hands.

Matches simple objects.

Touches fingers.

Is able to button and zip.

Builds with blocks.

Completes simple puzzles of up to five pieces.

Draws and colors beyond a simple scribble.

Controls pencil and crayon well.

Cuts simple shapes.

Handles scissors well.

Is able to copy simple shapes.

Social-Emotional Development

Can be away from parents for two to three hours without being upset.

Takes care of toilet needs independently.

Feels good about self.

Is not afraid to go to school.

Cares for own belongings.

Knows full name.

Dresses self.

Knows how to use a handkerchief.

Knows own sex.

Brushes teeth.

Crosses a residential street safely.

Asks to go to school.

Knows parents' names, home address, home phone number.

Enters into dinner table conversation.

Carries a plate of food.

Maintains self-control.

Gets along well with other children and plays with them.

Recognizes authority.

Shares with others.

Talks easily.

Likes teachers.

Meets visitors without shyness.

Puts away toys.

Is able to stay on a task.

Is able to work independently.

Helps family with chores.

Next stop, kindergarten.

7

THE KINDERGARTEN CONNECTION

Kindergarten is increasingly viewed as the start of formal schooling, but in many places this is a fairly recent development. As recently as 1974, only twenty-three states offered kindergarten programs to more than 90 percent of their eligible pupils. In 1985, twenty-eight states still allowed families to choose whether to send children to kindergarten, and in some of those states children could not be sent to kindergarten even if their parents so desired because the school districts were not required to offer kindergarten.

At least one out of every ten children across the country still does not attend kindergarten, not entering school until the first grade. The reason for this is that despite the fact that many of these youngsters live in school districts where kindergarten is now available, the law does not require their parents to send them to school until the age of six, and in some states, seven. There is not yet universal recognition of the enormous growth that occurs before the age of six and of the perils that face children who do not get adequate stimulation.

As awareness grows, however, not only is kindergarten likely to be offered, but the curriculum is apt to change. Until not very many years ago, ring-around-the-rosy, show-and-tell, finger painting, and perhaps a little counting were considered more than adequate fare for kindergarten. In that simpler, pre–"Sesame Street" era many more children than today arrived at kindergarten not knowing the letters of the alphabet. Formal teaching was once so frowned upon in kindergarten that in a state like New Jersey it was actually against regulations to teach reading in kindergarten. So diligent were authorities about enforcing this mandate that in kindergarten rooms with floor tiles that contained alphabet letters the tiles were removed and replaced with ones having no letters.

Where kindergarten once was seen as just another place for children to play, it is now increasingly considered an important rung on the educational ladder, so firmly entrenched in the regular program that for many people an elementary school without a kindergarten would be as incongruous as a bank without money. More and more, in fact, kindergarten has been transformed into a setting for academic work and some of the instruction that used to occur in first grade has now been moved down into kindergarten. The reasons for these changes are several:

• *Prekindergarten.* Child care and nursery school have become so prevalent that the majority of children now arrive in kindergarten fortified by school experience. The quality of the earlier programs varies, but many children nonetheless are no longer the wide-eyed innocents to whom everything in kindergarten is brand-new. In fact, some tykes show up downright jaded.

• *Television.* Whatever its shortcomings, television does have the advantage of opening a vista to the world. For small children this has meant early exposure to the lessons of life that used to be taught at later ages. They bring with them to kindergarten a level of information and a primitive sophistication that formerly was seldom possessed.

• *Toys.* Their playthings reinforce and extend the knowledge and sophistication that children get from television. Some youngsters even have toys as expensive and versatile as the computer. What is the school to do with children who consider the games of the old days passé?

• *Parents.* Like the children, the parents, too, are different. Being more educated, parents today have higher expectations of the schools and higher academic aspirations for their children. This new generation of parents is impatient if their children don't show sufficient progress.

• *Pressures.* Families are not as casual about the schooling of their children as they used to be. In a time of shrinking opportunities, the feeling is that the race is to the swiftest and that the fast track begins in kindergarten.

Yet, with proper attention, a family could probably still do just fine by its children if they were kept home until entering the first grade. It is within the power of conscientious parents to replicate much of what happens in kindergarten, enabling children from such families to start school at the first grade without academic deficits. This does not mean, though, that more parents should keep their children home instead of sending them to kindergarten. If nothing else, kindergarten is a place for social development, where children become accustomed to working and sharing with other children. The lessons they learn in this connection are invaluable for the remainder of their schooling.

Some kindergarten teachers say that helping children overcome aggressive tendencies is one of the most important functions of kindergarten. As a matter of fact, although today's children arrive at kindergarten with more facts in their little heads and a wider exposure to the world, there are teachers who say that the experiences make the students less disciplined and more difficult to teach.

Beyond the social dimension, kindergarten is important for what it means to a child's emotional, physical, and intellectual development. Again, while the home is a potentially adequate setting for the development of five-year-olds, the fact is that in today's society many, many children would be disadvantaged if they did not have kindergarten available to them.

Some need kindergarten more than others, not only because of differences in family background, but also due to the wide differences in their development at this age. Just look at a group of children in kindergarten and you can see these differences manifesting themselves. Some children are already bigger than others, even at this early age. Some are more social than others, butterflies who flit about the room talking to everyone, while the shyer children gravitate toward the edges of the group, seldom saying much of anything. Some can read and others barely know their last names.

The criterion that binds them is their birthdays, an ostensibly reasonable but actually imprecise way of grouping them. They are not even the same age, though it is common to think of them as all being five years old at about the time they enter kindergarten. State laws vary, but usually there is a cutoff date in the fall and because some youngsters just miss it, a kindergarten may end up enrolling them the next fall, when they are almost a year older than some classmates. Eleven months is not very meaningful if you are a month past your twenty-ninth birthday and your friend just turned thirty. But eleven months is almost 20 percent of a lifetime when you have been on this earth for only about five years. It is then a time period that can make an enormous difference between children.

Thus, the chronology that is used to determine entrance to kindergarten is misleading, and parents must be leery about comparisons of children in kindergarten. For this reason, parents should carefully weigh the consequences before battling to get a child who narrowly misses the cutoff date admitted to kindergarten a year early. That child might be better off waiting until the next autumn.

How do you know when your child is ready for kindergarten? The birthday is as reliable a guide as any. If your child turns five in time to meet the deadline for entrance, then probably he or she ought to begin. If the child seems particularly immature, the judgment of nursery school and preschool teachers might be helpful. There are tests, as well, but parents should regard the testing of five-year-olds with skepticism. Despite the hoopla about scientific accuracy, there are some respected experts in the early childhood field who question how much credence should be given to tests, particularly when children are so young.

Samuel J. Meisels, a professor in the Center for Human Growth and Development at the University of Michigan, challenged tests that determine whether young children are developmentally prepared for kindergarten. "These labels have been assigned on the basis of tests with unknown validity by testers who have had little training and usually no supervision," Meisels said.

One test that Meisels criticized is the Gesell School Readiness Screening Test, a widely used examination produced by the Gesell Institute in New Haven, Connecticut. There are other authorities, though, who find this test acceptable and use it extensively. One part of the test comprises various geometric shapes that the child is asked to copy freehand. These are the results, according to Gesell's findings:

• Easiest for four-and-a-half-year-olds is the circle, which 97 percent of the girls and 92 percent of the boys copy in recognizable form. When it comes to making a well-proportioned circle, however, only 35 percent of the girls and 25 percent of the boys are successful.
• Next easiest is a square, which 65 percent of the girls and 60 percent of the boys copy in recognizable form. A square in a well-proportioned shape is produced by 15 percent of the girls and 5 percent of the boys.
• Most difficult of these shapes for a four-and-a-half-year-old is a diamond in both a horizontal position and a vertical position. Many children are apt to shift the horizontal diamond to a vertical position in order to try to draw it. Ninety-eight percent could copy neither diamond acceptably, and the other 2 percent were able to copy only one of the two diamonds.

Another portion of the Gesell test is the Incomplete Man, a figure consisting of a small circle that is a head and, below it, a larger, incomplete circle that is the trunk of the body. A stick arm and a stick leg protrude from the larger circle, and the smaller circle, the head, has one ear drawn onto it, a few lines of hair on one side of the head, a line for a mouth, and another line for a nose. It is missing both eyes, an ear, and the hair on one side of the head. A line denoting one side of the neck connects the two circles and one side of a bow tie is intact. The child's job is to complete the drawing of the man.

The child is judged by how neatly he or she draws lines to complete the figure, by how well the parts added by the child match the ones that are already on the body, and by what the child does about the missing hair. These are the results of the test, which can be given to children from the preschool years through the early years of elementary school:

• Normally, the missing hair is not added by girls until they are four years old and by boys until they are four and a half. Up to the age of nine most children add too few hairs, and through five and a half, at least, hair tends to be too long in comparison to the hair that is already on the other side of the head.

• As early as five and a half, almost one-quarter of the children make a pupil in the eye and this is normal by the age of nine. Eyebrows are usually not added until the child is eight or nine, at which time children are likely to include pupils, lashes, and eyebrows.

• The missing ear is normally added by children at the age of three and a half, but the size, shape, and placement of the ear are problems to children until they are five or six.

• The missing arm and the missing leg are the two parts added at the earliest age. By the age of three, 70 percent of the girls and 55 percent of the boys can add an arm, and 75 percent of the girls and 62 percent of the boys add a leg. The placement and length of the limbs continue to be problems. An important consideration between the ages of four and five and a half is whether the child can draw a limb that properly meets the body line or crosses over it.

Whether or not a child can show by a test—any test— that he or she is ready for kindergarten, there is still apt to be some trauma associated with actually going off to kindergarten, especially for a child who has not had the experience of nursery school or child care. And even for those who have already spent time in such settings, kindergarten may nonetheless take on added significance. After all, there has probably been a good deal of talk about starting "real school," breeding all sorts of apprehensions about what lies ahead.

Kindergarten may be a time when pressures to succeed are welling up within a child. Gladys M. Stern, director of the Georgetown Day School in Washington, D.C., told of a four-year-old brought to the school for an interview in hope of gaining admission to the kindergarten for the following fall. When the mother had to go out to her automobile to fetch something, leaving the child behind with Stern, the anxious four-year-old took advantage of the moment to confide: "I don't think I can come to this school; I don't know how to read." Stern assured the child that she wasn't expected to know how to read yet.

The point is that children internalize pressures that parents may not realize they are communicating to their offspring. Even for youngsters who have been to nursery school or child care, going to kindergarten may be different in that it is housed in a regular school building, a place that to a child may feel as vast and bewildering as the Empire State Building. And, also, it is a place in which there are "big kids," too.

It is no wonder that when these circumstances are combined with the necessity to leave one's family—albeit if only for a few hours—some children grow tense. Separation can be difficult enough for adults, whose resources for adjusting are far greater than those of children. So it is easy to see that when children harbor anxiety over separation the experience can be positively devastating. These are some ways that parents can help head off this problem:

• Walking past the school building on occasion during the year leading up to kindergarten and talking about it as a place that the child will enjoy attending.
• Taking the future kindergartner inside the building now and then, perhaps to drop off or pick up an older sibling, giving the child a chance to regard the school as a familiar, nonthreatening place.
• Playing at home with some children of the same age who are likely to be classmates in kindergarten, so that there will be familiar faces from the very first day.
• Not saying anything to the child that will build up anxiety and make him or her feel that kindergarten is difficult or that the child will have to measure up to competition. Children are not innately school-phobic, but parents can make them that way.

When four-year-olds who are applicants for kindergarten at Georgetown Day School show up with their parents for a visit and interview, they are met in the corridor not only by the kindergarten teacher, but also by some of the kindergarteners. Each prospective kindergartener has a host who is in kindergarten and the instant acquisition of a friend makes the adjustment easier.

One of the first facts that a parent should want to know about the kindergarten a child will attend is the number of children in the class. Youngsters need close, individual attention in kindergarten, and monstrous classes should be avoided. Judging classes by their size may be as dangerous as judging books by their covers and so there is no number to use as a definitive cutoff point for class size. But a parent certainly ought to be concerned if there are more than twenty-five in a class, especially if there is no full-time aide to help the teacher.

Some of what children do in kindergarten they are doing for the first time. There has to be someone to ensure that they understand the concepts and to ascertain that they are carrying out the activities to their advantage. A teacher weighed down by the responsibility of caring for more than two dozen children has difficulty giving each the time he or she needs.

A great deal is said about the value of having children in kindergarten for a full school day instead of a a half day, but there are indications that class size—particularly when smallness becomes a basis for individual attention—is as important as the amount of time the child spends in class. In Chicago, children who went to kindergarten only a half day outperformed those who attended full-day kindergarten. What seemed to account for the difference between the two groups was class size. The half-day kindergarteners were in classes of sixteen, and those who attended full day were in classes of thirty. Researchers in Chicago concluded that having a small class was even more important than having a full day of kindergarten.

The finding in Chicago is significant in light of the debate today over whether children are better off going to kindergarten for a half day or a full day. One argument against all-day kindergarten is that it is taxing on little children to spend a whole day in school. An implication of the Chicago study is that a middle ground can be reached by giving them a half-day program with classes so small that they would get as much out of the experience as they would out of a full day of kindergarten. The quality of the time spent in kindergarten may be more important than the length.

Educational considerations are not the only ones that matter in this debate, however. Similar to the controversy over whether schools should start enrolling children at the age of four or at the age of five, a factor driving this debate is the desire of many working parents to have a reliable place to which to send their children during the entire workday. In examining the debate over full-day kindergarten versus half-day kindergarten, these are some of the points to consider:

For the Half-Day Kindergarten

- Children who are so young tire easily and need a shorter time in class to adjust gradually to the full day of instruction that awaits them in first grade.

- As the study in Chicago showed, it is better to have one teacher see children in groups of about fifteen for half a day than in groups of thirty for a full day, because it allows for greater individual attention without spending any additional money.

- Especially for children whose mother or some other adult is available in the home, a full day at school means that much less opportunity for family companionship and personal loving attention.

For the Full-Day Kindergarten

- So many children have experience with child care and other forms of preschool that they are used to spending as long as an entire day in a school-like setting.

- It is easy to schedule rest periods and snack periods that make the full day more tolerable for five-year-olds.

- Kindergartners have to spend so much time just getting ready for each task and cleaning up afterward that a half-day of school leaves little time for sustained activities.

- Field trips away from school are more practical with a longer school day, and the kindergartners are also on hand the entire school day to participate in the full range of activities in the school, whether they occur in the morning or the afternoon.

- Parents who work and have other school-age children can know that all the children will be on the same schedule, not necessitating special provisions during a portion of the school day for the kindergartner.

The weight of the argument and the trend itself indicate that full-day kindergarten is going to become increasingly more prevalent across the country, if for no other reason than the American philosophy that more is better. Half-day kindergartens still predominate, but the number of school districts with full-day kindergartens is growing. Full-day kindergartens are most widespread in Alabama, Hawaii, North Carolina, North Dakota, Colorado, Florida, Georgia, and Tennessee. In addition, as mentioned, someplace is needed to put all those children whose parents are at work all day.

One advocate for the full-day approach, Barry E. Herman, who organized full-day kindergartens for the public schools in New Haven, Connecticut, presents his side of the debate this way: "Children are ready for a richer and more diversified program, which an all-day kindergarten program can provide. The evidence clearly indicates that many young children, particularly our urban poor, will experience greater success in school if they are provided a well-planned, all-day kindergarten. . . . Establishing an all-day kindergarten will require careful research, systematic planning and community involvement. The payoff will be a stimulating and creative educational environment for young children, which serves as a basis for future school success."

The case for full-day kindergarten was reinforced by the findings of a study released in Indiana in 1988. The progress of students who had attended full-day kindergarten was traced through the eighth grade. It was found that they got higher marks and experienced fewer disciplinary problems than their peers who had attended half-day kindergarten. This finding was in line with research done by Vincent T. Puelo, who after reviewing many studies comparing half-day and full-day kindergarten concluded in *The Elementary School Journal* that "rarely are differences found in favor of half-day classes." He qualified his conclusion, though, with reminders about the importance of small class size and the ways in which time is spent.

Among some children the issue is not so much whether they can best handle a half day of kindergarten or a full day. They will have trouble coping with either, having not reached a level of development at the age of five that will enable them to feel comfortable with the expectations of the usual kindergarten. These children need special attention, whatever the duration of their kindergarten day. Here are signs that Maizie R. Solem said such a child exhibits:

- *Hyperactivity.* Cannot sit still and lacks organization. May be at one end or the other of the emotional spectrum, overaggressive or too shy.

- *Perceptual/Motor Deficiencies.* Poor coordination and clumsy in the use of pencils, scissors, crayons, and other implements.

- *Daydreaming.* Slow to react, fails to tune in.

- *Impulsiveness.* Does things without thinking, regardless of consequences.

- *Memory/Thinking Disorders.* Unable to recall. Makes inappropriate responses.

- *Perseveration.* Compulsively repeats a word, a phrase, a drawing and is unable to change activites readily.

- *Speech/Language/Hearing Disorders.* Reverses words, phrases, numbers, letters; speaks inarticulately, fails to comprehend or respond to verbal instruction.

- *Generally Poor Attitude Toward Self or School.* Seldom participates in instructional or social activities.

The problems suffered by some kindergarteners are reminders that such children may be best served by going on to a so-called transitional class after kindergarten rather than a regular first grade. A transitional class that is not quite a regular first grade can be a kind of incubator that provides children with the extra cushioning they need for a more gradual slide into first-grade work. It has advantages, but it also has some notable disadvantages. For one, there is the question of when the children will finally close the full gap between them and the children who went on directly to the regular first grade.

Also there is the possibility of placing a stigma on a child, since a transitional class can readily be regarded as a form of retention. Parents of children for whom it is appropriate ought to consider transitional classes where they are offered, but they should do so knowing that all will not be peaches and cream. Adding to the difficulty of deciding what to do about children who do not thrive in kindergarten is the troubling move in school districts to require large numbers of students to repeat kindergarten. In 1988, for instance, Georgia directed all of its school districts to consider the scores of kindergarteners on nationally standardized tests in deciding whether they should be promoted to first grade. Ninety-two percent of the children passed the test, but testing students this age to decide whether to promote them is a rather questionable practice, given developmental differences and the deficiencies of the test.

As for the academic expectations in kindergarten, much of what is taught involves readiness skills, the kind of preparation that educators say will make children "ready" for the basics that will be taught to them in the first grade. For example, a child who does not know the letters of the alphabet by the end of kindergarten will be at a disadvantage in learning to read. A child who cannot count and recognize numbers is not as ready to start adding and subtracting.

Children are made ready for school by an accumulation of experiences, not by putting them through drills. What is called "readiness" is simply normal development. It may seem appealing and efficient to provide formal instruction and it may even work, but such an approach is fraught with potential problems. For one thing, few children of kindergarten age have developed the attention span required for this kind of teaching. Just as with three- and four-year-olds, the formal approach is not an appropriate way to teach at this point in a child's development. It could backfire by inducing negative attitudes toward school among children forced into activities for which they are not ready.

A look at the activities in some kindergarten classrooms is provided by a survey of schools in California. The serious intent of the teachers was shown by the fact that 44 percent of the kindergarten teachers used reading workbooks or worksheets at least four times a week. Thirty-seven percent used such materials two or three times a week. Math workbooks or worksheets were used at least four times a week by 32 percent of the teachers and two or three times a week by 37 percent. While these activities may help prepare children for first grade, they also may impair their spontaneity and creativity. Similar objectives can be reached in less formal ways.

So, then, what should be expected of kindergarteners? What sort of curriculum should exist for them? This is a sample from the curriculum of one major school system, providing a list of some of the objectives and examples of how they might be realized, though all children are probably not going to be capable of all of the tasks by the time they finish kindergarten:

• *Oral language.* Identify rhyming words such as *can, man,* and *ran.* Differentiate among words showing position such as front and back, beginning and end, first and last. Distinguish and adopt patterns of standard usage—came, *not* comed; drew, *not* drawed; I haven't any, *not* I haven't no.

• *Listening.* Respond to a request for attention. Listen courteously, by learning to take turns and not to distract and interrupt others. Follow directions.

• *Composition.* Contribute ideas for group composition, doing so during discussions in complete sentences and logical order. Revise by taking part in discussions to help be sure that intended ideas are conveyed, repetitious sentences are deleted, and confusing sentences are reworded.

• *Interpretive and critical comprehension.* Select the most accurate analysis of a character's traits by choosing from among several examples (some of which could be pictures) after hearing a story. Identify plausible future events on the basis of information presented in the passage. After seeing a picture or hearing a story summarize it in just a few sentences. Differentiate between real and make-believe, knowing, for example, whether trolls really live under bridges or wolves really talk.

• *Word analysis.* Identify all uppercase letters of the alphabet. Identify all lowercase letters (this will probably be more difficult). Match uppercase letters with their lowercase letters. Recognize and name the sounds of letters at the beginning of words.

• *Mathematics readiness skills.* Sort and compare objects by color, kind, size, shape, and detail. Observe similarities and differences in objects.

• *Understand concepts related to whole numbers.* Use the counting sequence to determine quantity. Count on from a given number between 1 and 10 rather than always beginning with 1. Count backward. Make the connection between a quantity and the written numberal.

• *Demonstrate thoughtful behavior in solving problems.* Make and test predictions, say, by guessing which of two groups is a larger quantity and then counting the objects in each group. Learn from unsuccessful trials in mathematical situations. Develop strategies for solving problems.

Above all, kindergarten should be a happy experience, a place where children delight in spending time and evince no dread whatsoever. It would be nice, of course, if all of school—from the first day of kindergarten to the last day of twelfth grade—were this way, but unfortunately this is not the case. Parents and educators should at the very least keep kindergarten protected as turf where joyfulness rules.

Elizabeth Truax, a kindergarten teacher in Edison Local District, outside Steubenville, Ohio, said: "Kindergarten students are too young to do a lot of paper and pencil and workbook activities." That does not mean, though, that they are not ready to learn, according to Truax. "They are ready to learn a lot—numbers, letters, abstract ideas—but it is best to teach it to them through experience and through concrete objects," she said.

Truax suggested, for instance, using clay as a teaching vehicle, because it is easier for five-year-olds to handle than using a pencil. When children in her class learned the configuration of numbers they fashioned them out of clay.

Under her informal teaching technique, when Truax wanted to teach a new word to her kindergarteners, in this case the word *conspicuous,* she did it by telling a story about Victoria the "conspicuous hippopotamus." She never gave the actual meaning, but instead told how Victoria climbed out of the river and walked to town where she was "conspicuous." Everywhere the hippopotamous went in town people noticed her. Even when she tried to stand behind a telephone pole she was still "conspicuous." And so it goes in the informal manner that Truax employed.

A good kindergarten, though appearing informal to the untrained eye, is actually a place of purposefulness. It is just that the purposes are not at odds with what is appropriate for five-year-olds. Throughout the room there are stations where children can pursue playful activities that will promote their development in what will eventually be one of the skills they will study: in one spot, a display of picture books and a cozy rug on which to sprawl with a book; in a nearby corner, enough art supplies to make the heart of a budding Van Gogh jump with joy; across the room, counting rods and numerical games to introduce numbers in a delightful way; and elsewhere, a miniature play kitchen where they can learn the lessons of cooperation and take turns playing family roles.

Deborah Hillstead, a kindergarten teacher in Washington State whose classroom is filled with such stations, lets the children gravitate toward what they feel like doing at the moment. "If you leave them alone and don't criticize them they will learn," she said. And so a visitor to Hillstead's classroom might see a child sorting beads and arranging them in patterns, a group of three children sitting with the teacher adding and subtracting numbers, a few children looking at books, another one trying to print some words on a large page of paper, some other children coloring dinosaurs on a mural that is a project to which the entire class will contribute. Every chance she gets, Hillstead seems to be reading to some of them.

Using as a guide *The Position Statement on Kindergarten* adopted in 1984 by the Nebraska State Board of Education the desirable characteristics of a quality program include the following:

- A child-centered environment that encourages learning through exploration and discovery—not a sit-down-be-quiet classroom dominated by desks, paper, and workbooks.

- Access to multilevel experiences and activities of varying degrees of complexity—not all expected to perform the same task and reach the same level of performance.

- Choices and decisions within the limits of the materials provided—not largely teacher-directed.

- Learning there is often more than one right answer—not worksheets and discussions with predetermined answers.

- A daily story time, creative dramatics, and repeated opportunities to learn simple rhymes and other poems in order to develop appreciation of literary language—not told the day is too short for story time.

- Daily planned activities fostering both gross- and fine-motor development, including such activities as running, jumping, bouncing balls, lacing cards, hammering nails, playing with clay—not expected to sit quietly for long periods of time and perform fine-motor skills beyond their current ability.

- Development of mathematical understanding through use of familiar manipulatives such as sand, water, unit blocks, counters, and other concrete materials—not through marking an X on the right answer on a worksheet.

- Curiosity about natural, familiar elements forms the basis of scientific observation, experimentation, and conclusions—not science as a subject to be included only when time periods permit.

- Experimentation, enjoyment, and appreciation of varied forms of music are encouraged on a daily basis—not included only when time permits or when the music teacher works with the class.

- Many forms of art expression are encouraged through the use of a wide assortment of media integrated within the daily curriculum—not art that usually consists of copying a model, coloring a Ditto, or cutting and pasting a pattern.

- Activities planned to promote a positive self-image and attitude toward school and peers—not measuring a child only by the ability to conform to expectations.

With this kind of approach, children can experience kindergarten as the joyful adventure that it ought to be, a journey into learning in which the emphasis is on success, not failure. Parents should never forget that development among children, especially at five years of age, is uneven. The child who is unable to perform a given task this year will probably be able to do it next year or the year after. There is nothing wrong with desiring the best for one's child and trying to help the youngster get the most out of school. But concerned parents must resist the urge to exert pressure on the child or to instill any sense of failure over an inability to do work that is beyond the child's developmental level. Keep it fun—and the achievement will follow.

8

THE IMPACT OF
TELEVISION

Parents have ruefully conceded that the forces that influence their children outside the home are often beyond their control, but most parents would like to think that at least inside the home their influence on the upbringing of the children goes unchallenged. Wrong. There is one very powerful source of competition in the home that, if it does not offset the force of parents, does at least fully challenge parental authority: television.

Most children spend a great deal more time with a television set than they do with their parents, and probably no children in America hear as many words spoken by their parents as they do by the television set. It is a phenomenon that begins early, with infants peering at the glowing tube through the bars of a crib or through the netting of a playpen. By the time a child is ready for kindergarten, the average youngster has already viewed more than 7,000 hours of television, the equivalent of 10 entire months spent, night and day, in front of a television set. Once in elementary school, the average child watches at least 25 hours of television a week, almost as much time as is spent with the teacher.

Schools present one curriculum and television offers another, hidden though it may be. Drawing on both, a student is shaped in ways that go beyond anything the teacher or the parents may have desired. Attitudes, values, work habits—all are affected by television. What makes the whole process so troublesome is that after some forty years of living with television researchers still cannot say definitively what impact it has on children.

For families with children just entering school, television looms as a competitor with the classroom, making it important for parents to think about the implications for schoolwork. Such considerations may have seemed less important in the preschoool years, but now they take on fresh significance. Children who are allowed to watch television indiscriminately may find their schoolwork affected. Television exerts its influence both through the message it delivers and via the medium itself in terms of what is involved in watching a program, any program. These are some of the most important ways:

• *Time.* There is just so much time in the day, and the more television a child watches the less time there is for other activities. Reading, playing, interacting with family—all must compete with television. There is very little homework assigned in the earliest grades of school, and so television at this point is not likely to compete with homework. But as the homework load increases, children who have grown accustomed to long hours of viewing may find it difficult to tear themselves away from the set.

• *Learning style.* Passivity is all that is needed to watch television. A child can just sit back and let it happen. The active approach that characterizes games and sports is absent. The teacher-student relationship at its best requires active engagement. The best learning occurs when a pupil is involved in the process—reacting to questions, raising new questions, entering classroom discussions, looking up information. A student who is satisfied to be an inert receptacle, conditioned in that direction by television, will not get the most out of school.

• *Imagination.* Television leaves little to the imagination. Its portrayals can be so vivid and intimate that they literally jump into the viewer's head as full-blown images. This is both a strength and a weakness as far as young minds are concerned. Some experts maintain that children of previous eras were more creative because they used to make up their own games and listen to the radio, forming their own mental pictures rather than having them planted in their heads by television. This is debatable, but it is clear that the cultivation of imagination has taken new directions with the advent of television. And we are still discovering what this means to the growth of creativity.

• *Violence.* Every few seconds someone somewhere is killed or maimed on a television screen. It is the most violent of worlds and a steady diet of such programs would seem to inure children to violence. In some instances, lawyers have sought to defend clients by pleading that their criminal acts were so heavily influenced by what they saw on television that the perpetrators were not responsible for their acts. The courts will have to decide the veracity of such pleas, but surely parents would do well to consider that children who watch certain programs are being fed the belief that violence is acceptable. Whatever the lasting effects of such exposure, it is questionable whether parents want their children to have this kind of experience.

• *Health.* Television can contribute to making children less fit by keeping them physically inactive when they might otherwise be engaged in activities that provide exercise. Moreover, as almost any adult has unfortunately learned, sitting still in front of a television set is conducive to eating, even in the absence of genuine hunger, increasing food intake beyond what is needed. The result of too little exercise and too many snacks is readily apparent in some children.

• *Values.* Finally and inevitably, what all this leads to is the shaping of young, impressionable minds. The values that parents want to instill in their children are best taught through the example of the parents and by experiences that reinforce those closely held beliefs. To the extent that the depictions on television go in divergent directions, children are getting mixed messages and the goals of parents are potentially undermined.

What is most important as children enter school is that television no longer be—if it has been up to then—something to be viewed in uncontrolled fashion. There are very good reasons for setting limits and regulating the number and type of programs that children watch. If parents begin this practice in the preschool years it is easier to implement, but certainly they should act by the time children are in school.

Banishing television altogether, as a few parents have tried to do, is unrealistic. It also probably makes children even more determined to find ways to watch it. Bettter that they be permitted to view in moderation. Setting limits also affords the opportunity for children to make choices. If they are told how many hours a day they may watch television and permitted to choose among the programs, they will then get practice in decision making, which is always a good experience in preparing them for responsibility.

Joan Anderson Wilkins in her book *Breaking the TV Habit* sets down some rules that parents might follow in keeping television viewing by their children at a moderate level. Among them are that viewing be banned in the morning, immediately after school or before homework is done; no television sets be placed in bedrooms; certain nights be designated as off-limits for television viewing; a prescribed amount of time be devoted to exercise or reading in exchange for every half hour of viewing; the television not be used for background noise; and only previously selected programs be watched instead of turning the dial at random.

There is a temptation to use television viewing as a reward and, in turn, to withhold viewing privileges as a punishment. This may work in some families, but there are pitfalls. If there are more desirable ways for children to spend their time than in front of a television, it hardly seems reasonable to say that good behavior merits more viewing time. Why should that be encouraged? On the other hand, it makes sense to withhold viewing privileges if children are not doing their homework, especially given the likelihood that television is one of the main impediments to getting homework done.

There are some programs that can be beneficial to children, and wise parents will try to guide their children toward those programs, though still permitting children to exercise some choice. The best of the high-quality programs tend to be on public television stations, though commercial stations sometimes also have programs that are worthwhile for children.

One way to encourage children to watch some of the better programs that they might otherwise avoid is for parents to join the children. Forcing them to watch a certain program leads to the same problems as forcing them to practice a musical instrument, forcing them to read library books, or forcing them to kiss a despised aunt. They will rebel. Nonetheless, parents ought subtly to encourage their children to watch programs of high quality, recognizing that, just like travel or reading a good book, particularly good programs can be broadening.

Parents should make it a practice to join their children in watching not only the good programs but also the ones that are not so good, if those are the ones the children want to see. Research has shown that the attitude of children toward television and the amount of television they watch is somewhat modeled on the example set by their parents. Furthermore, according to the research, even where parents do little to control the amount of viewing by their children, they can still have an impact on the attitudes that children have toward what they have seen. Since so much time is spent in front of the television set, it might be a good place for parents to work on building bonds with their children. It also gives parents a better understanding of the kind of influence television is having on their offspring.

Occasional questions during and after a program can help a parent improve a child's thinking skills. "Why do you think she did that?" "What do you think is going to happen next?" "Which of those two characters would you have rather been?" Such questions, asked informally, can get a child thinking in ways that can be applied more generally.

So long as television is going to be watched by children, parents ought to do what they can to make the experience as beneficial as possible, recognizing that in the main television is, more than anything else, a source of entertainment. Having watched programs with their children, parents can hearken back to the content of the programs in succeeding days with questions and comments that will make more critical viewers of their children.

There is, in fact, growing interest by schools in promoting critical television-viewing skills in students. The idea is that—since television viewing is here to stay— schools should try to make it a more worthwhile experience for youngsters. The teaching of critical viewing skills focuses on specific points to which the attention of students can be drawn regardless of the quality of the program they have watched.

This means, for instance, getting children who have watched a particular show to discuss the characters, the story development, the ending, and many of the same attributes they are asked to study in a story that they read in a book. They may also be asked to compare how a presentation on television differs from the same story as told in a book. There are other forms of analysis that teachers get them to apply to news programs.

One area in which parents might especially want to encourage their children to apply critical viewing skills is in regard to commercials, which so often shamelessly seek to exploit youngsters starting at a very young age. Parents might want to discuss with their children some of the claims made in commercials on behalf of products that the youngsters ask to have bought for them. More often than not, the products are toys, a $12 billion industry that depends mightily on ads that flood the Saturday-morning cartoon slots, when children are apt to be the prime audience.

One challenge, so far as both the commercials and the programs are concerned, is making sure that the youngsters can sort out the real from the make-believe that they see on television. For some children, the artificial world on television has the ring of authenticity. The characters in such evening soap operas as "Dynasty" and such sitcoms as "The Cosby Show" are regarded with every bit as much verisimilitude as the cashier in the supermarket.

"Many of the children I talked to are morally certain that the 'real' world is much more like the world they have seen on TV than the one they can smell and touch," wrote Benjamin Stein. "More bizarre still, many of them believe that the world of 'Different Strokes' or 'Miami Vice' is the real world, every bit as authentic and available as Van Nuys Boulevard or their own kitchens." A measure of just how far this incorporation of the fictional into the real can go was what happened one summer a few years ago when magazines devoted space to articles speculating about who shot J.R., a character on "Dallas," who had been shot in the final episode of the series the previous season. Such articles appeared alongside those on topics from the real world. It's no wonder children become confused.

Sometimes the fiction of television becomes the standard by which actual experiences are gauged. I shall never forget when I, as a reporter sitting in the newsroom of *The New York Times*, watched a group of teenagers nearby on a tour, curiously noting how a newspaper operates. Seeing a reporter typing a story into a word processor, one young man said: "Look, it's just like they do it on Lou Grant's newspaper," alluding to the television show with Ed Asner. It was not that the fictional characters on Lou Grant did it like the real people at *The New York Times*, but the other way around. Television make-believe became the measure for the real world.

This is but one small example of the impact of television on the schoolwork of students. It has been documented that the lowest achievers in school tend to watch the most television and that, moreover, they gravitate toward the most inane programs. What isn't known, though, is whether heavy-viewing habits cause them to be poor students or whether the fact that they are poor students makes television more appealing to them and enhances the attractiveness of certain programs.

An organization that you can contact for information on how to deal with television's role in your child's life and to find fellow parents who want to work for better television for children is Action for Children's Television, 46 Austin Street, Newtonville, Mass. 02160. A source of information about appropriateness for children of upcoming broadcasts is KIDSNET, which is operated by the National Education Association, 1201 16th Street N.W., Washington, D.C. 20036. It is a national computerized clearinghouse for television and radio programs for children. KIDSNET, however, usually deals with libraries, schools, and teachers, so you might want to ask the librarian or teachers in your child's school to get on the mailing list for these guides.

It may be that television viewing in moderation is actually helpful to some children. At least research indicates that this is true of some younger children, as well as some older children who are less bright. Various studies have found that the academic performance of these two groups may be helped by exposure to television, enabling them, for example, to enlarge their vocabularies. So far as young children are concerned, this should come as no great surprise, given the praise that has been heaped on "Sesame Street" and other productions of the Children's Television Workshop. Gerald S. Lesser, the educational director of "Sesame Street," argued that the program was the "first real evidence" that young children could learn from television. He said the rate of their learning exceeded expectations.

Much is yet to be learned about television's effect on reading. A program such as "Sesame Street" that is essentially educational and is aimed at teaching fundamentals of the alphabet can be helpful. But most television programs are neither educational nor intended to teach the basics of reading, so the bigger question is what impact television in general has on the reading of schoolchildren. The more children read, the more likely they are to be good readers. That much is clear. And to the extent that television viewing takes time away from reading it has a negative impact on reading.

But who is to say that the child watching television would be reading if the set were turned off. After all, there are many other activities available, and children disinclined to read might be just as unlikely to read even if there were no television. Simply because of the time consumed, however, it is clear that the hours in front of the set are that many fewer hours that potentially are available for reading. Thus, the best course for parents is one that sets boundaries in recognition of the insatiability of television's demands on some children.

Also, you might want to piggyback on your child's interest in a particular television show to point out books and magazine articles on the subject of the program. There are many novels and nonfiction books on sports, for example, for a youngster who enjoys watching sports presentations. A children's book is available on almost any subject on television that piques a child's interest.

One way that television viewing affects schoolwork is in its impact on learning style. No teacher in a classroom presents a lesson the way it is given on television—even on the ostensibly educational programs of Children's Television Workshop. Children get used to the staccato of messages fired at them in rapid succession on television. The short, punchy format, packaged as it is in an attractive format, is at odds with the classroom, where the drab, slowly paced lessons must take account of the real learning needs of children. Furthermore, real teachers aren't entertainers and they have no one to choreograph their lessons for them.

On the other hand, it is about time that schools come to terms with what television has to offer as an educational medium and start doing more to exploit the magnificent teaching potential of television. Television has made hardly a dent in the way that educators approach teaching and learning. It is time to admit that there is absolutely nothing wrong with using television to provide some of the dramatizations that are in books and using television to see news footage that is now part of history. Television is an effective supplement to books for the teaching of thinking.

Television has become so much a part of the life of the young—and the lives of some not-so-young people as well—that the set is turned on almost as automatically as the light switch upon walking into a room. What such children and adults want is the background noise or the company of voices. It is a habit not terribly unlike that of someone who flips on a radio upon starting the automobile engine. Turning on a television is habitual with some people, whether or not they intend to give their attention to the program.

One group of researchers discovered in a study of children between the ages of two and five that only about two-thirds of the time that they were in a room with a television on were they actually watching it. They were playing the rest of the time. The researchers concluded that the statistics showing the amount of time that children spend watching television may, in fact, be somewhat misleading and that actual viewing is substantially less than the figures would suggest.

Some students can do their homework successfully while the television is on, just as many people seem to be able to work while plugged into a portable radio. This kind of distraction, once considered an obstacle to productivity, is increasingly being recognized as part of the working style of some children and adults. The Internal Revenue Service's huge regional processing center at Holtsville, New York, for instance, formerly banned Walkman-type radios, but now allows employees to use them because it does not seem to undermine their job performance.

Perhaps one of the most encouraging research findings is that the time children spend watching television declines with age. Whereas 30 percent of nine-year-olds say they watch six or more hours of television a day, the portion spending that much time in front of the set falls to 14 percent at age thirteen and to 6 percent at age seventeen. Parents can compare the viewing habits of their children against these findings by the National Assessment of Educational Progress, which asked children how much television they watched each day:

Age (Years)	0–2 Hours	3–5 Hours	6 Hours or More
9	32%	38%	30%
13	36%	50%	14%
17	57%	37%	6%

Coming to terms with the role of television in a child's life during the elementary school years is surely one of the most difficult challenges facing a parent. Each family will have to find what works best, a task complicated by the number of television sets in the house and the number of other children in the household. While it is laudable to try to get children to restrict their viewing to quality programs, it is probably unrealistic. Educated and refined adults who love classical music may at times listen to rock and roll or country music. They may supplement their viewing of public television with episodes from "L.A. Law" or reruns of "Hill Street Blues." They may read potboilers as well as good literature. Children can be expected to do no less.

Reasonable concern is probably a parent's best guide as far as television and children are concerned. Television is a powerful influence on the minds of children, and conscientious parents will try to intervene in ways that are protective of the welfare and school performance of their children, but do it in a manner that recognizes the realities of life.

9

READING:
THE GREAT
BEGINNING

The most important event that happens in all of education occurs in the first grade: most children learn to read books. This is the seminal experience of schooling, the basis for all that will follow. It is a natural outgrowth of the language development of the first six years of life, the fruition of a drive to make sense of the world that begins with the words heard by infants in the crib. Students who are successful at learning to read will be able to cope with school; those who falter may spend the rest of their education trying to catch up. Thus, once a child enters the first grade the focus of every parent's attention should be on making certain that the youngster becomes a sure and powerful reader, preferably one who enjoys reading and treasures books.

Children start first grade with vastly different levels of reading ability. They are strung along a continuum, some having advanced further than others in language acquisition during the years leading up to first grade.

Perhaps one out of five can pick up a first-grade primer and read it. At the opposite end of the spectrum are at least as many, or more, still struggling over virtually every word they see and barely aware of the sounds of the letters of the alphabet. And in the middle is a large group who are familiar with the alphabet and recognize some words they have memorized, but cannot yet make much sense of a printed page.

Teachers are not in the least daunted by the fact that the overwhelming number of children reach first grade unable to read. This is normal and not unexpected. Most people who today are physicians and lawyers, journalists and teachers, scientists and business executives did not know how to read when they entered first grade.

Children who are able to read when they begin first grade have a slight advantage over the others, but the edge is usually offset quickly by the rest of the class as they, too, join the great community of readers. I reiterate, there is no reason for parents to be alarmed if their children reach first grade unable to read. If a student is still at that point at the end of the first grade, that is a different matter. Then there is some cause for concern, though there are many children who will become perfectly capable students but will not read until they are in the second grade and, in some cases, the third grade. Children are individuals, not machines, and each develops at his or her own rate; there should be room to accommodate these differences without worry. Boys more often than girls are late to read. Parents should keep alert, though, if their children seem to be lagging seriously behind classmates.

Parents also have to look inward to see if conditions at home are slowing down their children as readers. For instance, watching a lot of television (for reasons discussed elsewhere in this book) could slow down a student's entry into reading. An absence of language stimulation in the home can have a retarding effect. Children who have the benefit of being talked to and read to are almost certain to have larger vocabularies and may read earlier than others, simply because more of the words make sense to them. One should not forget that words are used in a context, and children who spend the first six years of their lives in intellectually stimulating and psychologically supportive environments are apt to develop into readers with more ease than those who have not enjoyed these advantages.

A small number of readers seem to take to the printed word easily, making the most of just a little bit of coaching. They are precocious children whose curiosity and careful observation lead them quickly to break the mysterious code we call the alphabet. Most children, though, need more help in learning to read. They need more intense direction to guide them through the enigmatic symbols that represent our spoken language.

Remember when you learned to read? Chances are you memorized some words you saw regularly, like *stop* or *Colgate*. The context for your recognition was the traffic sign or the toothpaste tube. Some other words, like *cat* or *mother,* you sounded out, letter by letter, as you learned the alphabet and then remembered the word in its entirety, recognizing it easily when it was used in context.

Sounding out words is called phonics. The U.S. Department of Education, in its report on *What Works*, a summary of research findings about teaching and learning, stated: "Children get a better start in reading if they are taught phonics. Learning phonics helps them to understand the relationship between letters and sounds and to 'break the code' that links the words they hear with the words they see in print."

But it is important to point out that once people actually read they do not have to use phonics to figure out familiar words. Phonics, vital though it is, goes just so far; reading for comprehension requires one to derive inferential meaning from a text, not just be able to pronounce letters and words. Phonics is essential to enable students to decode the sounds of unfamiliar words, but phonics is best taught in conjunction with comprehension, not as a separate skill that has no relationship to meaning. If phonics degenerates into having children spend undue amounts of time reading pages full of, say, B's and saying "B . . . B . . . B . . . B," this is a poor approach. Instead, a school should teach sounds as much as possible through actual stories that use words with the sounds.

Learning to read, in the final analysis, is not simply a matter of being able to sound out words, but of knowing what they mean. Certainly phonics has a role. "No one imagines that children read without at least tacitly knowing the sounds of letters," said Richard Anderson of the University of Illinois, principal author of a major report of reading instruction in the United States sponsored by the federal government.

The reader constructs meaning, building on past exposure to the word and finding clues from the context of the accompanying words and phrases. If the reader has a weak vocabulary and limited experiences, then words will remain jumbles on paper, no matter how accurately they can be pronounced. It is clear that the children who have had the fullest background will be most adept at reading. Those who have been witnesses to and participants in rich conversation will be most familiar with new words they encounter. Language that children have acquired orally, after all, is what gives them the basis for learning to read.

Most important to each child in the first grade is that reading be at the core of the entire educational program and that comprehension be the goal. For a parent watching a child move through the first grade, there are sometimes questions about whether the student is making adequate progress and learning all that is needed to become an able reader. The best signs are that the child is eager and happy to read, proud of having some ability to read, and willing to read to a parent from the book used in school.

Most elementary schools in America use basal readers, special books for teaching reading, and have done so for decades. At their worst, these are contrived texts —"See Dick run. See Jane run"—devoid of real literature or with literature that has been edited in a heavy-handed way, supposedly to make it more readable. The poorest of the basals presume that learning to read is a matter of mastering a series of discrete skills. There is a focus on letters, syllables, and parts of speech, with words introduced and used and reused in a calculated fashion that is unrealistic and at odds with actual usage. Teachers are expected to follow these prescribed lessons without variation.

Work sheets and mastery tests, prepared to accompany the basal reader at each grade level, may emphasize this unnatural approach to language, giving insufficient attention to comprehension, reasoning, and other elements that actually constitute reading.

Another problem with the work sheets that accompany basal readers is that they tend to contain repetitious, boring exercises—"find all the words starting with *t"* or "add an *ed* ending to the appropriate words." Often, work sheets are assigned simply to keep students busy while the teacher attends to other matters. Children might be better off if the work sheets were used sparingly and more time were devoted to actual reading.

Increasingly, however, there are available improved basal reading series that are richer in their use of literature and edited with greater care. They do more to tie the teaching of reading to writing and other language experiences. While these newer basal readers tend to continue to present reading as a set of gradually more complex skills, they are more in tune than formerly with the idea that learning to read is a matter of dealing with language as a whole instead of in little parts. Furthermore, teachers are given greater leeway to deviate from the lessons in the basal reader and from the work sheets in order to incorporate other books and activities into the lessons.

Whatever changes may lie ahead in the teaching of reading, it is important that a parent be able to deal with the situation as it now exists. Therefore, you must know what to expect if your child is taught to read with a basal reading series, as will probably be the case.

A student who is keeping up with the class will, midway through the first grade, complete the one or two preprimers that are usually used in the first grade, as well as the primer itself, and be into the first of the two reading books that are generally used. If, as spring approaches, a youngster is still using one of the preprimers, which are most often softcover booklets, then that child is most likely lagging behind the class. Or, if the whole class has gone no further, it is a relatively slow class, which may or may not be the teacher's fault. By spring, the speedier readers may have completed the formal reading books and may have been allowed to move on to library books, though there are so many different ways to organize classes that this is not always the case.

Nicholas P. Criscuolo has set down several essentials that he maintains must be present in a good reading program in any school. He said the program should do the following:

- Strive for the reader's early independence.

- Involve parents.

- Teach reading sequentially.

- Encourage reading for pleasure.

- Allow adequate teaching time.

- Keep reading groups flexible.

- Let students read independently in class.

- Stock a variety of supplemental materials.

- Continue reading instruction in the upper grades.

- Adopt a statement of philosophy.

Reading should be taught as part of a so-called language arts program that includes instruction in writing, listening, and speaking, as well as in reading. The point is that these skills interlock and each complements the others. Enriching language experience should be the goal whether a student is producing language (writing or speaking) or consuming language (reading or listening). Each new word added to the vocabulary makes the student more capable in all four ways. One large school system includes the following activities related to speaking and listening in its first-grade curriculum:

- Learning how to respond to requests for attention and how to follow directions.

- Listening courteously.

- Establishing a purpose for listening (for example, being entertained, getting information).

- Pronouncing words distinctly.

- Speaking in sentences.

- Participating in large group discussions with the teacher.

- Responding to questions.

Reading and writing are directly related, inseparable as air and life, and the teacher should help students develop in both in concert. Students will be asked to do some writing even before they can read, the teacher taking down their dictation and reading their stories back to them. Eventually, the students themselves will take responsibility for more and more of the actual writing and may be asked to keep journals in which they write daily. The writing being discussed here is not penmanship, but composition—putting ideas and impressions to paper. The more writing the better. Parents should be concerned if there is not enough writing in a class, because reading will become more powerful with more writing. Writing is an activity that teachers in the first grade do not have children do as often as they might.

Traditionalists maintain that from the time students start writing, teachers should be sticklers for spelling, punctuation, and grammar. But there is abundant evidence that it is more important at the beginning to get youngsters to put words to paper without worrying too much about the mechanics. Proper form can be taught without making students worry about whether commas are in the right place, words are capitalized, and spelling is perfect. Inventive spelling can suffice at the beginning. Surely, at some point in elementary school, teachers should address these concerns, but there is nothing wrong if they first let students become enthusiastic about writing.

Reading instruction in school should be supplemented by a lot of reading at home. Just because a child has reached the first grade is no reason to think that reading will now be taken care of by the school. Trips to the library with parents after school and on weekends, gifts of books, the ritualistic reading before bedtime should all continue throughout elementary school. Parents cannot afford to leave this to chance. They must carefully plan their time and the schedules of their children to ensure that there is a thorough program of reading at home. The accent should be on enjoyment.

Reading out of school should not be onerous to a child or the battle may be lost. Parents also can contribute to the language development of children by talking with them about what they have read, in no way criticizing or judging them, but simply showing interest and helping the child reflect on what has been read. Thus, with some gentle guidance from a parent, a youngster should be encouraged to choose books for home pleasure reading. Parents who do not approve of the selections should not scoff. This is no time to turn off a student to reading. He or she should acquire the habit of pleasure reading and it should be just that—pleasure.

A report by the U.S. Department of Education, *What Works,* said: "Children improve their reading ability by reading a lot. Reading achievement is directly related to the amount of reading children do in school and outside. . . . American children do not spend much time reading independently at school or at home. In the average elementary school, for example, children spend just seven to eight minutes a day reading silently. At home, half of all fifth graders spend only four minutes a day reading. These same children spend an average of 130 minutes a day watching television." It is the job of dedicated parents to be sure that their children are anomalies to these sad statistics, but they should never force children to read.

The American Library Association has chosen these as notable books from among those published in 1987 for children from the preschool years through about the second grade:

Turtle Watch by George Ancona. Macmillan. This photodocumentary shows a team of Brazilian scientists working to save endangered sea turtles and the village children who help in the effort.

An Enchanted Hair Tale by Alexis DeVeaux. Pictures by Cheryl Hanna. Harper. The poetic celebration of a young boy's wild hair shows the joy of being different and accepted.

Granddaddy's Place by Helen V. Griffith. Pictures by James Stevenson. Greenwillow. Granddaddy first amuses, then wins an apprehensive Janetta's affection during her first visit to his farm.

In Coal Country by Judith Hendershot. Illustrated by Thomas B. Allen. Knopf. The daughter of a coal miner recalls her childhood, filled with coal dust and love, that Allen enhances with extraordinary pastel-and-charcoal illustrations.

The Wolf's Chicken Stew by Keiko Kasza. Putnam. A conniving wolf plots to consume an unsuspecting hen but is outwitted by her charming and numerous chicks.

I Want a Dog by Dayal Kaur Khalsa. Crown. Droll paintings illumine this tale of a determined little girl who "trains" a roller skate to prove her readiness to take responsibility for a dog.

A More Perfect Union: The Story of Our Constitution by Betty Maestro and Giulio Maestro. Lothrop. Clear text and large watercolor paintings trace the dramatic events surrounding the creation and ratification of the Constitution.

Bend and Stretch by Jan Ormerod. Lothrop.
Making Friends by Jan Ormerod. Lothrop.
Mom's Home by Jan Ormerod. Lothrop.
This Little Nose by Jan Ormerod. Lothrop.
Four cozy picture books briefly explore the tender relationship between a toddler and his pregnant mom.

All Fall Down by Helen Oxenbury. Macmillan/Aladdin.
Clap Hands by Helen Oxenbury. Macmillan/Aladdin.
Say Goodnight by Helen Oxenbury. Macmillan/Aladdin.
Tickle, Tickle by Helen Oxenbury. Macmillan/Aladdin.
An exuberant quartet of large-size board books features a multiracial cast of frolicking babies and toddlers with their caregivers.

Tasmania: A Wildlife Journey by Joyce Powzyk. Lothrop. Distinctive watercolors and a quietly poetic text bring to life the author's awe and delight in Tasmanian creatures.

Henry and Mudge under the Yellow Moon by Cynthia Rylant. Pictures by Sucie Stevenson. Macmillan/Bradbury. Young Henry and his huge, affectionate dog enjoy fall leaves, shiver through Mother's Halloween stories, and learn to appreciate Aunt Sally's annual Thanksgiving visit.

Oma and Bobo by Amy Schwartz. Macmillan/Bradbury. Alice's new dog shows little interest in obedience school or blue ribbons until Grandmother Oma takes charge.

Mufaro's Beautiful Daughters: An African Tale by John Steptoe. Lothrop. Lush watercolor paintings and a Zimbabwe setting distinguish this tale of two sisters and a wise king's search for the perfect wife. A 1988 Caldecott Honor Book.

Fox's Dream by Keizaburo Tejima. Putnam/Philomel. Memories haunt a fox's lonely journey through an ice-blue winter forest; presented in fine colored woodcuts.

Owl Lake by Keizaburo Tejima. Putnam/Philomel. Striking woodcuts and poetic text recount an owl family's nocturnal search for food.

Owl Moon by Jane Yolen. Illustrated by John Schoenherr. Putnam/Philomel. Delicate pen-and-ink lines over watercolors capture the wonder and intimacy of a father and child's moonlit winter search for an owl. The 1988 Caldecott Medal Book.

Parents can reinforce this out-of-school reading in various ways. Besides discussing a story and asking questions about it, a parent can invite the child to retell the story in his or her own words. Also, parent and child can sit with paper and crayons and draw pictures of the characters in the story. You might dramatize the story with your child, too, taking turns being the characters and perhaps giving distinctive voices to the characters. These activities not only heighten interest in reading but also help children attune to details and sequence. And, of course, they promote the exploration and development of language.

So far as what is happening in the classroom, it is desirable by the end of the first grade that students be able to read the most difficult of the two reading books that are usually introduced during the second half of the grade. A parent can take an informal reading inventory by asking the child to read aloud from a book like the one at school and observing whether the youngster moves fluidly through the sentences, pronouncing words accurately and with the kind of feeling that shows confidence and understanding. The ablest readers will be able to use phonics to figure out the pronunciation of almost all unfamiliar words of one or two syllables. Comprehension can be gauged by asking the child questions about what has just been read.

Pick out a passage of a few paragraphs that add up to about one hundred words. If the child can recognize and read aloud ninety-eight or ninety-nine of the words, then he or she is an independent reader at that level of difficulty. The child's comprehension can be gauged by asking about ten questions throughout the passage to see if the youngster understands what has just been read. Correct answers to at least nine of the ten questions indicate an independent reader at that particular level of difficulty.

The goal for children who are below the independent-reader level is to help them become stronger readers. However, a child who cannot reach the independent level with one book can make it with an easier book. Find out what level of book yields that result, and then encourage the child to read part of the time from that book and others of similar difficulty, even if the level is below that expected in the class. This will assure a successful reading experience.

A child who trips over words in every sentence is probably confounded by a lack of success and may well turn off to reading. An adult can best appreciate this frustration by trying to read about an esoteric subject like high-energy physics. If the child spends a portion of the time reading at a level that represents an independent ability—even if it is below the expected class level—the experience will be more satisfying and is more apt to breed confidence.

Gradually, the child's reading ability will grow and more difficult books will be less of an obstacle. Better to have a child reading books that might be considered too easy for his or her age than to have the child reading nothing at all because the only ones available are too difficult. On the other hand, you should not discourage your child from trying to read a book in which the child shows an interest, even if it is at a level of difficulty beyond his or her independent ability. There has to be room for experimentation and growth in reading.

Being an independent reader allows a youngster to enjoy reading and be successful at it. But just as important as the book being easy enough is the need for the book to be interesting. Reading is not promoted by books that can be read independently if there is nothing in those books that the person wants to read. So it is a matter of helping youngsters find books that are not only on the right level for them to read but on subjects that appeal to them as well.

The comprehension skills that were mostly literal in the first grade begin to require more subtle interpretation in the second grade, as students try to draw inferences. They look for clues to the content of the story in titles, note details in the text, and grow to understand that there is a logical order to the sequence of events in a story. Students gain a grasp of cause and effect and see that the main idea is stated and restated in different ways. There is also an introduction to the notion that there is a difference between an author's opinion and a fact.

Second grade is when teachers try to ensure that all members of the class have mastered the basics that they should have been able to handle by the end of first grade. A problem, however, is that in taking time to address the deficits of those who have lagged, the teacher may have less time to spend with the more advanced students and they may grow bored. Parents should be alert to this possibility and should seek to be certain that children who enter second grade as strong readers are allowed to soar ahead at their own pace, rather than being slowed down to wait for others. In encouraging children to read at home, parents can promote the ability of students to advance at the rate at which they are capable.

Vocabulary is the ammunition that the army of readers uses to advance from book to book. And vocabulary expands in the second grade as students widen their use of language to include more homonyms and antonyms, discover that the same word may have more than one meaning, and learn words that are constructed with such devices as apostrophes that are signs of either possession or contraction.

Usually, two reading books are used in the second grade, a so-called easy reader and a so-called hard reader. Children start with the easy one, with its simpler, less involved stories, and work their way into the hard one, in which stories get longer and more complex, dealing with more intricately shaped characters. There is more plot to follow. The average child completes both readers before the end of the second grade and moves on to supplementary readers and library books. If a school restricts the reading program—even for students who are not high achievers—to only these two books, then parents should press for more variety. Otherwise there is the danger that students will get bored.

By the second grade in most schools it becomes apparent that testing is used frequently in connection with the instructional program. Students in almost all schools will be given reading tests supposedly to measure their progress and/or to determine their special needs. Parents should not regard the scores as infallible. The parents' own observations from reading done by children at home and the judgments of teachers should be given greatest consideration.

If a norm-referenced, nationally standardized test is used, as in most school systems, the score is supposed to indicate how the student compares with others in the same grade around the country. It is important to remember that the midpoint average that represents the grade level is found by giving the test to a representative sampling of students nationally and finding their average score. Therefore, by definition, all the students in the country cannot be at grade level, since grade level is the point at which half are above and half are below.

It cannot be said too often that despite the importance attached to reading tests parents should realize that these tests have shortcomings. The results are subject to manipulation when lessons are taught specifically to help students get better scores, and the questions sometimes are flawed by the possibility that answers deemed wrong are in fact reasonable. In the earliest grades, low scores on reading tests can cause unnecessary alarm about a child's progress.

A letter raising some of the concerns that surround reading tests was sent a few years ago to Nathan Quinones, then the school chancellor in New York City, by a group of professors at Bank Street College of Education who were worried about the school system's testing program. They stated:

From research and from our own experience as educators working with children and teachers, we know that six- and seven-year-old children who are within the scope of normal development demonstrate wide developmental differences. These differences can be seen in all areas of development, including physical growth, psychological maturation, language development and the ability to recognize symbolic representations. Because of these differences we acknowledge that children acquire reading skills and become proficient readers at different rates and in different ways. Children taking longer to learn will naturally score poorly on formal reading tests. This does not necessarily demonstrate a deficiency in learning to read; yet this will be the interpretation.

Yet reading tests are widely used, and for all their faults they do have relevance to the ability to read.

Under circumstances in which students have not been coached in advance on the questions it is a safe bet that children who get higher scores are generally better readers than those who get lower scores. One of several major norm-referenced, nationally standardized reading tests is the California Achievement Test, published by CTB/McGraw-Hill. Here are samples of questions (the correct answers checked) from that test. These particular questions deal with word analysis and the information in the parentheses under the incorrect answers—which does not appear on the actual test—tells the nature of the wrong response.

First Grade
Single Consonants/Oral

Find the word that has the same *beginning* sound as "feet."

vase	fan	tell	tree
○	✓	○	○
(sound confusion)		(begins with ending sound)	(same medial sound)

Second Grade
Compound Words

Find the word that is a compound word.

corner	finding	goodness	airplane
○	○	○	✓
(embedded word)	(affixed word)		

Second and Third Grades
Root Words, Affixes

Find the *suffix* of the underlined word.

played	ed	yed	pl	lay
	✓	○	○	○
		(affix and part of root)	(part of root)	

Second and Third Grades
Short Vowels

Find the word that has the same *vowel* sound as the underlined part.

hill   line   ice   first   pin

                ○   ○   ○   ✓

            (long vowel sound)   (r-controlled vowel sound)

The third grade is generally considered the last year of the teaching of reading fundamentals. In many schools, the students still use an easy reader and a hard reader during this year. As in earlier grades, the readers are accompanied by work sheets and specific tests based on the basal reading series.

More than in the first or second grade, students in the third grade use reading to study other subjects. They no longer just read stories, but do more and more of their reading for subject content of the sort regularly presented in science and social studies in the fourth, fifth, and sixth grades. They may, for instance, read facts about grasshoppers rather than just reading a story about a grasshopper.

Third grade tends to be the final point at which there is emphasis on decoding, that is, figuring out words by the sounds of their letters. Students are supposed to master that skill by the end of the third grade and, theoretically, should be able to pronounce from print almost any word of as many as three syllables, whether or not they know its meaning. Of course, these word-attack skills for sounding out words should be taught in the context of comprehension, so that students know the meaning of what they are reading and are able to use context to figure out the meaning of unfamiliar words. Certainly, parents should give special attention to the problem if a child approaching the end of the third grade is still struggling with decoding.

Students by the third grade are more adept in dealing with prefixes and suffixes and, increasingly, they delve into word origin, exploring the Latin and Greek roots of familiar words.

What is expected of a student's reading ability in the third grade? Perhaps you can get some idea by looking at the following passage that is a sample from a test known as the Degrees of Reading Power. It should be reasonably easy for an able third-grader. The test was developed for the College Board and New York State Education Department by Touchstone Applied Science Associates and is a type of examination now mandated for schools throughout New York State:

Dogs help blind people. Many blind people stay home. They won't go out alone. They are afraid to go out because they cannot see. They think they may fall. They think they may get lost. Such fears are not foolish. There really are many ____1____. Blind people often do need help. But they may not want to ask anyone to help them. They may get a dog instead. It is called a seeing eye dog. It sees for them.

1 a) dangers   b) masters
  c) jobs   d) expense
    e) tests

The ____2____ helps a lot. It is a guard. It is a leader. It is a friend. The dog and its owner go out together. The dog looks. It listens. It thinks. The dog makes sure the way is safe.

2 a) color   b) doctor
  c) animal   d) sound
    e) exercise

The dog must obey. But it must also know when not to obey. Good _____3_____ is important. The owner may say "Go." But a car may be coming. Then the dog must not go.

3 a) progress   b) sense
    c) company   d) food
      e) health

Most dogs cannot be seeing eyes. They would not be able to do this work. They would _____4_____. Seeing eye dogs must be smart. They must be true. Few dogs are chosen for this work. Those that are picked go to school. They have good teachers. They are trained. They work hard. And they _____5_____. Soon they know what to do.

4 a) jump   b) search
    c) hear   d) fail
      e) approach

5 a) drink   b) hunt
    c) learn   d) bark
      e) approach

Many blind people want seeing eyes. But there are very few of these dogs to be had. Somebody who wants a dog must ask for one. Then the person must _____6_____. It may take a long time to get a dog. Months may pass.

6 a) wash   b) dress
    c) wait   d) finish
      e) improve

The dog and its owner will work together. They will live together. So they must get along well. All dogs are not the same. Neither are all people. The dog and its owner must suit each other. For this reaon, the dog must be chosen carefully. A blind person can't be given just any seeing eye dog. It must be the _____7_____ one.

7 a) fastest   b) first
    c) largest   d) right
      e) youngest

Students learn to read more critically in the third grade. They are supposed to be able to read for deeper meaning. They should start exploring the nuances in texts. Increasingly, they look at character development and mood and hidden meanings. Why did the character say this instead of that? What do you think the author was trying to say? Why didn't the story end with this paragraph instead of the next one? They think more seriously about the "clue words" that indicate the sequence in the story and the "clue words" that signal cause and effect. A good reading program has had them digging in to this kind of comprehension since the first grade, but the effort takes on notably more sophistication in the middle elementary grades.

Also, third graders are learning the art of skimming and scanning that adult readers take for granted. They find out that it may not be necessary to read every word of the text to get the meaning. They discover that there are key phrases and that often these phrases are introduced by tip-off words. In other words, in many respects they begin to take on the characteristics of adult readers. The best students are on the verge of reading some rather complex juvenile novels.

By the end of the third grade, students can pronounce aloud the vast amount of what is printed on the front page of a newspaper, pausing perhaps at words like *Chernobyl*. If all has gone well, reading can now be used for obtaining information or entertaining one's self. As Indiana University's Roger Farr put it, the poor readers still think that what reading is about is pronouncing the words correctly and the good readers are reading to find out what is going to happen next.

Parents should continue to supplement the school's effort by discussing with children the books the children have read. Adults must be careful, though, that their questions do not have the quality of a third degree administered at a police station. Reading is supposed to be fun. The kinds of questions to ask are those like: What do you think will happen next (during the reading)?

What did you like about the story? Did you like the idea of the main character wearing the kinds of clothes that the author said he was wearing? How did it make you feel when that happened? That was scary, wasn't it?

Here is a list of books published in 1987 that the American Library Association recommends for students beginning in about the third grade:

Anno's Math Games by Mitsumasa Anno. Putnam/Philomel. Bright, small-scale paintings enliven a creative introduction to mathematical concepts.

Sketching Outdoors in Spring by Jim Arnosky. Lothrop. An artist journeys through spring woodlands with sketches and comments on how to draw subjects in nature.

The Naked Bear, edited by John Bierhorst. Illustrated by Dirk Zimmer. Morrow. An unexpectedly humorous collection of Iroquois legends accessible to a wide range of readers.

Maggie by My Side by Beverly Butler. Dodd. Butler shares the triumphs and woes of training and adjustment when she replaces her recently deceased guide dog.

The Blossoms and the Green Phantom by Betsy Byars. Delacorte; distributed by Doubleday. Junior is building a UFO and needs all the help he can get to launch it—so his family rallies around.

These Small Stones. Poems selected by Norma Farber and Myra Cohn Livingston. Harper/Charlotte Zolotow. Fifty-seven short poems from a variety of sources praise the virtues of small things from marbles to shells, paper clips, and lentils.

Shh! We're Writing the Constitution by Jean Fritz. Pictures by Tomie de Paola. Putnam. A lively, detailed, and compelling account of the conflicts and compromises involved in the Constitution's creation.

From Hand to Mouth; or, How We Invented Knives, Forks, Spoons, and Chopsticks and the Table Manners to Go with Them by James Cross Giblin. Harper/Crowell. The development of eating utensils and why they are used—East and West—are presented in this entertaining, informative history.

An Actor's Life for Me! by Lillian Gish. As told to Selma G. Lanes. Illustrated by Patricia Henderson Lincoln. Viking Kestrel. Gish's beguiling memories of life as a child actress and pioneer film star provide a fascinating glimpse of early-twentieth-century America.

Harry's Mad by Dick King-Smith. Pictures by Jill Bennet. Crown. Harry's legacy from a great-uncle—a parrot called Madison—amazes everyone with his extensive vocabulary and winning personality.

Hating Alison Ashley by Robin Klein. Viking Kestrel. Set in Australia, this funny, sensitive novel portrays an insecure girl's determination to outshine an attractive new classmate who seems to have everything.

Dinosaurs Walked Here: And Other Stories Fossils Tell by Patricia Lauber. Macmillan/Bradbury. Clear color photographs accompany a lucid description of how fossils reveal information about prehistoric plant and animal life.

Tales of Uncle Remus: The Adventures of Brer Rabbit by Julius Lester. Illustrated by Jerry Pinkney. Dial. Forty-eight lively and well-researched tales in modern language are enhanced by jocular illustrations in color and black and white.

Cat Poems, selected by Myra Cohn Livingston. Illustrated by Trina Schart Hyman. Holiday. The many moods and manners of cats are captured in poetry and pictures.

If You Didn't Have Me by Ulk Nilsson. Illustrated by Eva Eriksson. Translated from the Swedish by Lone and George Blecher. Macmillan/Margaret K. McElderry. Amusing episodes chart the subtle growth of a small Swedish boy as he spends the summer on his grandmother's farm while his parents build a new home.

Finn MacCool and the Small Men of Deeds by Pat O'Shea. Illustrated by Steven Lavis. Holiday. Finn and a team of remarkably talented small men solve a giant's problem in fine, high style.

Jump Again! More Adventures of Brer Rabbit by Van Dyke Parks. Illustrated by Barry Moser. HBJ. Witty, evocative watercolors accompany spirited retellings of the well-loved trickster tales.

The Invisible Hunters by Harriet Rohmer. Illustrated by Joe Sam. Children's Book Press. A bilingual retelling of a Nicaraguan folktale symbolically recounts the tragic clash of indigenous and Western cultures.

Fran Ellen's House by Marilyn Sachs. Dutton. The rebuilding of a dollhouse parallels the mending of a newly reunited family first introduced in Sachs's *Bear's House.*

Whales, the Nomads of the Sea by Helen Roney Sattler. Illustrated by Jean Day Zallinger. Lothrop. Personal experience, up-to-date information, and outstanding illustrations combine with a long, much-needed dictionary of the species.

Mars by Seymour Simon. Morrow. Striking, full-color photographs accompany a compelling description of the red planet.

The Friendship by Mildred D. Taylor. Illustrated by Max Ginsburg. Dial. The four Logan children witness a cruel, racist attack on the dignified, stubborn Mr. Tom Bee.

The Z Was Zapped: A Play in Twenty-six Acts by Chris Van Allsburg. Houghton. In dramatic black and white, sculptured letters meet their unexpected fates onstage.

10

GETTING STARTED
IN MATHEMATICS

While the reasons for emphasizing reading in the primary grades are so obvious, parents often find it more difficult to see why mathematics is fundamental. And even if they pay lip service to the importance of math, they are not as zealous about promoting it in the home, doing less than they might to interact with their children in ways that make mathematics pleasurable and part of the everyday natural experience.

One need not search for an explanation for this behavior. Reading is relatively painless for most adults and a tool that they use repeatedly each day. On the other hand, math is not only uncomfortable and baffling for many people, but also fraught with unpleasant memories of lessons not understood and tests that made one feel stupid. Many adults approach mathematics with trepidation, and only with special effort is this negative attitude not passed on to children.

But your offspring deserve and need something better. They should not be saddled with early prejudices against a subject that, along with reading, will be the backbone of their education. Parents must strive to help children gain favorable attitudes toward mathematics and confidence in their ability to solve math problems. This is especially important as far as little girls are concerned. While it remains to be determined whether the higher scores that boys get on standardized tests in mathematics is owed, in part, to any biological distinctions between the sexes, it is beyond dispute that at least a portion of the gap is traceable to differences in the ways boys and girls are treated by their parents.

Parents who are more inclined to discuss mathematical matters with sons than with daughters sow the seeds of this problem. Both mothers and fathers must make extra attempts to include their daughters in any discussions of mathematics or any allusions to math that are made in conversation. Nothing must happen in family settings to lead daughters to conclude that mathematics is a province primarily of boys. The impact of the difference can be readily seen by the time students reach high school, when boys are more likely than girls to take such subjects as calculus and physics. Math anxiety, which affects both males and females, is generally worse among females.

In an era in which technology wields so powerful an influence over human life, it is vital that people be sufficiently comfortable with math to understand and cope with the world around them. Furthermore, the range of occupations for which a basic grasp of math is fundamental is so vast that anyone who shuns math limits career possibilities. Discomfort with math even keeps many people away from computers, an irrational fear in the many instances in which all one has to know to use a computer is how to read the keyboard.

Clearly, math has not been taught as well in schools in the United States as it has been elsewhere, and this is probably why so many people—male and female—are ill at ease with math. On tests given to eighth-grade students in sixteen countries, Americans ranked eighth in arithmetic, ninth in algebra, and thirteenth in geometry.

Harold W. Stevenson, a psychology professor at the University of Michigan, tells us that math problems begin early for children in the United States. By the age of five they are exceeded by their peers in Japan in knowledge of concepts and basic skills. And the difficulties continue. Stevenson and his colleagues tested representative samples of students in the Japanese city of Sendai, the Chinese cities of Beijing and Taipei, and in Chicago. The top 5 percent of a total of 3,500 fifth-graders in the four cities contained only 2 American children, and of all the children in the bottom 5 percent only 13 were *not* Americans.

Predilections are formed in the early grades of elementary school, when pupils set the stage for their level of achievement in math. Wise parents, looking toward the elementary grades, are already—during the preschool years—thinking about the role that math will play in their children's lives. Parents should treat math much as they do reading by making conscientious efforts to build a foundation during the preschool years.

The U.S. Department of Education, in its booklet *What Works,* proposes that learning to count everyday objects, be they buttons in a sewing kit or automobiles on the highway, is an effective basis for early arithmetic lessons. "Just watching the enjoyment children get from songs and nursery rhymes that involve counting is ample evidence of their natural ease," observes the booklet from the federal government. "But counting is not limited to merely reciting strings of numbers. It also includes matching numbers to objects and reaching totals. Children learn to do arithmetic by first mastering different counting strategies, beginning with rote counting and progressing to memorized computations. As children learn the facts of arithmetic, they also learn to combine those facts by using more sophisticated strategies."

Patricia C. Kenschaft, a mathematics professor at Montclair State College in New Jersey and the author of three college textbooks, incorporated math into the lives of her two children from the time they were in diapers, to make it a source of fun and to provide them with a sound start. The approach, along with the genes that their parents provided, must have been right. Her daughter made the highest possible score on the advanced math achievement test of the College Board at the age of sixteen and her son got an A in a college calculus course at the age of fourteen.

What happened in the Kenschaft home? For one thing, the children were encouraged to feel comfortable with math when they were very young. "I explained why x times y equals y times x to both of them while changing a diaper," Kenschaft said. "Of course, I didn't use x's and y's. I asked them to think of two dogs standing in line and consider how we would count the total number of legs. There are two 'fours' of legs, the right legs and the left legs. Or we can think of there being four 'twos' of legs, the front pair of the first dog and the back pair of the first dog, the front pair of the second dog and the back pair of the second dog." After the diaper was changed, Kenschaft said, "I got a piece of paper and showed the child that there was nothing special about two and four; the same thing is true of three and four. Three rows of four dots will equal the same number as four rows of three dots each."

And so it went in the Kenschaft household, where learning early that two fours is the same as four twos was not itself the key that unlocked the path to math achievement, but was characteristic of the kind of interaction that regularly took place. This household with its two gifted children was not the normal family, but nonetheless the Kenschaft experience exemplifies a conceptual approach that parents of all children can present at appropriate times in the development of their children. Kenschaft recalled how her young daughter was once wondering how many holes there were on the door of the clothes dryer. "I showed her how she could count only the number of rows and the numbers of dots in each row and use multiplication to find the number much faster," Kenschaft recalled. "She was so excited that she will always remember the moment."

Math is nothing if not a system of logical thinking. It is best imagined as problem solving. Numbers are manipulated toward a purpose; math is not an idle exercise. Numbers are simply the alphabet of the language of mathematics as letters are for the language in which we read and write poetry. Knowing math makes life easier, just as a calculator makes math itself easier. But a person who has no understanding of concepts is at loss even with a calculator.

The National Council of Teachers of Mathematics, in a working draft it developed for a model curriculum in mathematics, proposed six underlying assumptions for the math instruction during the first four years of school.

The organization said the curriculum during this period should:

- *Be conceptually oriented.* Enable children to acquire clear and stable concepts by constructing meanings in the context of physical situations and allow mathematical abstractions to emerge from empirical experiences. Emphasizing mathematical concepts and relationships means devoting substantial time to the development of understandings.
- *Actively involve children in doing mathematics.* Teachers need to create an environment that encourages children to explore, develop, test, discuss, and apply ideas. K–4 classrooms need to be equipped with a wide variety of physical materials and supplies.
- *Emphasize the development of children's mathematical thinking and reasoning abilities.* The curriculum must take seriously the goal of instilling in students a sense of confidence in their ability to think and communicate mathematically, to solve problems, to demonstrate flexibility in working with mathematical ideas and problems, to make appropriate decisions in selecting strategies and techniques, to recognize familiar mathematical structures in unfamiliar settings, to detect patterns, and to analyze data. Developing these characteristics in children requires that schools build appropriate reasoning and problem-solving experiences into the curriculum from the outset.
- *Emphasize the application of mathematics.* In order for children to view mathematics as a practical, useful subject, they must understand that it can be applied to a wide variety of real-world problems and phenomena. One major purpose is helping children to understand

and interpret their world and to solve problems that occur in it.

• *Include a broad range of content.* Students must possess knowledge of such important branches of mathematics as measurement, geometry, statistics, probability, and algebra. Inclusion of a broad range of content in the curriculum allows children to see the interrelated nature of mathematical knowledge.

• *Make appropriate and ongoing use of calculators and computers.* Calculators enable children to explore number ideas and patterns, to have valuable concept development experiences, to focus on problem-solving processes and to investigate realistic applications. Calculators do not replace the need to learn basic facts, to compute mentally, or to do reasonable paper-and-pencil computation. The power of computers also needs to be utilized in contemporary programs.

Throughout elementary school, computation of numbers is at the core of the math curriculum. Children gradually gain a sense of numeration and grasp the basic concepts of operations involving numbers—adding, subtracting, multiplying, and dividing. They come to see the patterns and relationships between and among numbers. At first, it is essential that students become comfortable with numbers so that counting, grouping, and place value concepts will mean something to them.

Teachers talk of children who come into the first grade spouting such slogans as "three and two is five," but have no understanding of the addition inherent in their words. A teacher at the Trinity School, a leading private school in New York City, remembers an entering first-grader who thought the number 20 was arrived at by combining a 2 and a 0. In kindergarten and first grade the task is to get children to think of numbers not as abstractions, but as representations of quantities. A 5, for example, represents five objects, and when some of those objects are removed the number itself changes.

Teachers should try to get children at this age to recognize and anticipate patterns of numbers that repeat themselves so that they can, for instance, look at 2, 4, 6 and recognize that 8 comes next, or look at 1, 3, 5 and recognize that 7 comes next. In its earliest form this may be pursued with colors, so that the logic is reinforced even if the child is not yet conversant with numbers. Eventually, though, the goal is to get students to recognize regularities in sets of numbers and the relationships of numbers so that youngsters can bring more intuition to their work in mathematics. In their recognition of what quantities equal each other are the seeds from which a knowledge of algebra will grow.

Part of the attempt to instill orderly thinking includes exercises in matching and sorting, determining which objects are alike and which are different. Students are encouraged to see that the same objects can be classified in several different ways. One time a pile of buttons might be sorted by color, another time by shape, and still another time by the number of needle holes in the buttons. Again, the aim is to inculcate concepts and it is but a short step from classifying buttons to classifying groups of numbers.

Geometry, probability and statistics, measurement, estimation, fractions, and decimals fill out the curriculum in the early grades, appearing in only the most rudimentary form in the beginning and, like a balloon into which one blows air, gradually taking familiar form in the upper grades. To the greatest extent possible, everything should be taught in the context of problem solving and reasoning. Mathematics ought to be depicted as just another form of communication.

One example of how a child's knowledge accumulates into the understanding of a mathematical topic can be seen in the approach to geometry. It starts with the recognition of such shapes as circles, squares, triangles, rectangles, cylinders, and spheres. Parents and teachers can use everyday objects as illustrations. For example, the top of a juice can is the perfect circle that can be used to reinforce the lessons that children are given when introduced to geometrical concepts.

Looking at shapes and thinking about them gives children the opportunity to observe, describe, analyze, and test hypotheses. "Parents can ask their children to list objects in the room that are square, round, rectangular, and triangular," suggested Bob Davies, coordinator of mathematics for Stamford Public Schools in Connecticut. "Then parents can discuss the differences among the various shapes with the children. What characteristics does each shape have? What are the relationships between the edges?"

By the second and third grade students will be dividing and combining shapes and figures into smaller and larger units and relating geometric concepts to measurement. They will not actually take a course in geometry until high school, but their success at that point will depend on the background they got in earlier grades.

This approach to building a foundation for further study in mathematics characterizes the entire mathematics curriculum in elementary school. Kindergarten is the formal starting place. By the conclusion of kindergarten, according to a consensus of the curriculums of several school systems, it is desirable that a student be able to do at least the following, though some children will enter kindergarten already having acquired some of these abilities and others will not do so until the first grade:

- Recognize, count, and write numbers from 1 to 10.

- Count backward.

- Have a sense of "greater than," "less than," and "the same as."

- Arrange sets of up to six objects in numerical order.

- Add one or two objects to or take one or two objects from a set of objects and name the number of the resulting set.

- Recognize pennies, nickels, dimes, and quarters.

- Relate some meaning to the concepts of time, weight, length, and volume.

- Read a rudimentary picture graph and make a simple bar graph.

First grade, above all, is a time of adding and subtracting. Students learn to add and subtract both one-digit numbers and two-digit numbers. Some schools limit first-graders to operations that do not require regrouping, or what was once referred to as borrowing and carrying, and do not teach regrouping until the second grade.

It is a time for memorizing "basic facts" so that a child can know, once the underlying concept has been learned, without even having to think about it that 12 minus 7 is 5 or that 4 plus 5 is 9. These facts are to be learned in a way that they come to mind as automatically as those in the multiplication table that they will start memorizing in the second grade.

A key to teaching such concepts is the materials that are used. Books are basic to teaching, but a school that does not make lavish use of blocks, rods, and other tangible items that children can manipulate to visualize the concepts they are trying to learn is not doing all it can to impart concepts.

There is nothing watered down about using manipulative materials, and a school that eschews manipulatives to concentrate exclusively on textbooks and workbooks is not operating in the best interests of the students. Manipulative materials should be extensively available in kindergarten and first grade. They have a place also in second and third grade, and some experts advocate using such materials through the upper elementary grades and into junior high school to enable students to visualize concepts and keep them in mind more easily.

The goal is to provide a concrete representation of an idea, whether it is letting students see what it means to take two away from five or to help teach the meaning of each place in relation to the decimal system. Manipulatives make abstractions and procedures accessible to children by illustrating them. Students see concretely in using a set of Base Ten blocks, for instance, the rationale for regrouping that they must perform in arithmetic and subtraction.

"Learning theories suggest that children whose mathematical learning is firmly grounded in manipulative experiences will be more likely to bridge the gap between the world in which they live and the abstract world of mathematics," said Leonard Kennedy, an education professor at California State University, Sacramento.

On the other hand, just having a lot of materials in the classroom for children to manipulate is not sufficient unless the teacher makes them a purposeful part of instruction. They should be used in ways that are connected to concepts, not as toys. Students should be shown that the outcome is the same and that the concept identical whether the problem is being worked out in a book or with manipulative materials. It is up to a good teacher to be certain that the connection is made.

Ultimately, then, what should a student learn in math during the first grade? Much of the activity will be about putting children at ease with numbers, in much the same way as they grow comfortable with the alphabet in their reading. Numbers, just as letters of the alphabet, should become like old friends to them, breeding the sort of familiarity that will make math a pleasant experience.

Students get to see quantities in sets, as groups of twos and groups of four, for instance. They start thinking of counting by twos or by threes, as well as counting by ones. First-graders are also taught about place value so that they come to understand, for example, in the number 18 that the 8 is in the ones place, the 1 is in the tens place. The stage is set for fractions, even this early, as students are encouraged to think of the halves and quarters that make up a whole object. Also, students get their first taste of ratios, proportions, and percentages.

An important basic concept for first-graders to comprehend is the meaning of the equals sign. They must come to realize that = does not mean "the answer is," as many are inclined at first to think. When they see $5 + 3 = 8$ they must realize that the equals sign means that the numbers on each side of the sign represent the same quantity. Teachers get students to count sets of objects so that they are impressed with the fact that four toy trucks are equal in number to four pencils, for example, and that all sets containing the same number of objects are equal.

First-graders come to understand that they are learning about numbers because numbers help them in their everyday lives. Good teachers should connect mathematics to normal experiences. Measurement takes many forms and six-year-olds pursue most of them—measuring money, time, capacity, weight, temperature, distance. They see that numbers can mean "more than," "later than," "fuller than," "heavier than," "longer than," "hotter than," and "farther than." As adults we take such concepts for granted, but these ideas represent a grand awakening for six-year-olds.

Parents should seize the many opportunities in the course of each day to build on these lessons in measurement through activities with their children. The use of measurement is perhaps one of the earliest ways that children make use of math in their daily activities. Children can be encouraged to measure almost anything in the home. And it does not matter what standard of measurement they use. A child can measure how many steps it takes to walk across the living room and compare that with the number of steps required to walk across a bedroom. The number of spoons, set end to end, that it takes to cover the length of the kitchen table can be compared with the number of spoon lengths required to cover the dining-room table. Once children get to think in terms of units of measurement, it is easy enough for a teacher to move them along to measurement done in feet or meters.

The first-grade curriculum also introduces children to charts, graphs, and statistics. They start organizing information by use of these devices, so that they can understand that there are various ways to represent what numbers are saying. Another facet of the curriculum deals with estimation and probability and statistics, concepts that have gained a firm foothold in the lowest grades in recent years.

Students should see that the worth of estimating is that objects do not have to be counted one by one. They should grow familiar with strategies that allow them to make reliable estimates, just as an adult, looking at an egg carton known to hold a dozen eggs, can tell at a glance when only six eggs remain. Parents can incorporate estimation into many of their conversations with children. How many cups of water do you think are in that pitcher? How many towels do you think that shelf will hold? How many pencils do you think are in that drawer? How many pennies does it look like there are on the dresser?

To reemphasize the point made earlier, much of what pupils do in math from the beginning is oriented toward problem solving. That is perhaps what is most different in today's mathematics from what was taught in many schools a generation ago. The emphasis on problem solving is a tacit statement that math has a purpose and that its usefulness is determined by the extent to which it helps us to make sense out of everyday life. The ways that parents point out mathematical applications to their children will reinforce this point.

There are untold opportunities for parents to make these connections. Little children who help set the dinner table can figure out how many utensils the family will need. As they get old enough to go to school they can be asked to help figure out how much money will be needed for small items they wish to purchase. Once they begin moving through the elementary grades they can be increasingly drawn into conversations involving jobs around the house: when it must be determined how much paint is needed for a room that is to be re-painted, or how much carpeting is required for a floor that is to be covered. Increasingly, parents can cast these questions in the form of problems that are to be solved.

Using problem solving as the context for teaching skills helps motivate students because they can more readily see the reason for learning the skills. The development of reasoning ability is, of course, closely tied to problem solving.

It is desirable that by the end of the first grade a student is able to do the following, though not all children will progress at the same rate:

- Identify the numbers that come before and after any given number from 1 to 100. This, in particular, varies from school system to school system, and some very good systems expect that first-graders' familiarity with numbers will go only to 20.

- Arrange sets from 0 to 10 objects in sequential order.

- Count by twos, fives, and tens to 20.

- Recognize and explain place value of numbers up to 20, in terms of tens and ones.

- Add and subtract single-digit numbers and some two-digit numbers that do not require regrouping.

- Understand the concept of one-half.

- Be able to tell time to the nearest half hour.

- Compare the weights of objects in terms of "heavier than" and "lighter than," and the lengths of objects in terms of "longer than" and "shorter than."

- Write and solve number sentences for number stories.

- Solve word problems involving addition and subtraction facts through the quantity of 10.

In second grade, students build on the lessons in addition and subtraction that were taught in the first grade. An important new feature—though some will already have picked it up in the first grade—will be regrouping to carry numbers when they add and borrow numbers when they subtract. Having started to learn about the place values of numbers in the first grade, they will more easily understand why it is necessary to regroup in order to add and subtract. Knowing the basic concepts of adding and subtracting, they add longer columns of numbers in the second grade and subtract larger numbers. They grow accustomed to having addition problems presented to them not only vertically but horizontally as well, a step toward the form they will see in algebra.

Parents who keep up with what is occurring in mathematics instruction will notice that there is always lots of review—two steps forward, one step backward, two steps forward, one step backward. New math information is parceled out in small quantities and lots of time is spent going over what was taught before—yesterday, last week, last month, and even last year. Should it be this way? Probably so. There must be an element of review in the curriculum since it is the nature of the mind to learn in only small doses and to forget over a period of time. Mathematics being sequential, with one lesson building on another, requires understanding of the last lesson in order to understand the new one.

Review may be approached in different ways, though. A teacher who strives to keep students interested in material that they have already covered can package the numbers in a fresh wrapping. In other words, instead of being given rows of numbers to add and subtract, the student can be presented with a situation confronting a child trying to handle change to make a purchase at McDonald's. The addition or subtraction facts are the ones that are supposed to be reviewed, but the setting of the problem makes it more challenging and less boring.

When is too much time being spent on review? When your child is consistently bored. If this happens, talk to the teacher and see if some of the work can be individualized to prop up your child's flagging interest. On the other hand, if some other children do not get enough review, their parents must be sure that somehow these students shore up their foundation so that they do not fall behind and fail to understand the new lessons. For these children, this could be the time to think about hiring a tutor, and this is discussed in Chapter 25.

Remember, it is not easy for a teacher to deal with the diverse needs in a class of a couple of dozen children when they are progressing at different rates. Once the teacher introduces a new concept to the class in a group lesson, there is usually a need for a great deal of individualization, and parents should monitor the instructional program to be certain that that is happening.

Second-graders are usually introduced to multiplication, and less often to division, leaving the third grade as a place for a full-scale examination of both operations. Because students in the average class move at different rates, some students proceed at a slower pace and may get only a smattering of multiplication in the second grade.

But with at least average progress, the second grade should be a time when students grow comfortable with multiplying all of the numbers up to 5 by each other— $2 \times 2, 2 \times 3, 2 \times 4, 2 \times 5, 3 \times 3, 3 \times 4, 4 \times 5, 5 \times 5$— and begin knowing the product without even thinking about it. Similarly, in division, they should be familiar with twos through the number of twos in 10, threes through the number of threes in 15, fours through the number of fours in 20, and fives through the number of fives in 25.

Essentially, by the end of the second grade it is desirable that a student be able to do the following, though not all will be able to do so:

- Read and write every number up to 100.

- Compare and order whole numbers up to 100.

- Count by ones, twos, fives, and tens to 100.

- Count by odd and even numbers to 100.

- Recognize the pattern of counting by threes.

- Find the sum of three single-digit numbers up to a total of 18.

- Add two multiples of 10 totaling sums up to 90 (for example, 30 plus 50).

- Add two two-digit numbers totaling less than 100 that require regrouping.

- Add three two-digit numbers totaling less than 100 that do not require regrouping.

- Solve addition equations containing a missing addend.

- Subtract two-digit numbers requiring regrouping.

- Subtract two-digit multiples of 10 (for example, 60 minus 20).

- Subtract a one-digit number from a two-digit number when given the problem in horizontal form.

- Solve subtraction equations containing a missing subtrahend.

- Multiply any two numbers up to the number 5.

- Have a sense of symmetry and congruency in shapes and figures.

- Be able to tell time to five-minute intervals.

- Answer questions about information contained in a picture graph.

- Answer questions about the days of a month by looking at a calendar, and use a scale to find the weight of objects.

It is in the third grade that students delve deeply into multiplication and division. An aim is get them to see that multiplication and division are akin to each other, having the same inverse relationship as addition and subtraction, a point that should have been made when they began adding and subtracting in the first grade. One constant throughout the generations has been the memorizing of multiplication tables. Parents may wonder why in the era of calculator there is still the emphasis on rote learning. Isn't it an anachronism?

This is a natural question and educators have good answers. They point out, first of all, that a calculator is not always available. But this is not the most important reason. Students who rely fully on calculators without having committed the basic facts of multiplication to mind are less likely to realize when they have pressed the wrong buttons on the calculator and the device is giving them a wildly wrong answer. Quick mental calculations are a part of everyday life, and having committed the multiplication tables to memory is part of what allows mathematically competent adults to function as smoothly as they do in many situations.

Anyone, child or adult, who does not automatically know the outcome of manipulating certain basic numbers is at a disadvantage, unable to estimate at a glance whether an answer is right, unable to check on the calculator, which is no more accurate than the buttons that are pressed. Thus, students in many schools are asked to memorize the multiplication table through 12×12.

The comprehension that comes from being able to do basic operations by hand gives a student more insight into what directions to punch into the calculator in trying to solve a problem. Calculators definitely have a place in school, though many experts feel that they should be used sparingly before the third or fourth grade, so that students will spend more time performing the operations themselves. After that point, though, calculators can relieve students of tedious calculations in longhand and allow them to use more of the time for thinking about mathematics and solving problems. Also, the calculator tends to motivate many youngsters because it gives them power and relieves the monotony. They can verify computations and better understand computational algorithms by repeated operations on the calculator.

The public schools in Chicago began in 1987 to give calculators to students as they entered the fourth grade. Officials made clear that students would still be expected to be able to perform basic calculations without calculators and would periodically be tested to demonstrate that ability. Parents who are uneasy about the idea of their children using calculators in mathematics should be reassured by the position of the National Council of Teachers of Mathematics, which recommends that "calculators should be available for appropriate use in all mathematics classrooms."

The third grade is when the universe of numbers explodes beyond the hundreds and into the thousands, for many exercises. Students deal with place values in numbers of up to and including five digits. They round off numbers to the nearest tenth or the nearest hundredth. Counting by twos, threes, fours, fives, and tens is part of the routine. Numbers are grouped by tens and by hundreds. Computation continues with the addition and subtraction of four- and five-digit numbers.

Fractions and decimals are important features of third grade. Students add and subtract fractions with like denominators. A good deal of manipulation of fractions is standard in the third grade and students get used to seeing numbers like ½, ⅓, ¼, ⅕, and ⅙. They see that ½ and ²⁄₄ are the same thing, and that ³⁄₃ is the same as 1.

A third-grader should gain a clear notion of exactly what a fraction means in its representation of part of a whole. A good teacher should be relating fractions to familiar aspects of students' lives so that they can more readily understand the concept. For example, the coin we call a quarter is ¼ of a dollar and the half-hour television show is ½ of an hour. Fractions are seen as related to decimals, so that students begin to establish connections between these two systems. A student who recognizes that ¾ is the same as .75 can more easily comprehend that .65 is a little less than ¾ and that .85 is a little more than ¾.

Measurement, too, becomes a bit more complex in the third grade, as the metric system, to which students may or may not have already been introduced, is used increasingly on an interchangeable basis with the nonmetric system. Weight is expressed in kilograms and grams, as well as pounds and ounces, and length is expressed in meters and centimeters, as well as yards, feet, and inches. Some of the measurement is used in a geometric mode, as students learn more about shapes and areas.

A word about the metric system. The United States has given lip service to metrics but remains the only one of the world's major countries that continues to resist full-scale adoption of the system. Instead, an archaic system that borrows and combines imprecise measurements from the Babylonians, the ancient Hebrews, the Egyptians, the Romans, the Vikings, and the English of the Middle Ages produces a crazy quilt of rods and furlongs, feet and inches, pints and pecks. A standard length used today in the United States may be based on nothing more than the distance from the tip of the nose to the extended fingertips of a fourteenth-century English king. While you may not want to convert your thinking to metrics, it is to the benefit of your child for him or her to learn the metric approach.

Besides studying metrics, third-graders are encouraged to become more sophisticated in their use of graphs and charts, setting up their own word problems that can then be put into visual form. Estimation is applied to questions of dimension, distance, quantity, height, and time. Strategies are developed for applying estimation to quantities, measurement, computation, and problem solving. Students come to recognize that estimation gives them the power to know if they are roughly correct or way off base.

Somewhat related is their exploration into the world of statistics and probability. Students take on projects in which they collect, organize, and record information activities that may very well be assigned in the context of a scientific experiment. What is important is that they learn how data is collected and discover that the way that it is organized and recorded is crucial to what can be done with it. In a good classroom there is a spirit of exploration surrounding the use of statistics, as students collect, display, and analyze data. They use statistics to apply the lessons of measurement and their computational ability. Soon it becomes apparent how hypotheses are formed, and they are into studying probability.

This is what it is desirable for students to be able to do by the end of the third grade, though not all will be able to do so:

• Write three-digit numbers in words and numerals.

• Identify place value for numbers below 1,000.

• Add two three-digit numbers that require regrouping.

• Subtract three-digit numbers requiring regrouping.

• Check subtraction by addition.

• Multiply a two-digit number by a one-digit number with regrouping.

- Divide a two-digit number by a one-digit number with a remainder.

- Have an idea of the concept of fractions from ½ through ⅛ and a sense of which fractions are greater and smaller than each other.

- Identify the operation used to solve a word problem.

- Find the missing addend in a number sentence in which the sum is not greater than 50.

- Solve addition and subtraction problems involving dimensions expressed in the metric system.

- Have a sense of the difference between solid figures and plain figures.

- Measure lengths and weigh objects in both American and metric measures.

- Tell time to the minute.

- Be able to compare time between time zones.

- Read both Celsius and Fahrenheit thermometers.

- Add coins and paper money up to a value of $5.00.

- Have a sense of estimating the approximate value of small sums of money without actually adding.

- Have a sense of the decimal system on which money is based.

- Round off numbers to the nearest 10 or 100.

- Solve word problems involving the addition and subtraction of amounts of money.

- Identify the parts of a geometric figure that has been divided into thirds, fourths, or sixths.

- Read graphs and tables for the purpose of gleaning information.

- Do rudimentary coordinate graphing.

Much of the math that follows in the upper elementary grades will essentially be based on these fundamental lessons of the first, second, and third grades. Even the secondary school mathematics curriculum hearkens back to the basic skills acquired in the primary grades. It can readily be seen then that gaining a sound understanding of the math taught in the first three grades is essential to later success in school.

Children who do not attain this grasp may well spend the rest of their days, right into adulthood, struggling with mathematics. And, unfortunately, despising and fearing math. They will avoid advanced courses in mathematics in high school and college. Career options will be closed to them. Thus, parents cannot do enough to make sure this doesn't happen to their children.

11

WORKING WITH
THE STAFF

Helping your child get the most out of school has to mean learning to work with the professional staff at the school to get the most out of them. Ideally, the principal, the teachers, and others in the school will be turned into advocates for your child. As obvious as this may seem, it is not taken to heart by parents to the extent that it ought to be. Thus, while you may think that every set of parents in your child's class is competing for the attention of the teacher, this is seldom the case. A large number of parents, including many who are well educated and should know better, are apathetic or too busy to get involved with the school.

Don't be shy about it; most teachers will welcome your inquiries and will try to cooperate with you. A teacher usually looks favorably upon children whose parents show interest in their education, so long as the parents are not aggressive.

A word about teachers. More than those in most

white-collar occupations, teachers do not feel appreciated. They are paid an average annual salary of $28,085 (salary statistics are from the American Federation of Teachers), and in most cases the conditions of their employment are difficult and somewhat unpleasant. An elementary school teacher especially has almost no free time and seldom gets the kind of breaks during the working day that other kinds of workers take for granted. This is a situation inconceivable to the many workers accustomed to jobs in which they can strike up occasional conversations with fellow employees, grab a cup of coffee now and then, and perhaps take a stroll down the hall for a breather.

For elementary school teachers, there are no strolls, no coffee breaks, and, except for lunch, few conversations with other adults. While a teacher has considerable freedom in running a classroom, the teacher, nonetheless, is confined to that room and must be constantly vigilant to the needs of twenty-five to thirty children. Few teachers are ever released to attend professional conferences during the day, and they almost never travel in behalf of their work as so many other professionals do.

A poll of the nation's teachers by Louis Harris and Associates in 1986 showed that teachers were so dissatisfied that 55 percent of them seriously considered leaving the field for another occupation. As for steps that might encourage able teachers to remain on the job and attract additional good people into teaching, "providing a decent salary" was mentioned by 94 percent of the respondents. Seventy-nine percent said that smaller class size also would help, a not surprising response considering the large number of children for whom they are asked to be responsible.

All in all, teachers have little power over the circumstances in which they labor. They realize they are not held in high esteem by a society prone to measure accomplishment in terms of dollars. Their morale often sags because they do not end up feeling good about themselves. They are not even able to keep up with developments in their field the way they would prefer and are sensitive to the possibility that their professional knowledge is not as current as it should be.

Parents, then, should be aware of these enormous pressures on the men and women who teach their children. In their dealings with teachers, parents should remember that they are talking to very beleaguered people who will respond well to a pat on the back, people who want to cooperate if shown the respect they crave. Teachers get little recognition for the important contribution they make and sometimes wonder if anyone really cares about the work they do.

A parent's main reason for keeping in touch with the school and with the teacher should be to keep track of how a child is doing in coping with the curriculum. Parents who really want to get involved in the education of their children should strive to learn about the curriculum in each subject, getting a sense of approximately what sort of work their children are doing in a particular subject at any given time. This is the key to helping children with homework. It also is an important way of monitoring a child's progress to be sure that the child is not having a problem that is going unattended.

By contacting the teacher at the start of the school year, a parent can learn of the lessons for the weeks ahead and get some understanding of what is to be covered. Then, by keeping an eye on papers and assignments that the child brings home, the parent can see how the child is doing. Telephone calls to the teacher every few weeks can be helpful in remaining up-to-date. Some parents might even want to meet with the teacher every month or so and go through the pages of the books in the various subjects with the teacher, so as to have an idea what their children will be facing.

Remember, though, any conferences with a teacher, by phone or in person, should be at the teacher's convenience, not the parent's. There is little flexibility in an elementary school teacher's schedule to allow conferences or meetings with parents during the school day, except on days that have been designated for this purpose. Thus, let the teacher tell you what might be the best time for a meeting. The early morning, before the school bell rings, or the late afternoon, after dismissal, are probably convenient for the teacher. Some teachers are amenable to telephone conversations from their homes in the evening, but contacts of this sort should be at the option of the teacher. If the teacher says it is all right to call at home in the evening, then go ahead and do it, but don't take advantage.

Conferences with the teacher about a student's progress are valuable and parents might wish to seek such meetings—at least by telephone—more often than they are formally scheduled by the school. Some schools build periodic teacher-parent meetings into the schedule each time grade reports are released. In fact, at some elementary schools the conferences substitute for report cards.

A list of suggestions to help parents make the most of conferences with their children's teachers was prepared by the National Education Association and the National PTA. These groups recommend that parents talk with their children before the conference to find out which subjects the children like and dislike and why. Also, children can be asked what they would like their parents to discuss with teachers. These are questions that the NEA and the PTA propose that parents ask of teachers in conferences:

- Is my child in different groups for different subjects? Why?

- How well does my child get along with others?

- What are my child's best and worst subjects?

- Is my child working up to his or her ability?

- Does my child participate in class discussions and activities?

- Have you noticed any sudden changes in the way my child acts? For example, have you noticed any squinting, tiredness, or moodiness that might be a sign of physical or other problems?

- What kind of testing is being done? What do the tests tell about my child's progress? How does my child handle taking tests?

- What specific suggestions do you have to help my child do better?

Open-school night is the time when parents play students and settle in at their children's desks to be addressed by the teacher. The many divorced parents awkwardly try to cooperate in pursuit of their children's best interests, and the teacher looks around the room trying to connect the faces of the parents she sees with the faces of the children lodged in her memory. Afterward, the parents flock around the teacher at the front of the room, seeking tidbits of information about their children. That is a mistake.

Such a gathering is an inappropriate forum for intimate conversation about an individual child. Parents who try to use it in that way put the teacher on the spot and rudely rob other parents of the time they might spend greeting the teacher. Open-school night is a time only to shake hands, say hello, issue a few thank-yous, and say that you will be in touch. Leave it at that.

In addition to whatever other contact a parent has with a teacher, it is worth trying to get admitted to the classroom to observe during the regular school day once or twice a semester. Some teachers are comfortable with this and others find it disruptive and perhaps even a threat. Broach the idea and then take your cue from the teacher. Don't try to force your way into the classroom, because this could be counterproductive.

Once in the classroom, sit quietly and be as unobtrusive as possible, participating only to the extent that the teacher solicits your involvement. The experience of spending an hour or two in the classroom should be revealing, though the presence of a visitor inevitably has some effect on the ambiance and certainly on the deportment of one's own child that day. Nonetheless, it soon becomes clear what sort of rapport the teacher has with the students and what the teacher's teaching style is like. The lessons being taught tell parents more about the class than they are likely to learn from asking their children. Allan Shedlin, Jr., executive director of the Elementary School Center, based in New York City, offered these questions to bear in mind when assessing an elementary school:

- Do the children and adults seem happy—that is, generally pleased to be in the school?

- Are differences in children's learning styles, developmental levels, and interests considered in terms of teaching styles and curricular adaptations?

- Do students and adults within the school have mutual regard and respect for one another?

- Does the pace of the school day allow time for relaxation, for imaginative activities, and for pondering?

- Is the process of learning valued as much as the outcome?

- Is there an interest in fostering cooperation and collaboration?

- Does the physical environment indicate an appreciation of children and their work?

- Does the teacher take advantage of opportunities to interrelate and interconnect different areas of the curriculum to show that they are interdependent?

- Do the teachers and principal appreciate and encourage the parental role?

- Is the principal's presence felt and perceived as supportive, enabling, encouraging, firm, kind, and consistent?

- Are school rules and regulations clearly stated?

Observations, conferences in person and by phone, and casual contacts all help build a relationship between parent and teacher. Occasional notes to the teacher raising questions, remarking on the child's progress, complimenting the teacher's work, or making suggestions may also be part of the process. It is almost certain that a parent who is better known to a teacher, who has worked at showing an interest, being supportive and building a relationship, is going to have an entrée to a teacher when it is needed. And the learning needs of a child of such a parent may well get a little more attention.

The National Committee for Citizens in Education, an advocacy group to help parents in dealing with schools, prepared a list of the following steps that parents can take to help motivate teachers:

- Be sensitive and responsive to the needs and values of the individual teacher.

- Give teachers recognition for the good things that they do.

- Make educator-of-the-year awards a common practice in the school district.

- Attend parent-teacher conferences and school functions on a regular basis.

- Treat school personnel as professionals and appreciate the complexity and importance of their work.

- Organize social activities for parents and teachers in settings where they can talk to each other.

- Establish teacher appreciation programs at each school.

- Write letters of appreciation to teachers who show a special interest in their students.

• Write letters to the editor of your newspaper, stating what's right with schools and teachers.

In all of the ways that parents choose to be involved in the school, especially in dealings with their children's classroom teachers, there is a line they must be careful not to cross so that they do not end up being aggressive. Common sense ought to indicate the location of that boundary, and parents would be wise to respect it. To exceed the line might mean running the risk of making one's self and one's overtures unwelcome.

Unfortunately, there may come a time when a parent finds a reason to doubt a teacher's judgment, when a parent is unsure that the child is progressing as he or she ought to be. Usually, a teacher can be counted on to give a fair and accurate appraisal of each student, but independent feedback from someone other than the classroom teacher may be needed when a parent doesn't feel right about the opinions of the teacher.

One way to get such feedback is to take your child to a private educational psychologist who will conduct an independent appraisal, based mostly on interviews and tests that the psychologist will administer to the child. The procedure costs several hundred dollars. You might also want to talk with the psychologist about strategies the school ought to be following to be more helpful to the child. Another possibility is to hire a tutor to meet with the child after school (more about this in Chapter 25). An experienced tutor, who usually checks with the teacher about the material being covered in school, can often be helpful to a parent in determining whether the child's needs are being properly met at school.

One problem with all this is that the child's regular teacher, on finding out what the parent is doing, may be uneasy with the notion of being checked up on. Like most people, teachers do not like having their expertise doubted. Thus, a parent should be cautious in this sort of intervention, trying to minimize any ill feelings by the teacher. The child, after all, must spend the rest of the term with the teacher and resentment against a parent could very easily affect the teacher-pupil relationship.

In normal circumstances, the student's deportment in class has much to do with the tenor of that relationship, and it is worth the time for a parent to talk with a child about how well he or she is getting along with the teacher. A teacher's interest in a student is reinforced when the child is cooperative and shows an interest in school. The teacher wants to feel that his or her effort is not for naught. Good conduct in class and doing homework assignments are important ways that pupils can impress teachers with the seriousness of their intent.

Showing up on time for school and being absent as seldom as possible also have a favorable effect on a teacher's attitude. Youngsters should learn to take responsibility in these areas, but parents can help their children develop positive attitudes toward school. Talking favorably about the teacher at home is important, for example, as is the need for parents to be up with the child in the morning to make certain that the child is not running late and is setting off for school in a good frame of mind.

Every parent ought to consider not only joining the school PTA, but taking an active role in it. The school's formal parents' group has the potential to be a significant force in the operation of a school, though more often such groups tend not to assert themselves. But if the time ever comes that cooperative action by parents is needed, it will be easier to get something done if a potent organization is already in existence. If parents do not give their time to such an organization they will not have a collective voice in the school.

This is not to say that principals and teachers all welcome such activism by parents. Enlightened educators realize that involved parents can be an asset, but some less secure educators feel it just adds to their headaches if parents are embroiled in school affairs.

A survey of the attitudes of parents and elementary school principals found that many of the kinds of activities in which parents were interested in becoming involved were not considered to be useful to the school by the principal. For instance, 72 percent of parents thought there should be a role for parents in evaluating the teachers and principals, but only 23 percent of the principals considered this useful. Fifty percent of the parents thought there should be parental input in hiring a principal, but only 11 percent of the principals agreed. Eighty-two percent of parents were interested in a role in evaluating the learning of their children, but only 31 percent of the principals thought this useful.

Finally, from the view of self-interest, individual parents gain from being active in such an organization as a PTA, because they have one more way to exert influence on behalf of their children. Getting involved in the PTA is akin to Teddy Roosevelt's admonition of speaking softly and carrying a big stick. The school personnel know very well which parents are influential, and usually it is not necessary for those parents to speak very loudly in order to be heard.

Which brings us to the principal, a kind of odd-man-out in all this. The principal has to contend with the parents on one side and the teachers on the other. It can be a rather lonely and isolated job. Like the classroom teacher, the principal should be cultivated as an advocate for your child. This is not a matter of being manipulative or thinking you are Machiavelli, it is an acknowledgment of reality.

Each principal operates a sort of fiefdom, paying tribute to the superintendent, but having considerable latitude in running the school. The children in an elementary school are powerless; they are not even big enough to intimidate anyone. School systems are like the Kremlin in their hierarchical nature. The power flows down from the top. Almost none of it—in an elementary school especially—gets to the students, who occupy a role not unlike the serfs in the Middle Ages. So the lowly little student in an elementary school needs allies wherever they can be found. The principal is a good one to have on the side of any child.

A parent dissatisfied with some act by a teacher should be wary, though, about going to the principal about the matter. Such contact should be held in reserve as the ultimate weapon, to be put into service only after the barricades have given way and there seems to be no other way to protect the child. No teacher is going to be pleased with a child whose parent takes a complaint to the principal, just as no worker in any job welcomes someone going to the boss about his or her performance. Such intervention may be appropriate in unusual situations, but parents should carefully gauge when those moments have arrived.

On some issues, though, a parent should not hesitate in dealing with the principal. For example, the principal is the one to approach in the spring for a conversation about getting your child assigned to a specific teacher for the following fall. Parents should be assertive about this when they have good information that allows them to determine that a child's needs will best be served in a particular class.

Also, the principal can help get special services to which your child is entitled, whether it means making sure the bus stops at a certain corner or getting the child an appointment with one of the system's speech therapists. The principal can explain the procedures for securing extra services for a student, or at least refer the parent to the proper person. You should not be bashful about seeking such services; they are available to youngsters who qualify and the school system budget covers the costs.

When all else has failed and a parent cannot get satisfaction from the teacher or the principal, it is probably time to turn to the superintendent or a member of the board of education. The board members are the private citizens appointed or elected to perform in their positions as a kind of public service. The superintendent is the professional educational executive the school board hires to run the school system. Neither the superintendent nor a member of the school board should be contacted for help except as a last resort.

Finally, a parent who can find no source of redress in a local school system might want to turn to a national organization. This is not likely to happen, but in case it ever does—or if you simply are seeking general information—these are some groups to contact:

American Civil Liberties Union, 132 W. 43rd Street, New York, N.Y. 10036

Children's Defense Fund, 1520 New Hampshire Avenue N.W., Washington, D.C. 20036

Council for Exceptional Children, 1920 Association Drive, Reston, Va. 22091

Mexican American Legal Defense Fund, 145 9th Street, San Francisco, Calif. 94103

NAACP Legal Defense and Educational Fund, 10 Columbus Circle, New York, N.Y. 10019

National Committee for Citizens in Education, 410 Wilde Lake Village Green, Columbia, Md. 21004

United States Department of Education, Office for Civil Rights, 400 Maryland Avenue S.W., Washington, D.C. 20202

This chapter has tended to portray the parent as an adversary of the school system, but this is only because of the importance to parents of understanding what they can do when the needs of their children are not being met. In general, schools and the people who work in them tend to cooperate with the families they serve. But parents must be prepared to act on those occasions when the response from the school is unsatisfactory.

12

SCHOOL POLICY AND EDUCATIONAL PHILOSOPHY

Schools are governed by rules, sometimes arbitrary, affecting most facets of life in the building. Teachers are told what to teach and how to teach it. Procedures stemming from collective bargaining contracts dictate the maximum number of students in each class and the extent to which teachers may be assigned extra duties. Rules outline the ways to deal with pupil absences, and report cards are distributed at prescribed intervals. A schoolwide testing program mandates certain tests on certain days, whether or not teachers want them.

In other words, a tightly woven web of regulations provides the framework within which teaching and learning occur. This is not to say that creative teachers have no room to influence what happens in their classrooms. The degree of restrictiveness varies from school to school and most teachers have leeway for maneuverability. Some, though, are so accustomed to being told what to do that they do not recognize and exercise the flexibility available to them. Others who might prefer to be creative have been thwarted so often by unreasonable administrators that they have resigned themselves to maintaining the status quo.

Furthermore, the force of the regulations is not always what it might appear at first glance. Some policies are so capricious that a serious challenge would expose the subjectivity on which they are predicated. In this category, for instance, are questions of whether a student is promoted or has to repeat a year.

Though certain rules for running the school may be arbitrary, there is a need for governance of some sort to assure that a structure exists within which education may take place. Rules regarding absences and tardiness, for instance, are necessary. Though parents may not agree with the way the school deals with absences and tardiness, it will make life a lot easier for their children to adhere to the rules. Anyway, being late to school or absent without cause is not in a child's interest and parents ought to strive to see that neither happens.

Students in elementary school are still so dependent on their parents that essentially it is the parents, not the children, who are responsible for making certain that children are at school on time and not absent without cause. In high school, when students are older and relatively independent, it is another matter and the students themselves should assume much of the responsibility for their attendance.

In essence, this means that parents must instill good habits in their children so far as attendance is concerned. They should help children see that getting to school on time and not missing school is a matter of being responsible. It is desirable to help youngsters establish routines that they can follow at night just before they go to sleep and in the morning right after they awake to ensure that they will have enough time to get to school. Furthermore, children should learn that going to school is their job at this point in life and that a worker does not miss a day at the job without cause.

The school keeps records on your child, listing information not only about attendance, but also concerning test scores, teachers' observations, special requests made by you to the school, and reports on the child by members of the staff, including psychologists and social workers. Increasingly, these records are kept by computer. Schools use the data to monitor the student's performance so that teachers can ensure that the child is making suitable progress and receiving appropriate services. You have a right under federal law to examine your child's records. If a school does not have such records and does not know how its students are doing, then it is not fully serving them.

In part, this record keeping involves keeping track of the student's scores on tests administered periodically to see how the student is doing compared with peers. Parents should realize that there is a tendency in many school districts to administer nationally standardized tests more frequently than necessary. While it is good to assess students and to monitor their progress, there are limits to the usefulness of these tests, especially before the fourth grade.

First of all, valuable instructional time is lost to district-wide or statewide tests, which may eat up several days of instruction over the course of a school year. Furthermore, most nationally normed, standardized tests reveal very little about the individual child that is used in a diagnostic way. Finally, the tests are somewhat flawed even in what they say about your child. The test may be

outdated or students may have received so much practice preparing for the test that it is no longer a measure
of achievement.

There are several ways in which scores on national
tests might be reported:

• *Grade equivalent.* This is an indication of the grade
level represented by a student's performance on a test.
The scale ranges from 1.1 for the first month of the first
grade to 12.9 for the last month of the twelfth grade. A
score of 2.8 for a second-grader who took the test in April
means the child is exactly at the average of the national
student population on which the test was normed. The
2 means second grade and the .8 means the eighth
month of the school year, which would be April. A score
of, say, 3.7 for the same child means he or she reads at a
level ahead of the average second-grader, which—based
on the number of correct items beyond the average—
has been extrapolated to represent a third-grader in the
seventh month of the school year. But this extrapolation,
whether the score is above or below grade level, is
merely an imprecise indicator of being above or below
average.

• *Percentile ranking.* A score at the 50th percentile is
exactly at the midpoint for all students in the grade in
the normed population. Anything higher than this score
is therefore above average. A score at the 62nd percentile, for instance, means the student did better on the
test than 61 percent of the students in the same grade in
the country and worse than 38 percent. In contrast, a
score of 45 percent means the student did better than 44
percent of the students in the same grade in the country
and worse than 55 percent. Because the score is based
on a national population and not the student's class-

mates, it is possible for a student to score at the 70th percentile, exceeding 69 percent of the students in the country, and still have the lowest standing in his or her class, if everyone in the class scored at the 71st percentile or higher.

• *Stanine.* This reporting method divides the range of scores along a continuum of nine parts, with the lower scores in the first stanine and the highest in the ninth stanine. The first, second, and third stanines are below average; the fourth, fifth, and sixth stanines are average; and the seventh, eighth, and ninth are above average. Of course, the eighth is further above average than the seventh, and the ninth is further above average than the seventh or the eighth. Many experts regard stanines as the most meaningful way to report nationally normed standardized test results.

• *Criterion-referenced.* These scores are reported in terms of ability to perform specific tasks. For example, it might be reported that 63 percent of the students in a particular grade around the country knew the definition of a particular word or that 41 percent of the students could answer correctly a question intended to reveal understanding of a passage they read. A student who answers the question on the definition correctly, for example, knows that this was a question that 63 percent of his or her peers got right.

Tests and the teacher's judgment about performance in class determine whether a student is to be promoted at the end of the school year from one grade to the next. Some school systems use test scores as a basis for holding back students, declaring that those who cannot attain a minimum score must be retained to repeat the grade.

Sometimes it is beneficial for a student to repeat a grade, but more often it is a detriment. Parents should be chary of allowing their children to be retained in a grade. Statistics show, for one thing, that children who are held back become the ones most likely to drop out of school. Also, because development is so uneven in the early years of elementary school, it is unreasonable to expect that elementary school children of the same age will exhibit the same rate of academic proficiency. An elementary school should be sufficiently attuned to individual differences to accommodate variations in achievement. Students who develop more slowly should be given time to catch up with their peers without having to hold them back, though there are some occasions when retention is necessary.

One way for a school to deal with the uneven rates of development in the early elementary years is not to organize the school into first, second, and third grades. Instead, the children can be assigned to classes in which the age groups are mixed and each youngster advances through the curriculum at his or her own rate.

What counts is that by about the end of third grade all students have exceeded the same point of minimum achievement to assure that they can handle the curriculum in the upper grades. Few school systems offer this nongraded approach, but where it exists, parents should give it serious consideration. Non-gradedness is a more realistic approach to teaching and learning and makes it unnecessary to be concerned about questions of promotion before the fourth grade.

The marks used to rate students and determine their promotions are another aspect of imprecise measurement. How much difference is there really between a pupil who gets a B and one who gets a C, or one who gets a 72 and one who gets a 67? No matter how much authority a school seeks to give to these marks they are no more than rough ratings. A very strong case can be made for not assigning marks in the lower elementary grades.

A danger involving marks is that the self-image of students is at stake. Those with the lowest marks may come to see themselves in ways that make it increasingly difficult to achieve. Parents should do all they can to bolster the confidence of youngsters who get low marks. However, while parents should not put too much emphasis on marks, they should not disregard them either. As long as the school takes marks seriously, students must attach some importance to them. It is certainly preferable that a child have good marks than bad ones.

Particular attention should be paid to a child's achievement in the third and fourth grades. Teachers find that some students go into a prolonged slump in the grades midway through elementary school. Speculations vary as to the causes. One explanation has to do with the fact that in many schools the work tends to get more demanding as students move from having mastered the basic skills in the lower elementary grades into more actively applying them to complex problems in the upper elementary grades. Perhaps the emotional needs of youngsters start to change more profoundly at this point, too. In any event, it is a time when parents must keep especially close tabs on the progress of their children and respond quickly to signs of lagging motivation.

How the teacher deals with a student's self-image has a great deal to do with the student's attitude. A teacher should be looking for ways to help children find and enjoy success. Such a teacher uses praise, but not in a lavish and unrealistic manner so that it becomes meaningless. Children should be made to feel as though they belong and are fully accepted members of the class. When they misbehave or make errors the teacher corrects them in a positive and supportive manner. These are characteristics of teachers who do *not* motivate students, and parents ought to keep close watch on such teachers:

- Rigid and narrow concept of education and teacher duties.

- Belief that learning is attained only through hard work and that learning need not be enjoyable.

- Belief that the disposition to learn is solely up to the student.

- Lessons that appeal only to intellectual concerns and ignore drama and emotion.

- Limited variety of teaching strategies.

- Lack of student-centered activities.

- Narrow means for students to demonstrate competency.

- Lack of preassessment prior to providing instruction.

- Infrequent provision for individualized and personalized instruction.

- Preoccupation with standards.

- Inflexibility.

- Emphasis on power and control by the teacher.

- Ignoring the needs of the nonachiever.

The instructional philosophy in the school will help determine whether students remain motivated throughout their elementary years. A school that acknowledges the differing rates of development in elementary-age children will create a climate in which students are encouraged to work at their own level and enjoy what they are doing. The teacher will use the interests of individual students to help guide each in a direction that will lead toward effective learning.

Parents may find that students are taught to read in groups arranged according to how advanced the children are. Those who read best may be in one group, those who read worst in another, with the remainder in groups in between the extremes. This homogeneous grouping makes it easier for the teacher and may be beneficial to students, since children are more likely to get the attention they need if the range of reading ability in a group is narrowed.

But parents should monitor the use of grouping to make certain it is not used to the child's detriment. When there are reading groups at several different levels in a class, there should be sufficient flexibility that a student who improves has the chance to move up to another group. Too often students in the lower groups get less demanding work and cover less material than those in higher groups. As a result, the neediest students are deprived of the depth they need to keep from falling further behind, creating a self-fulfilling prophecy, in which lower-achieving students are doomed to achieve less because they are given less. Grouping can be an effective instructional device, but it must be meticulously monitored.

Also, parents should object if the school is assigning students to classrooms based on reading ability, putting the worst readers in one classroom for all their subjects and the best readers in another classroom for all their subjects. Instead, parents should seek classes that have a wider range of abilities and where grouping for all subjects is not based solely on reading ability.

Another important aspect of class organization has to do with the amount of time devoted to instruction. A significant portion of the time students spend in class has little to do with learning their subjects. Teachers are taking attendance, giving instructions about how to walk down the hall to the cafeteria, collecting signature cards that parents were supposed to sign, handing out papers, waiting for students to put on coats and take off coats, directing students to put away the books and materials for one subject and take out those for another subject.

Experts who have monitored classrooms have found that huge chunks of time are lost to these noninstructional activities. Some of this time loss is inevitable, but much of it can be avoided. It is up to teachers to try to minimize the loss of instructional time and to try to ensure that the time devoted to learning tasks is protected from erosion by housekeeping activities.

Thus, each classroom bears some resemblance to a small business. It has a culture of its own, with a pervading tone set by the teacher, who is analogous to the boss or chief executive officer. There are expected patterns of behavior. The workers, who are the students, must follow rules for performing the various tasks, and if they do not they are subject to reprimand.

Good bosses tend as much as it is practical to let each employee act as a self-employed entrepreneur, so long as the employee produces and works within the rules. Good teachers, no less, should let students be independent and lead them to take a good portion of the responsibility for their own learning.

13

THE GIFTED AND TALENTED

Having a gifted or talented child confers a special responsibility on a family. It is akin to owning a rare plant that should receive intensive nurturing. Parents must take on much of the responsibility for ensuring that the special needs of their gifted and talented children are taken into account by the school. Most children, after all, are not gifted and schools are set up to serve the average child.

Experts remind us that giftedness takes many forms and that it is a mistake to think of it only in terms of a high IQ. The U.S. Department of Education proposed a wider definition for the gifted that has now become generally accepted and includes the talented. In addition to those of high intellectual ability, the grouping comprises children who have unusual attributes in a specific academic subject, or creative thinking ability, or leadership ability, or special talent in the visual or performing arts, or unusual physical abilities.

A theory gaining wide attention in regard to the variegated forms of giftedness is that of Howard Gardner, a psychologist at Harvard University and author of *Frames of Mind: The Theory of Multiple Intelligences.* As the title of the book implies, Gardner maintains that intelligence can manifest itself in a variety of ways. Parents would do well to take note of this theory, because they might otherwise tend to overlook signs of giftedness in their children.

Some of the kinds of intelligence Gardner describes, for example, involve spatial intelligence that allows one to use art to re-create, transform, or modify visual perceptions; music intelligence that gives one unusual sensitivity to melody, rhythm, tone, and pitch; and kinesthetic intelligence that leads to using the body in extraordinary ways. In other words, an Andy Warhol or a Vladimir Horowitz or an Earvin "Magic" Johnson has gifts that are every bit as notable as those that show up on the standard paper-and-pencil tests of intelligence. Many talents do not lend themselves to measurement on an IQ test.

A special word about intellectually gifted children. They often bear an extra burden, differing from their peers in ways that may cause them to incur the displeasure of other children and sometimes of adults, too. Parents of such children usually have a notion of their children's specialness even before they start school. Intellectually gifted children are apt to perform feats that set them apart when they are still of preschool age. By drawing comparisons with other children of the same age, parents may see that their youngsters speak in more complex sentences and use more extensive vocabularies. They may also read earlier and show an unusual amount of curiosity. They recognize cause-and-effect relationships to which their peers are largely oblivious.

A goal should be to make sure that giftedness gets the attention it should at school. There is a difference between being smart and being intellectually gifted. One measure—and by no means the only one—of giftedness is a score on an IQ test. Under most circumstances, a score of 135 is on the threshold of giftedness and any child with at least that score ought to be further examined by experts to determine whether or not the youngster is gifted. Similarly, there is a large difference between being a child who likes to draw and one who exhibits rare promise as an artist.

Even the young Albert Einstein was not immediately recognized as gifted. All too often, a child's extraordinary promise is overlooked. A gifted or talented student who is shy, for example, may not allow his or her talents to flourish, and one who is bored may falsely be labeled as lazy.

For intellectually gifted children, especially, knowledge is its own reward; creativity is often their hallmark. From the very beginning they are unlike other children. Once they reach school, their attention span is longer, their learning rate is faster, their potential for abstraction is greater, their sensitivity is keener, and their need for exploration in depth is overwhelming. They flourish in the classrooms of teachers who engage them in critical thinking and encourage them to go off in whatever directions their curiosity provokes. Their drive for perfection makes them fearful of mistakes and they are discomfited by the mental capacities they possess but do not yet fully comprehend.

Gifted children often perform difficult tasks more easily than their classmates and are able to do work equivalent to that being done by older children. By the upper elementary grades many gifted children often are able to do work well beyond their grade level. Thus, if their special abilities have not been recognized they are probably not being adequately stimulated. Boredom is a problem for gifted students of all ages when they are not challenged. Teachers who emphasize drills and leave little room for creativity rob the gifted of their motivation.

Giftedness should be cultivated. Parents should do all they can to make sure the school gives such children room to flourish. They must not be stifled. There is evidence that failure to nurture high intellectual ability can cause it to wither. Some fifteen years ago, a commissioner of the U.S. Office of Education, Sidney P. Marland, Jr., concluded in a report to Congress: "We are increasingly being stripped of the comfortable notion that a bright mind will make it on its own. Intelligence and creative talent cannot survive educational neglect and apathy."

In practice, this should mean that when gifted and talented children enter school, their special nature is recognized and the school does what it can to stimulate their unusual attributes. Be wary of a school that says it gives no extra attention to the gifted and talented. Parents of such students should expect that the school will offer their children the opportunity to go as far as their abilities will take them. Giftedness must never be converted into a liability.

An obstacle confronting parents of the gifted and talented is the attitude of those who feel that students of exceptional promise should not get attention that is not bestowed on all children. Lewis M. Terman, the pioneer in education of the intellectually gifted, who began a long-term study of gifted children in 1921, remarked more than fifty years ago that "it is a curious fact that special classes for bright children are strenuously opposed by a few of the country's leading educational authorities. Their opposition seems to derive from an extreme democratic bias."

Society has no reservation about spending some $4 billion a year on remedial education for the disadvantaged. In turn, there should be no qualms about extra funds for the gifted. There are national organizations that are advocates for the gifted and talented, and parents who are stymied in efforts to get a proper education for their children or need more information of any kind should consult one of these groups:

Council for Exceptional Children
The Association for the Gifted
1920 Association Drive
Reston, Va. 22091
703-620-3660

Gifted Child Society, Inc.
190 Rock Road
Glen Rock, N.J. 07452
201-444-6530

National/State Leadership Training Institute on the
  Gifted
642 S. Grand Avenue
#1007
Los Angeles, Calif. 90017
213-489-7470

Gifted Children Advocacy Association
P.O. Box 115
Sewell, N.J. 08080
609-582-0277

National Association for Gifted Children
4175 Lovell Road
Suite 140
Circle Pines, Minn. 55014
612-784-3475

MENSA Gifted Children Program
5403 1st Place North
Arlington, Va. 22203
703-527-4293

In addition to the above-mentioned groups, there is in the education department of each state government a person who oversees programs for the gifted at the state level. The name and phone number of this person can be obtained by calling the office of the state superintendent or commissioner of education.

Parents who suspect their children are gifted should ask school personnel to interview the child, observe the child in class, and administer appropriate assessments. Incidentally, more than testing should be used to identify the gifted. If the school refuses to use such measures then parents should take their children to private psychologists for evaluation.

Joseph S. Renzulli of the University of Connecticut, an authority on the gifted, suggests that giftedness should be seen in terms of the convergence of three traits: above-average general ability, task commitment, and creativity. The test scores of gifted students are not necessarily extremely high, because sometimes giftedness may not be easily measured by tests. But they do have general abilities that are above average. The gifted have the capacity to get absorbed in tasks that interest them to a degree far beyond that of most people. Gifted people are not merely smart and accomplished; they possess an originality of thought and an ability to make fresh connections in their insights.

Educators debate the question of how best to serve the gifted and talented in elementary school. There is no one way and these are some of the main possibilities:

• *Acceleration.* Students can be allowed to skip to higher grade levels than their age would normally dictate.

• *Enrichment.* Students can remain in the age-appropriate grade, but be given instruction, assignments, and freedom that enable them to go into greater depth and move further along than others of the same age. In theory, it is possible for this to happen without removing a gifted or talented child from the regular class.

• *Homogeneous grouping.* Students can attend separate classes or special schools limited to gifted and talented students so that what they study is, where appropriate, accelerated and enriched in the normal course of events. A related approach is to bring together gifted students in a regular class as a group, separate from the rest of the class, part of the time.

There is no strict rule as to which of these approaches is best for a student in elementary school. What is vital is that the child is challenged and develops to the fullest extent that his or her gift allows. But to compel a gifted or talented student to attend a strict regimen of ordinary classes with the standard curriculum may not permit giftedness to blossom.

Ideally, one style of teaching would be used for all students and it would allow each youngster to thrive, whether or not gifted. There would be no need for separating the gifted or doing anything for them that would not be done for all students, because the curriculum would be presented in ways that challenged every student at his or her own level. There would be adjustments to meet individual learning needs and each student would have the leeway to go just as far just as fast as he or she wanted. In such a school there might well be no need for special attention for the gifted since, essentially, what is best for the gifted is best for all students.

Unfortunately, there are few such schools. Most students in most elementary schools get little opportunity to advance deeper or further than the curriculum dictates. Thus, parents of the gifted, unless their children attend the small number of ideal elementary schools, should seek special programs that single out the gifted for the kind of attention that, if this were a perfect world, all students would receive. Ordinarily, no parent of a gifted or talented young child should be satisfied with a program that does not embrace some aspect of acceleration, enrichment, or homogeneous grouping.

The point is—and it cannot be made too emphatically —that schools as they are usually constituted are not geared to serve the needs of individual students, so it is a cinch they are not going to serve the gifted without special provisions. It is not that students having other kinds of needs should get less, but that society should realize the extraordinary potential for loss when giftedness is ignored. The possibility of such loss is greatest among the children of poor, less educated parents. Gift-edness frequently goes unrecognized in such children and their families are less apt to act independently of the school in the child's behalf.

Ultimately, the key to any program for the gifted and talented is the teacher. This is true whether the student is kept in a regular classroom or assigned to a special class. Many teachers simply do not know how to work with gifted and talented children. Some make the error of thinking that the idea is to heap extra homework on the gifted; others think it is enough merely to teach the gifted from the standard curriculum that would be used by older students. In general, teachers in elementary school fail to engage the gifted in dialogue—just as they fail all children, not understanding the need to cultivate curiosity and deeper thinking.

Spending more money is not the solution to accom-modating the needs of the gifted and talented. It helps, but the same per pupil expenditures can be made in behalf of the gifted as for other students. What makes the difference for the gifted are the instructional meth-ods and the ways the classes are organized.

Authorities recommend that any instructional pro-gram for intellectually gifted children in elementary school should have these characteristics:

- Encouragement of children to pursue a chosen inter-est in depth.

- Learning based on needs rather than on predeter-mined order or sequence of instruction.

- Activities that are more complex and require more ab-stract and higher-level thinking processes.

- Greater flexibility in the use of materials, time, and resources.

- Higher expectations for independence and persistence to tasks.

- Greater encouragement of creative and productive thinking.

- Recognition of the child's greater interest in interpreting the behavior and feelings of self and others.

- More opportunities to broaden the base of knowledge and enhance language abilities.

- Encouragement to take intellectual risks.

- Many opportunities for decision making.

- Lots of problem solving.

- Interdisciplinary work that recognizes that learning more often than not depends on combining skills drawn from several subjects.

All in all, parents of the gifted and talented must be prepared to advocate for their children at every turn, even more than other parents, because the chances are so great of the children's needs not being taken into consideration by the school. Just as all parents of school-aged children should seek to become experts of a sort on elementary education, the parents of the gifted and talented must add an extra layer of expertise. One way to begin is by reading books such as these that were identified by E. Paul Torrance of the University of Georgia as particularly valuable:

The Creatively Gifted Child: Suggestions for Parents and Teachers by J. Khatena. Vantage.

Does This Mean My Kid's a Genius? by L. P. Moore. McGraw-Hill.

The Gifted Child, the Family, and the Community by B. S. Miller and M. Price. Walker.

Guiding the Gifted Child by J. T. Webb, E. A. Meckstroth, and S. S. Tolan. Ohio Publishing.

How to Be a Gifted Parent by D. Lewis. Norton.

Is Your Child Gifted? by G. Ginsberg. Simon & Schuster.

Somewhere to Turn: Strategies for Parents of Gifted and Talented Children by A. J. Tannenbaum and E. Newman. Teachers College Press.

Your Gifted Child and You by F. Kaufmann. Council for Exceptional Children.

Another useful book is *Parents' Guide to Raising a Gifted Child* (Ballantine) by James Alvino, who issued the reminder that parents—not teachers—most often identify gifted children first and most effectively. Thus, he said, "it is important that parents be aware of relevant facts, fictions, and current debates concerning identifying giftedness."

14

THE HANDICAPPED

ntil the mid-1970s, public schools often re-
fused to enroll handicapped youngsters,
forcing parents to place such children in
special private schools if they wanted to see
them educated. The small number of handicapped students admitted to public schools would usually be banished to out-of-the-way classrooms where
they had no contact with students who were not disabled. If parents of the handicapped did not like the
treatment their children got, that was too bad; school
officials could set the rules and they were accountable
to no one.

Today, the situation is vastly different as the result of
the passage of the Education of All Handicapped Children Act in November 1975. An intricate system of rules
and regulations assures the rights of the handicapped to
a free and appropriate education. Furthermore, because
the law was enacted by Congress, parents have recourse
in the federal courts to back up claims in behalf of their

children. No parent of a handicapped child should settle for less than the law provides.

Approximately 10 percent of all students in the country, more than 4 million children, get services in connection with the legislation for the handicapped. The federal government has disbursed about $10 billion since 1975 to help pay for these services. An even larger amount has been provided by the states and local school districts specifically for handicapped students. Paying for special education of the handicapped remains a key difficulty for school districts. For instance, New York City estimated the extra cost of educating its 116,000 handicapped students at more than $300 million annually.

But the important fact for parents of the handicapped is that families are not required to pay a cent out of their own pockets for the additional services to which their children are entitled. Basically, the same procedures are in effect everywhere in the country to identify and diagnose handicapped students and to establish and monitor individualized programs for their education. There are almost 16,000 school systems in the United States, and in each, with small variations, parents will find that the mandate of the law is carried out in similar ways. These are the procedures that public school systems are obligated to provide:

• *Referral.* The parents or the school may initiate the process. For a youngster just entering kindergarten it is the parents who might bring to the attention of the school a situation already familiar to family. On the other hand, once a student enters school, a teacher in the kindergarten or first grade may suspect a problem that had previously gone undetected. Also, on some occasions the referral might be made by a physician, a court officer, or a representative of a welfare or health agency. Parents are to be notified in writing when a child is referred for evaluation by the school or by some outside party.

• *Evaluation.* Psychologists and other experts test and assess the student to determine whether there is a handicapping situation. It is a comprehensive assessment of the child's skills and abilities, including a physical examination.

• *Recommendation.* The evaluation must be followed by a conference with the parents to describe the findings, talk about the implications, and recommend whether or not special education is appropriate. If special education is in order, then a main aspect of the meeting is the writing of an Individualized Education Plan (IEP) specific to the child. It details the youngster's current level of achievement, the educational goals for the child, and the services to be provided. The plan cannot be implemented unless the parents give their written permission.

• *Implementation.* A child for whom an IEP has been created is placed in the kind of setting appropriate to the disability.

• *Annual assessment.* Parents are entitled to meet with a school representative each year to review the child's progress, modify the IEP if necessary, and discuss whether or not the student should be kept in special education.

• *Revised IEP.* At least every three years, if not more frequently, a school representative must meet with the parents of a special education student to write an entirely new Individualized Education Plan.

At every point along the way, parents are assured of due process; the law provides for a hearing or appeal if parents are not satisfied with what the school is doing. In essence this means that at each step parents must be kept informed of all actions involving their children and offered the opportunity to participate in the decision making. Parents may challenge decisions and follow a prescribed route of appeal when they are dissatisfied with what is happening.

At the outset, parents who do not want their children evaluated to see if they are handicapped may refuse a request for evaluation that is initiated by the school. The school must then follow a due process procedure if it wants to override the parents' objections and get permission from the state to evaluate the child.

Parents who object to the sort of placement proposed for a child or to the details of the IEP also have channels of appeal. The school is required, if asked by parents, to follow up its evaluation by another evaluation by an independent expert not on the school staff. If still dissatisfied, the parents may have a hearing before an impartial examiner, at which parents have the right to have a lawyer attend. Or if the parents want to skip the independent evaluation, they may go directly into the hearing process.

If dissatisfied with the decision of the hearing officer, parents may file an administrative appeal with the state's Department of Education, which will then make its own adminstrative review of the case. Then, if the finding by the state's Department of Education is unsatisfactory, parents may sue in federal court or request a federal investigation by the U.S. Department of Education's Office of Civil Rights or its Bureau for the Education of the Handicapped.

Though it is not prescribed by law, mediation has been adopted in a number of states, including Massachusetts and California, as an alternative to hearings or trials for resolving disagreements concerning handicapped students. Parents are not obligated to use mediation in those places that recognize it, but it might be preferable to the more protracted process.

The requirement to provide services for handicapped students can be liberally defined, as was demonstrated when the U.S. Supreme Court upheld the plea of parents in Texas that a nurse be made available by the school for daily catheterization of a disabled child who otherwise could not make it through the schoolday. The courts have also upheld the right of parents to be reimbursed for attorney fees by the school district if they sue and win their case in behalf of a handicapped child.

There is a limit, though, in just how far the judiciary will go to enforce the rights of the handicapped. This was underscored by a 1982 verdict in which the U.S. Supreme Court found in favor of a school district in New York State that was sued by the family of a deaf first-grader whose lawyer argued that even with the extra services being provided she was "not learning as much or performing as well academically as she would without her handicap." The family wanted the school to provide a sign language interpreter for her. The Supreme Court held that the extra services already being rendered were sufficient and that the law did not obligate the school district to do more.

The law and the regulations surrounding it have established that handicapped students are entitled to a whole range of support services, many of which are non-academic in nature, because without such help the children would not be able to function in the academic setting. Thus, depending on what is found in the evaluation and what is prescribed in the individualized education plan, your child may get the services of a nurse, psychologist, physical therapist, speech therapist, audiologist, or counselor.

All aspects of the program in which their handicapped child will participate should be carefully considered by parents, but there are several areas that merit especially close scrutiny. The New York State Education Department took note of these areas in a booklet prepared for parents of the handicapped:

• *Curriculum.* For the most part, curriculum content in special education should be equivalent to the content in regular education. Most students with handicapping conditions are able to accomplish the goals and objectives of the regular curriculum. Parents should be careful that participation in special education does not cut off their children from the mainstream, except to the extent absolutely necessary. Ideally, special education is designed to modify or adapt regular teaching strategies so students can participate in the mainstream as much as possible.

• *Grouping.* When handicapped students are grouped together for teaching, the curriculum and instruction should be consistent with the individual needs of the handicapped child.

• *Scheduling.* The student's schedule should be coordinated with the regular school day so that the youngster has opportunities, whenever possible and appropriate, to participate in art, music, and other subjects and activities in which the handicapping condition will not normally be an issue.

• *Testing and remedial programs.* Handicapped students should not be barred from the regular testing programs that identify the extent to which the students are meeting the goals expected of all students, nor should they be denied regular remedial services.

• *Extracurricular activities.* The full range of activities should be open to all students to the extent possible.

• *Second language instruction.* A handicapped student who is interested and capable should be allowed to pursue foreign language study.

• *Computers.* The chance to work with computers should be available even if it means special devices and applications for students who are orthopedically or sensorially impaired.

Transportation to and from school must be provided for a physically disabled student, even if this means sending a specially outfitted van with a wheelchair lift to the home, if that is what is needed. Parents should be sure that such service is spelled out in the IEP just to be certain there is no dispute. Moreover, the school district cannot charge extra for this service.

Two years before passing the Handicapped Act, Congress enacted legislation—Section 504 of the Rehabilitation Act—requiring any public or private organization receiving government funds to eliminate physical barriers that blocked the participation of the handicapped. Thus, many schools and other buildings have had to install such devices as ramps and elevators for those of limited physical mobility, and audible signals and braille signs for the blind. The school system is obligated to make available for your child a regular school building that is fully accessible; it is illegal in this connection to try to meet the mandate by using a separate facility just for the handicapped so that other buildings do not have to be adapted.

School districts have enlarged their capacity to provide a full range of services to children with even the most severe handicapping conditions. Therefore, parents today seldom have to use special private schools for the education of disabled youngsters. If, however, the school district finds that the student's needs exceed the available services, then there is an obligation for the school district to pay for private placement, as might be the case for a child who is profoundly handicapped, both mentally and physically.

In some cases, a child whose needs the school district claims it can serve is nonetheless placed by parents in a private school. The school district is not required to pay the costs in this instance, unless the parents can establish through the appeals process that the school district was incorrect in its assertion that it was able to serve the child. In a Massachusetts case that went all the way to the U.S. Supreme Court, it was ruled that parents who unilaterally take their handicapped children out of public schools and place them in private schools can be reimbursed for tuition if such transfers are later determined to have been in the children's best interests. But the court decided that parents are not entitled to such reimbursement if hearing officers or judges ultimately find that placement in public school was appropriate.

Parents do not have to wait until their handicapped children are of kindergarten age to begin receiving services under the auspices of a public school system. Handicapped youngsters are eligible from the ages of three through twenty-one, and parents should check with the public schools about how to get services before a child enters kindergarten. Furthermore, a section added to the Handicapped Law in 1986 opened the way for the federal goverment to assist states that voluntarily offer programs for "developmentally delayed" infants and toddlers before the age of three.

The range of handicapping conditions is wide and some disabilities are not as readily apparent as others, so parents should not hesitate to consult a physician or some other expert if they suspect that their infant or toddler may in some way be disabled. In fact, the most prevalent of all handicaps, learning disabilities, may not be recognized by parents before their children enter school.

So common are learning disabilities that 1.8 million of the 4.1 million handicapped students fall into this category. In other words, of all those students classified as handicapped, 44 percent are learning-disabled. Among the remaining students classified as handicapped, 27 percent are speech-impaired, 15 percent are mentally retarded, 8 percent are emotionally disturbed, 1 percent are deaf or hearing-impaired, 1 percent are orthopedically impaired, 1 percent are multiple-handicapped, and other categories—including the blind—make up less than 1 percent each.

The most prevalent of the handicaps, learning disability, is certainly the most controversial. The term was unknown when the parents of today's students were in school. What are now called learning disabilities did not become widely recognized by that name until the 1970s.

A host of conditions with familiar names are included under this rubric: hyperactivity, dyslexia, minimal brain damage, dyscalculia, dysgraphia, perceptually handicapped, neurologically handicapped. Speculation on causes of learning disabilities range from food additives to environment to ear infections to genetics to head injuries. Whether for developmental reasons or other reasons, the overwhelming portion of students afflicted with learning disabilities are boys. When the federal government needed an all-encompassing definition so that the public schools would know whom they were to serve as learning-disabled, experts struggled until they finally produced a definition that is little more than a reiteration of the conditions that are supposed to be defined:

Children with special learning disabilities exhibit a disorder in one or more of the basic psychological processes involved in understanding or using spoken or written languages. These may be manifested in disorders of listening, thinking, reading, writing, spelling, or arithmetic. They include conditions which have been referred to as perceptual handicaps, brain injury, minimal brain dysfunction, dyslexia, developmental aphasia, etc. They do not include learning problems which are due primarily to visual, hearing, or motor handicaps, to mental retardation, emotional disturbance, or to environmental disadvantage.

Just because a student is a slow learner does not mean that the child is learning-disabled; conversely, a learning-disabled child can with great effort compensate sufficiently to perform above grade level, but this should not obviate the need for special attention.

It is unfortunate that the stigma of a label must be placed on learning-disabled students in order for them to get the extra attention that should be theirs merely on the basis of need. A compelling argument has been made by some critics who charge that the learning-disability category has no firm neurological basis and is more a way of the school making an excuse for not doing a good job of educating some students who are, for one reason or another, more difficult to teach. A decade ago in the *Harvard Educational Review*, Gerald S. Coles of the Rutgers Medical School argued that "the success of learning-disabilities specialists in remedying the problem results from their ability to use general remedial techniques and not from the special knowledge of neurological dysfunction."

Some parents may bridle at the idea of having their children called "handicapped" to qualify them for aid, since once the label is affixed it is difficult to remove. Furthermore, the label affects the self-image of the child, as well as the way that the child is viewed by others. But the struggles of such children to learn are real enough, and to block the designation of learning-disabled simply for appearance's sake may not be to the benefit of the student. The alternatives should be carefully considered.

If your child is in any elementary grade and having trouble beyond what you consider normal, but has not been classified as learning-disabled, you might want to ask the school to conduct an evaluation. These are some of the signs—not all of which are likely to be present in any one child—that may be exhibited by a learning-disabled child, according to an article in *Today's Education*, published by the National Education Association:

- *Classroom behavior.* Moves constantly, has difficulty beginning or completing tasks, often tardy or absent, generally quiet or withdrawn, difficulty with peer relationships, disorganized, inconsistent behavior, misunderstands oral directions.

- *Reading.* Loses place, repeats words, confuses similar letters and words, uses fingers to follow along, does not read willingly.

- *Arithmetic.* Difficulty associating numbers with symbols, cannot remember math facts, difficulty with story problems, fails to understand concepts.

- *Spelling.* Uses incorrect order of letters in words, difficulty associating sound with appropriate letter, reverses letters and words.

- *Writing.* Cannot stay on a line, difficulty copying from board or book, poor written expression for age, slow in completing written work, uses cursive writing and printing in same assignment.

- *Verbal.* Hesitates often when speaking, poor verbal expression for age.

- *Motor.* Poor coordination, problems of balance, confuses right and left, lacks rhythm in movements, poor muscle strength for age.

One of the most notable features of the Handicapped Law is its requirement that every disabled student be educated in "the least restrictive environment." This has been interpreted to mean that children must be accommodated—to whatever extent possible—in the mainstream of the school's program with nonhandicapped students. This is an attempt to avoid the segregation of the handicapped that was so often the rule in former years.

Mainstreaming, however, does not have the same effect for every handicapped student. Those whose handicap is most slight may be in a regular class and follow a regular schedule except for a periodic visit to a speech therapist or a psychologist. The most profoundly handicapped may be totally separated in a self-contained classroom in which fellow students are all afflicted with similarly severe handicaps. In between the two extremes are some students who spend part of the day in a regular class and part of the day in a class for the handicapped. For most learning-disabled students there is a resource room to which they go for a portion of their instruction, maybe once a day, maybe only once a week.

Parents who feel that their children are not being sufficiently mainstreamed should take up the matter with school authorities. Mainstreaming is an important consideration for parents to bear in mind during the writing of the individualized education plan. A distinct advantage to students when they are in a class with other handicapped students is that there are fewer students per teacher. This is the main reason why special education is more expensive than regular education. It allows teachers to give students the extra attention that is considered necessary in light of the handicapping condition.

But having to be classified as handicapped is a large price for a child to pay to get the kind of close attention that ideally would be provided to every student. While there has definitely been progress by schools in serving the handicapped and parents have reason to be thankful for the improvement, the education of such children should still be closely monitored by their parents. If parents generally must be prepared to act as advocates for their children, then parents of the handicapped have double the responsibility.

15

SCIENCE

O f the major subjects, science has certainly been the most ignored at the elementary school level. The scientific illiteracy of so large a portion of the adult population is largely owed to a poor education in science, a deficiency that for most people begins in the earliest grades of school. One indication of the low regard the schools sometimes have for science was seen in Connecticut, where a survey released in 1987 found that more than half of the state's elementary school students were using books in science that were outdated, books that did not take note of the latest scientific advances. Poor teaching of science in elementary grades sets the tone for negative feelings about science in high school and adulthood.

Many students do not take advanced science courses in high school because their early experience has made them fear or dislike the subject. For example, though 96 percent of the country's high school students attend schools where physics is offered, only 20 percent enroll in physics, according to a survey by the American Institute of Physics. Students with a weak background in science become adults who are uncomfortable with scientific and technological topics, not understanding them and deferring more than they should to experts.

The best way to combat the problem is to teach science from the very earliest grades and to do so in ways that make the subject attractive and interesting. Educators are ever more frequently coming to this conclusion, and a growing number of schools are paying greater attention to science. You should be unwilling to accept a curriculum for your child that gives short shrift to science or a curriculum in which science is not taught as a vibrant subject that excites children in elementary school.

The biggest advance in science education is the "hands-on" approach that calls for the active participation of students in scientific inquiry as early as kindergarten and first grade. Individual children and groups of children conduct their own experiments, rather than serving as an audience to the teacher. It is a highly desirable approach that fires up motivation and enhances learning. Science, especially in elementary school, must not be reduced to memorizing facts. That is a way to turn off youngsters. It is more important that they become familiar with the scientific process and know how to pursue discovery on their own.

"Students are given a distorted view of the nature of science when they are presented only with facts, definitions, numbers, and the local processes of the scientific method," said a statement from the American Chemical Society. "Students seldom see that science is also a creative endeavor."

Hands-on science might mean a pail of water for each student in which to immerse various objects to see which float and which sink. It might mean a collection of rocks for each child to sort in order to identify the geological characteristics they have in common. It might mean enough wire, bulbs, and batteries for each child to construct a bulb holder and discover the properties of electricity. At Crabtree Elementary School in Alberta, Canada, it could even mean going to the library to check out a rabbit or a gerbil or a mouse to take home and observe for a week or two.

"If kids touch it, lift it and manipulate it, they learn whether it is hot or cold, big or little, heavy or light," said Thomas Fitch, professor of education at Illinois State University, in an article in *Instructor* magazine. "And kids then can begin to make estimations, measure and calculate. That is how science works. You cannot rely only on textbooks."

The magazine article, recognizing that hands-on science can take many different forms, proposed, nonetheless, that there were qualities that programs should share at all elementary schools. They are these:

- *Time.* Science once a week isn't enough. There should be the equivalent of at least three to five periods a week of twenty to thirty minutes each.
- *Doing as well as reading.* Rather than just read about a topic, students should have a chance to conduct experiments. They should observe, describe, compare, classify, measure, use numbers, predict, and create graphs.
- *Organization.* Hands-on science is not sufficient without an organizational scheme to the activities. The lessons should have a focus and a goal and should not simply be busywork.

• *Activities and enforcement.* Hands-on experiments should usually be followed by lessons involving reading and/or lectures by the teacher so that students understand what they have been doing.

• *Measuring learning.* A teacher should assess how much each student learns from the hands-on experience. Assessment ideally should not be limited to paper-and-pencil tests, but should include having students performing activities and describing what they have learned.

The approach to science in elementary schools throughout the United States is so varied that there is no way, unlike the situation in reading or math, to list achievements for science by grade level. In fact, the emphasis for students in elementary school should not be on learning scientific laws, but on becoming familiar with the scientific process. The goal should be to arouse their curiosity and inquisitiveness about scientific matters. The rest will follow naturally.

The teaching of science can stem from the interests of the children. In an open-ended approach, a room rich in potential areas of investigation—animals, earth, water, batteries, wires—can be a mother lode of discoveries that children pursue at their own choosing with the teacher providing appropriate intervention. The idea is to cultivate inquisitiveness. A guiding philosophy is that inquiry occurs best at the child's own pace and that the observations and conclusions of the child should not be dictated by the curriculum. Children should be free to make discoveries. It is an approach that calls for better-trained teachers, because they must be able to operate independent of a curriculum that tells them what to do each step of the way.

Whether or not the curriculum is specific, there should be the aim of familiarizing students with the scientific method so that they come to take an organized approach to the process of solving scientific problems. They learn to form hypotheses and to test them in order to make judgments. Step-by-step, this means students learn to observe, measure, classify, record, predict, and interpret. They must develop the ability to define terms, use space and time relationships, draw inferences, and recognize variables.

The Model Science Curriculum developed by the California State Department of Education gives an idea of the possible scope of science at the elementary level. The program has components in biological science, earth science, and physical science, breaking these topics into subcategories that are covered in a gradually more sophisticated way in each grade. For instance, earth science deals with astronomy, geology and natural resources, and oceanography and hydrology. Meteorology is added in the fourth grade.

Astronomy, as one example, is studied from kindergarten through the third grade by an examination of six postulates. These have to do with the sun and the heat and light it emits; the moon and its role as a satellite of the earth; the earth as one of nine planets revolving around the sun; the sun as the center of the solar system; the rotation of the earth and the differences in the length of daylight periods in the summer and winter.

In looking at the sun as the center of the solar system, kindergarteners and first-graders may use the occasion of various holidays such as Christmas and Easter to take note of the time required for the earth to revolve around the sun in that season of the year. Second- and third-graders may simulate the rotation by setting up the

classroom with a bulb for the sun and a revolving bas-
ketball for the earth, observing the simultaneous rotation of the earth on its axis and its revolution around the
sun.

The model curriculum in California takes students
through such topics in ways that build on what was
taught earlier and deals with increasingly complex
knowledge in each grade.

During the fourth, fifth, and sixth grades, the curriculum calls for students to delve more deeply into astronomy. They learn how the earth's rotation, revolution,
and axis tilt cause specific climatic changes in the north-
ern and southern hemispheres; how the moon's rotation,
revolution, and reflection of the sun's light cause pre-
dictable changes in the moon's phases as well as
eclipses; that the sun is a massive sphere of hydrogen
and helium that releases energy; that in addition to
planets and their moons, the solar system contains asteroids, meteoroids, comets, and a host of smaller particles,
and that astronomers identify star groupings as constel-
lations and galaxies.

California's model curriculum is one possible approach. There is more than one way to teach science
effectively to elementary-age youngsters. Some experts
maintain that the curriculum need not be as specific as
that developed in California. Whatever approach is
used, there is a growing awareness of the need to inte-
grate the teaching of science in elementary school into
other subjects, an admirable idea that underscores the
reality that science does not stand alone, divorced from
the rest of human endeavors. Science is about knowing
the math that is essential to the physical sciences; it is
about knowing how to read the many articles and books
on scientific topics for both information and enjoyment;

and it is about being familiar with the history and politics that affect decisions involving science and the geography that affects natural phenomena.

A good example of a school district that has recognized such interrelationships is the Fairfax County system serving suburban Washington, D.C. In addition to the regular reading program in the Fairfax elementary schools, there is a special reading program that uses books on scientific subjects. The collection of 140 different titles includes books suitable for all reading levels from kindergarten through sixth grade. An activity card has been developed to accompany each book, so that students can ask themselves questions about what they have read. Besides this link to the reading program, science in Fairfax is generally coordinated with the math that is being taught at the particular grade level.

Parents interested in compiling their own list of books on science that their children can read at home should consult the September 1987 issue of *Young Children* magazine published by the National Association for the Education of Young Children. The magazine is in most libraries that carry educational journals, and the organization can be contacted at 1834 Connecticut Avenue N.W., Washington, D.C. 20009.

Concern with integrating science into other subjects, as exhibited in Fairfax County, should carry through all the grades of elementary education. It is imperative that science be a regular and strong part of the curriculum by the upper elementary grades, when students should be able to draw on a solid science education that was provided during the early grades. The National Assessment of Educational Progress found that more than 80 percent of the country's fourth-graders knew the following:

- A caterpillar will grow up to look like a butterfly, not a grasshopper, a bat, or a praying mantis (91 percent).

- Roots, not leaves, stems, or flowers hold plants in the soil (88 percent).

- How to read a simple bar graph (85 percent).

Sixty-one to 80 percent of fourth-graders knew:

- How to apply their knowledge of ecosystems to an understanding of why populations will stop increasing in size when there is a limited amount of food, space, and air (77 percent).

- Given a list of common instruments, that a telescope is the instrument used to view the planets (71 percent).

- Whether a cat, a ship, a pencil, a bush, a fish, a television, or a chair belongs with a group of animals or inanimate objects (67 percent).

- That in summer there are more hours of sunlight, not the same or fewer hours than in winter (61 percent).

Forty-one to 60 percent of fourth-graders knew:

- Sugar will dissolve faster in hot tea than in iced tea (56 percent).

- That certain objects had been categorized to emphasize the concepts of hardness and softness, rather than the concepts of dangerous and nondangerous, or metallic and nonmetallic (52 percent).

- A year is based on the amount of time it takes the earth to revolve around the sun, not the time measured by a clock, the phases of the moon, or the time it takes light to travel (51 percent).

- How to apply their knowledge of nutrition to select a balanced menu over menus that emphasize mainly carbohydrates and fats, protein, or carbohydrates alone (46 percent).

Twenty-one to 40 percent of the fourth-graders knew:

- Given a list of options, that an egg and a bean seed are alike because both contain stored food (36 percent).

- How to apply their knowledge of the directions "right" or "left" and "front" to draw and label a diagram (24 percent).

- The normal body temperature is 98.6° Fahrenheit (23 percent).

Twenty percent or fewer of fourth-graders knew:

- The biological role of the male in human reproduction is to fertilize the egg, not protect or provide for the female or give her the egg (19 percent).

- How to apply the principle of condensation of water to examples that illustrate the cooling and heating processes (19 percent).

- Given a list of five common instruments, that a barometer is used to measure atmospheric pressure (16 percent).

- Water displacement is dependent on the size of the object, not the shape or weight of the object (7 percent).

Students are not going to know more about science until they spend more time with the subject and until it is taught better. The average fourth-grader spends 28 minutes a day on science, compared with 34 minutes on social studies, 52 minutes on mathematics, and 100 minutes on reading, according to the Association for Supervision and Curriculum Development. Of course, in a good school there should be overlapping time when science is integrated into math, social studies, and reading.

Part of the difficulty is that so many teachers have not been adequately prepared to teach science and may even be apprehensive about it. Only 27 percent of elementary school teachers deemed themselves "very well qualified" to teach life science, and only 15 percent to teach physical science, in the National Survey of Science and Mathematics. You should ask what your school district is providing by way of in-service training to help elementary school teachers improve their command of science.

Parents can also aid their children by getting them subscriptions to science magazines. Some of the better ones aimed at older elementary school students are the following:

3-2-1 Contact
Children's Television Workshop
One Lincoln Plaza
New York, N.Y. 10023

National Geographic World
The National Geographic Society
17th and M Streets N.W.
Washington, D.C. 20036

Odyssey
1027 N.W. 7th Street
Milwaukee, Wis. 53202

Wonder Science
The American Chemical Society
1155 Sixteenth Street N.W.
Washington, D.C. 20036

The hands-on approach that is appropriate in the lower grades should be just as prominent in the upper elementary years. A school should not make science a subject taught only from books. Some of the best hands-on experiences don't even require the acquisition of equipment. Urban schools situated near parks and schools that are in suburban and semirural settings have learning opportunities almost at the doorsteps. Teachers should be able to take students outside for life science lessons about trees and insects, ponds and lakes, and birds and small animals. Students should make field trips and visits for physical science lessons at generating plants and airports, factories and dams.

In the classroom itself, one example of a commercially available hands-on program is Science Curriculum Improvement Study (SCIS II), which is widely used throughout the country. It consists of twelve units, one in life science and one in physical science for each of the six elementary school grade levels. An extensive variety of hands-on activities accompany all the lessons and the program—operated by Delta Education in Nashua, New Hampshire—even sells the schools all of the supplies, animals, and living organisms that students will need for their experiments.

At the fourth-grade level, for instance, the physical science concentrates on measurement, motion, and change. Students are introduced to techniques for dealing with spatial relationships of both stationary and moving objects. They learn about some basic weather phenomena. The life science unit is devoted to environments and the study of such phenomena as seasonal change, temperature, and the response of living organisms to environmental changes. They learn, for example, what range of temperature is tolerable. Observing life in a terrarium is one of the hands-on experiences that enhances the lesson.

The fifth-grade physical science deals with energy sources, continuing the development and application of the systems concept, identification of variables, and interpretation of data that students themselves record. Students are introduced to examples of energy sources, energy chains, and energy receivers—leading to the overall concept of energy transfer. Meanwhile, the life science unit is concerned with communities, and by concentrating on the transfer of food in the community it provides a companion to the physical science lessons about energy transfer. The subjects of the communities unit are producer, consumer, decomposer, food source, food transfer, raw materials, reproduction, food cycle, and photosynthesis.

In the sixth grade, there is both a climax to the early studies and a start toward the advanced studies of secondary school. A look at modeling systems in physical science introduces the concept of scientific model and opens a new level of data interpretation and hypothesis making. Students relate matter and energy to electrical, magnetic, and atmospheric phenomena, acquiring a basis for developing a model of the atmosphere. The life science unit is devoted to ecosystems, integrating units in the earlier grades in both physical and biological science, as students investigate the exchange of matter and energy between organisms and their environment. Included are a look at the water cycle, oxygen—carbon dioxide cycle, food-mineral cycle, evaporation and condensation.

All of this is not to say that every school should use the SCIS II approach, or that no other program is as good. There are other fine programs, but with so many different approaches to science it is not possible to say what students should have done or what should have been learned by a particular grade. Any of the units mentioned above, for example, could actually be taught at any grade level, but obviously it would have to be taught differently at each grade, and the students would get different things out of it at different ages.

What may turn out to be one of the most important events in improving the teaching of science in elementary schools is the creation in 1985 of the National Science Resources Center, a joint enterprise of the National Academy of Sciences and the Smithsonian Institution in Washington. The agency is devoted to helping the schools in science and mathematics, and one of its main activities is to develop and disseminate resource materials. These are some of the issues and recommendations that were identified when the Center brought together a hundred experts for a National Conference on the Teaching of Science in Elementary Schools:

- Participatory activities should be at the center of an elementary science program.

- Hands-on science programs can be implemented in both large and small school systems and can be operated with a modest allocation of school system resources.

- Most successful hands-on elementary science programs are based on a series of modular units. Each module includes the instructional materials and apparatus needed to investigate a particular science topic, plus clearly defined lesson plans for six to eight weeks of student activities.

- The school systems with exemplary elementary science programs usually do not limit themselves to the materials developed by any one of the nationally developed elementary science programs, but instead use an eclectic approach to develop a science curriculum that includes a variety of nationally and locally produced units.

- Creative, well-prepared teachers are the most important element of an effective elementary science program.

- Elementary science instructional materials need to be relatively easy for teachers to use and should not require large amounts of teacher preparation time.

- Elementary school teachers will spend more time teaching science if science activities emphasize the development of skills that are important in other areas of the curriculum, such as writing, reading, applied mathematics, and artistic expression.

- There is widespread concern that standardized achievement tests do not do a good job of assessing what students learn in elementary school science.

SCIENCE

The progress of students in science is difficult to gauge because there is no wide-scale agreement on what ought to be taught in elementary school science and what subject matter should be mastered.

Actually, this could be turned to a real advantage. Without having to worry about standardized achievement tests and the pitfalls that accompany them, teachers could be free to concentrate on real learning in their students. Science is an elementary school subject that can stress deeper meanings and problem solving, playing down the rote learning that so often is encouraged by standardized achievement tests. Furthermore, the symbiotic relationship of science to math and reading can provide an opportunity to use science to teach reading and math just as reading and math can be used as a chance to teach science.

Ideally, the scope of the science program in elementary school will cover the full array of categories—life science (plants, animals, and ecology), human biology and health, earth science (geology, weather, and astronomy), and physical science (light, sound, electricity, chemistry, energy, heat, density, magnetism, forces, and motion and equilibrium).

What parents ought to watch for is that science is a part of the curriculum in every grade and that it is taught in an active way that involves the students. It should get sufficient time and be presented in an interesting manner. Students should acquire an understanding of basic concepts that will be explored in greater depth in secondary school. They should develop a favorable attitude toward science and want to learn more about the subject.

16

SOCIAL STUDIES

Parents who get aroused about their children not learning to read properly or being insufficiently grounded in mathematics seldom evince the same indignation over the inadequacies of education in the social studies. The subject usually does not stir passions and parents are apt to pay scant attention to what is being taught in social studies or to how well their children are learning it.

You can get a sense of the level at which your child ought to be able to read at the second grade, the fourth grade, or any other grade in elementary school. Similarly, you have a notion of the kind of work a student ought to be able to do in mathematics, knowing, for instance, that if a fifth-grader cannot divide 20 by 2 there is cause for concern. While specific skills that might be expected to be learned in science at a given grade are less recognized, parents are aware that they should expect children to be doing experiments involving growing seeds, measuring water, and finding out about the rudiments of electricity.

What about social studies? What should students learn in a given grade? How does a parent determine if a child is progressing properly in social studies? In fact, what in the world is social studies?

At its core, social studies is history. But history is only one of the subjects that make up social studies. Woven around history and through it are sociology, anthropology, psychology, social psychology, economics, political science, geography, and several other disciplines that are otherwise separate unto themselves. How a topic is treated in social studies depends on the grade in which it is presented. The same topic can be used for lessons for second-graders or for sixth-graders, but the approach depends on the knowledge and ability of the class. A lesson delving into the legislative process, for instance, would be rather different for second-graders and sixth-graders.

What is most surprising about social studies is the similarity of the curriculum in elementary schools around the country. Wherever students attend school they are likely to follow more or less the same path through the social studies, year by year, though the details vary from school district to school district and from state to state. Much of this conformity is owed to the influence of textbooks.

Basically, social studies is taught in what is known as an "expanding approach." It starts in kindergarten with the child learning about herself or himself—undoubtedly the most interesting topic there is for a small child still at a very self-centered point in personal development. Gradually, grade by grade, the subject expands in ever widening circles, from self in kindergarten to family in the first grade and to neighborhood in the second grade. The curriculum stretches to embrace the entire city in the third grade. What begins in a very cursory fashion in the early grades is pursued in greater depth in the upper grades, when students can read better and bring more experience and sophistication to the topics.

Typically, when kindergarteners and first-graders start studying themselves and their families they do very little of it through reading. They use posters, they look at pictures, they dress up in costumes. The emphasis is on the role of the youngster as a member of a group, a basic kind of social psychology though it does not carry that label. These are children who are learning to get along with others and to interact in ways that are productive for themselves and other children. The goal is to give them a firmer sense of self by leading them to examine their roles in the group.

Some children need such lessons more than others. Most kindergarteners today have already spent a year or two or even longer in group situations at child care centers, nursery schools, and preschools. Despite having been in groups before their formal schooling began, some kindergarteners and first-graders still function in ways largely oblivious to others, unless space is infringed upon or someone tries to play with one of their toys. Students tend to pass through the period smoothly enough, learning about themselves, growing comfortable as members of the class "family," and becoming eager to learn about those beyond their immediate circle.

In first grade, they are taught about the family of which they are part. They study the roles of fathers and mothers, brothers and sisters, grandparents, uncles, and aunts. There is a generous dose of sociology here, and anyone who has taken a college sociology course on the family has dealt with some of the same issues as the first-grader, but of course in greater depth.

In the second grade there is the neighborhood, and in the third grade the moment comes to reach out and study the larger community. Students tend to learn about the systems of transportation and communications and the public services that link households and neighborhoods to the city at large. This is prime time for visits to the police station, the fire station, city hall, and the local newspaper office. For some youngsters in suburban school systems surrounding such cities as Washington, Chicago, and Philadelphia, the first trip on a subway line may be taken at this time.

In Palo Alto, California, the unit at this point is called "Megalopolis—Bridges to the Bay" and involves studying the entire Bay Area surrounding San Francisco, learning about the network of bridges that transverse the waterways of the region, including the magnificent Golden Gate Bridge. Such an approach provides a basis for delving into the geography of the area, the history of the bridges, the anthropology of the groups that settled the area, and the environmental science of the Bay Area —all on an intellectual level that a third-grader can grasp.

Very often study of the community is followed by study of the state, which usually comes in the fourth grade. Many states require that students have a unit on the state and this may provide the focus of social studies for the entire year. As in studying their local community, students tend to view the subject matter through the prism of a variety of disciplines.

It is also around the third or fourth grade that geography looms larger in the curriculum, though it is by no means the only time the topic is taught. Geography has not disappeared from the elementary school curriculum as some critics charge, but it no longer is accorded the importance it once had.

Colorful globes still sit on tables in the corners of classrooms and maps hang from the walls, as indeed they should. Good teachers continue to make use of such aids. If your child's elementary school does not include geography in the social studies curriculum, then there is reason to complain. Geography should be a part of social studies, grade by grade. There is no reason why it cannot be pursued in terms of neighborhood, community, state, country, and world.

In Newton, Massachusetts, where geography is the mainstay of the social studies curriculum in the fourth grade, the year is spent largely looking at the "People of America." The sources of immigration, the routes of immigration, and the locales where immigrants settled all lend themselves to geography at this time.

A place can be made for geography at each grade level if a school truly wants to make it a continuing and enduring part of social studies. The Joint Committee on Geographic Education prepared guidelines that would allow this to happen. A sample of the outcomes for which the guidelines provide are the following:

Kindergarten Through Second Grade

CENTRAL FOCUS: SELF IN SPACE

- Knows and uses terms related to location, direction, and distance.

- Recognizes a globe as a model of the earth.

- Recognizes and uses terms that express relative size and shape.

- Identifies school and local community by name.

- Recognizes and uses models and symbols to represent real things.

- Makes simple observations and describes weather, seasons, the school, the neighborhood, and the route to school and to home.

CENTRAL FOCUS: HOMES AND SCHOOLS IN
DIFFERENT PLACES

- Knows geographic location of home in relation to school and neighborhood.

- Uses simple classroom maps to locate objects.

- Identifies state and nation by name.

- Describes characteristics of seasons and discusses their impact on people.

- Distinguishes between land and water symbols on globes and maps.

- Relates location on map/globe to location on earth.

- Describes similarities and differences between people in their own community and in other places.

- Observes, describes, and builds simple models and maps of the local environment.

CENTRAL FOCUS: NEIGHBORHOODS—
SMALL PLACES IN LARGER COMMUNITIES

- Makes and uses simple maps of school and home neighborhoods.

- Interprets map symbols using a legend.

- Knows and uses cardinal directions.

- Identifies a variety of types of transportation and communication within the community.

- Describes effects of seasonal change on the local environment.

- Explains that neighborhoods depend on other neighborhoods to satisfy their wants and needs.

- Traces routes within and between neighborhoods using a variety of maps and models.

- Compares pictures and maps of same area.

Grades Three and Four

CENTRAL FOCUS: COMMUNITY—SHARING WITH OTHERS

- Prepares physical and human profile of community including ethnic diversity and some historical dimensions.

- Compares community with other communities.

- Compares rural and urban environments.

- Analyzes various environmental situations in terms of positive/negative consequences.

- Describes how people depend on each other in communities.

- Describes interaction in community in terms of transportation/communication.

- Describes how community interacts with other communities and areas.

CENTRAL FOCUS: THE STATE, NATION, AND WORLD

- Interprets pictures, graphs, charts, and tables.

- Works with distance, direction, scale, and map symbolization.

- Uses maps of different scales and themes.

- Discusses how regions are defined.

- Compares and contrasts major geographical features and regions using case studies of countries having different peoples, cultures, and environments.

- Notes how regions change through time.

- Describes how people have adapted to and modified their environments.

- Discusses how personal behavior could be changed to solve a particular environmental problem.

Grades Five and Six

CENTRAL FOCUS: UNITED STATES, CANADA, AND MEXICO

- Works with latitude and longitude.

- Uses maps, charts, graphs, and tables to display data.

- Maps the correspondence between resources and industry.

- Compares physical and cultural areas and regions within the United States.

- Describes how there has been environmental deterioration in the United States, Mexico, and Canada related to industrial growth and prosperity.

- Comprehends how the United States, Mexico, and Canada grew into the present territorial areas.

CENTRAL FOCUS: LATIN AMERICA, EUROPE, U.S.S.R., MIDDLE EAST, ASIA, AND AFRICA

- Gains insights about the interaction of climate, landforms, natural vegetation, and other interactions in physical regions.

- Examines human-land adaptations in difficult environments.

- Perceives and analyzes migration patterns.

- Maps trade routes.

- Divides several large regions such as the U.S.S.R. or Africa into smaller regions based on race, language, nationality, religion, or some other cultural characteristic.

- Identifies important global problems with geographic dimensions, that is, deforestation, desertification, pollution, overfishing.

In either the third or fourth grade social studies may, in part, concern itself with government and/or economics. Some schools that use the fourth grade to emphasize geography provide doses of government and/or economics in the third grade. Again, the disciplines cannot always be discerned by the label. Government for children this age means getting a notion of the legislative apparatus for running the locality, the state, or the country and an introduction to the process of enacting and implementing laws. Economics may mean a look at goods and services and the rudiments of market forces. It is a time in their education when youngsters get a larger sense of their role in a democratic society in which the rules of law and the rules of the marketplace affect so much of their lives.

Government is likely to be taught more competently than economics by elementary school teachers. Too often teachers feel uncomfortable with economics and lack a grasp of the subject, even for teaching it to young children. A good elementary school should provide its teachers with opportunities to learn more about economics. In turn, these are some of the economic subjects that the teacher might teach students between third and sixth grades:

- The effect of advertising on sales.

- The need for currency in developing trade.

- The impact of supply and demand.

- The distribution, importance and conservation of natural resources.

- How individuals and societies make choices based on limited resources.

- The ways in which economics are affected by geographical features.

- A rudimentary exposure to comparative economic systems.

More often than not, grade five is the place for American history, which in most school systems in the United States will reappear in the eighth and eleventh grades. While some schools try to cover the entire sweep of the history of the United States in the fifth grade, the more prevalent approach is to concentrate on the colonial and revolutionary periods. This is the time when elementary schools do most to try to inculcate students with national traditions and to give them a feel of what it means to be an American. Thanksgiving is very, very big in the fifth grade, coming as it does just after the Pilgrims have been studied.

On paper, the fifth-grade curriculum may call for marching the students through the entirety of American history, but this is an unrealistic goal. There simply is not enough time to cover so many years in a meaningful way, especially when much of the material is new to the students. Parents should neither expect all of American history to be covered in the fifth grade nor be disappointed if it is not. It is far better for the students to get a decent grounding in at least one period of American history. If the material is conveyed with a sense of excitement and the teacher draws them into it through discussions and activities, the children will retain some of what they have been taught and want more.

The heavy concentration in history in the fifth grade underscores the paucity of history in other grades. Social studies in American public elementary schools is often a grab bag of subjects lacking coherence. Students don't get the substance they might in a curriculum in which the focus was on history in every grade and such topics as economics, sociology, and political science were offered in a historical framework. Such a curriculum might also be more closely wed to literature, with students using the biographies of such figures as Napoleon, George Washington, and Harriet Tubman as vehicles for learning history. But this is generally not the case—except in some of the good private elementary schools—and so parents must try to see to it that their children get the most out of the social studies curriculum as it is constituted.

After being provided with a glimpse of the United States, most students are given a worldview in the sixth grade. Chances are that as your child studies other countries the emphasis will vary from school district to school district in terms of the amount of history, culture, and geography provided. In Fairfax County, Virginia, for instance, sixth-graders study Western civilization from classical Greece and Rome through the Middle Ages and the Renaissance, as well as contemporary non-European countries.

A recent trend in elementary and secondary schools has been toward global education, an attempt to infuse the social studies curriculum with a deeper appreciation of the world community of which the United States is part. Some political conservatives object to this practice, charging that it leaves less time for learning about the United States and that it weakens the loyalty of students to their country if they are led to look at social studies through a world lens.

If handled sensibly and sensitively, the global approach can be valuable. In a world in which the population of the United States is such a small part of the whole, it is folly to be myopic. Furthermore, some educators maintain that the scanty teaching about other countries in American schools has left students somewhat xenophobic, distrustful, and uncomprehending of non-American cultures. In districts that lean toward a global approach, one possibility is for students to learn about other countries and other cultures as they learn about the United States. When third-graders in Newton, Massachusetts, study their hometown area, for example, they draw comparisons with Nairobi and Tokyo.

The teaching of values is discussed in a separate chapter of this book, but it is worth noting here that social studies is a main vehicle through which values are imparted. Students cannot help but come away from the subject with their attitudes affected in regard to capitalism, democracy, and the role of the United States in the world. To get an idea of the kinds of ideas being taught, parents ought to read the books and materials assigned to their children, review the papers that their children write, observe an occasional class, talk with the teacher, and, according to what is being taught any particular term, ask their children some pointed questions about what they have learned.

Parents rightfully should be concerned that children get a sense of history as they move through the grades, even if much of what is taught to them under the rubric of social sciences is not labeled history. It is important that students acquire a feeling for the meaning of change and continuity, a notion of chronology, and an appreciation of what can be learned from the past.

Several ways of making the social studies curriculum history-centered were proposed by the Bradley Commission on History in the Schools. This panel of school-teachers and scholars issued a report in 1988 entitled *Building a History Curriculum: Guidelines for Teaching History in Schools.* One approach would piggyback on the existing curriculum, but push it beyond "my" family, "my" neighborhood, "my" community. In kindergarten, when children learn about themselves, there would also be teaching about children in other places at other times. The units in the first grade would include a history of the family. Then the second grade would include local history and the third grade would include lessons on how cities began and grew. State history would continue in the fourth grade, history of the United States—dealing with the period through the end of the Civil War—in the fifth grade and world history in the sixth grade.

Another possible approach recommended by the Bradley Commission would replace the existing social studies curriculum with one drawing largely on historical and literary sources. Children would study folktales of different cultures, novels that provide a taste of history, biographies, poetry, songs, and books that help them understand such complicated subjects as the U.S. Constitution. Good teachers already use some such materials in social studies, but many less imaginative teachers seldom deviate from the textbooks.

Textbooks generally do not play as prominent a role in the social studies during the first three or four grades as they do in the upper grades. This is true not only because the students are not yet strong readers, but also because the curriculum and the subject matter in the earlier years more readily lend themselves to less formal materials. Even if teachers don't use social studies textbooks very much, however, they tend to follow the scope and sequence of the curriculum as presented in the textbooks.

A danger of too heavy a reliance on textbooks for teaching social studies in elementary school is that some of the books are just not very good. Imaginative teachers often can develop lessons that are more apt to motivate students in social studies and to lead to the students learning more. David Elliott, Kathleen Carter Nagel, and Arthur Woodward reviewed ten of the leading social studies series for elementary school and found these six major problems:

1. Rather than providing a good, basic underpinning in the subject, building concepts and skills from grade to grade, the books in each series were a collection of separate, unrelated topics that often were little more than lists of dates, events, and names.

2. The emphasis was on the United States even when an international or cross-cultural understanding was supposed to be the goal.

3. The approach in the textbooks assumed that teachers would use recitation, reading, and simple exercise, and only occasionally were there case studies or activities that required the use of higher-order thinking skills. Seldom were concepts involving anthropology, sociology, or economics brought into play.

4. Many topics were covered superficially, with some subjects just mentioned and dropped because publishers tried to cram the books with as much content as possible.

5. Representations of women and minorities were unrealistic, making the books still largely accounts of white male achievements.

6. Skills emphasized were generally those most easily tested, such as map reading. Although publishers claimed they integrated higher-order thinking skills into their series, these were primarily relegated to occasional appearances in chapter and unit review exercises, not used to underpin the main discussions of the topics.

Books of all sorts figure into social studies in another way. Social studies and language arts are seen as companion subjects, and this makes sense as long as the content of social studies does not get underemphasized. In other words, if a goal of the school is to teach reading, then why not use reading in the social studies as a way that reading gets taught? At the same time, reading is the heart of social studies and it should be seen as a subject that is very much related to the main focus of school.

Whether students read, hear lectures, watch videotapes, or go on field trips, it is difficult to say just what it is that students ought to learn in the social studies during these elementary school years. Standardized tests in reading and math can be based on discrete skills that students are expected to master at each grade level for sequential progression through the subject. Social studies does not lend itself to this kind of testing. There is no discrete body of skills in the social studies that an elementary school pupil ought to master by a certain grade.

One measure of knowledge in social studies is provided by the National Assessment of Educational Progress. The only grade tested at the elementary level was the fourth grade, and these were some of the results:

• In identifying by name whether rivers were in the United States, the Mississippi River was recognized as an American river by 84 percent, the Ohio River by 71 percent, and the Missouri River by 66 percent. Sixty-six percent knew that the Amazon is not in the United States, and 72 percent knew that the Rhine is not in the United States.

• Presented with a list of several states and asked which was a southern state—Connecticut, Idaho, Minnesota, Mississippi, and Ohio—42 percent knew that Mississippi is in the South.

• Given the names of five European countries, 40 percent knew that England is the one that had the most influence on the United States during its early history.

• On a question dealing with technological development, 62 percent knew that guns existed at the time of Columbus.

• Asked to write a short definition of democracy, fewer than 3 percent were able to do so correctly, as compared with 42 percent of eighth-graders and 74 percent of high school seniors.

There is an unfortunate tendency to try to reduce social studies to a set of facts on which students can more easily be tested, a practice that the National Assessment —with varying degrees of success—tries to resist in its tests. The overemphasis on dates and names traditional to the teaching of history and social studies generally is a product of the questionable stressing of facts. Mindless memorization is required in some places. Geography, for instance, in this kind of approach becomes a collection of the names and populations of capitals instead of an examination of how day-to-day life of people might be influenced by the location of deserts and mountains.

It is not that facts are insignificant, but that ideas and concepts are more important. Knowing the exact populations of India and China is not as vital as understanding how the countries are affected by policies dealing with population growth. Knowing the names of the United States senators and representatives from Illinois is not as crucial as knowing why there is a bicameral Congress and how the powers in the two houses differ. Knowing the names of the founders of Rhode Island is not as meaningful as understanding why the state's founding was important in the development of religious freedom in the colonies.

Social studies, and history in particular, can be one of the most exciting subjects offered in elementary school and the fact that so many children end up hating history attests to the failure of the schools to teach social studies as well as it ought to be taught. Parents can supplement the teaching of history in the schools by doing some of the following with their elementary-aged youngsters:

• Giving them biographies of famous people to read at home.

• Suggesting that they conduct tape-recorded interviews of grandparents and older relatives, asking about their experiences as children.

• Taking them on a trip to Washington, D.C., to visit the White House, the Capitol, the Washington Monument, the Lincoln Memorial, and other sites that would appeal to a young child.

• Visiting Colonial Williamsburg, in Virginia, a remarkable restoration of life during the colonial period. Similar experiences are available on a more modest scale at such regional re-creations as Old Sturbridge Village in Massachusetts.

• Making weekend excursions to historic landmarks near home.

Perhaps parents should be guided by the definition of social studies presented in 1986 by the National Council for the Social Studies:

The purpose of social studies for young children, as for all age groups, is to enable them to understand and to participate effectively in their world. Social studies explains their relationship to other people, to institutions and to the environment. It equips children with the knowledge and understanding of the past which is necessary for coping with the present and planning for the future. It provides them with the skills for productive problem solving and decision making, as well as for assessing issues and making thoughtful value judgments. Above all, it integrates these skills and understandings into a framework for responsible citizen participation, whether in their play group, the school, the community or the world.

17

THE ARTS

he arts get a great deal of attention when students begin their formal schooling in kindergarten. They paint with watercolors, draw with crayons, and model with clay. They dance and sing and enjoy watching their classmates perform. Once they enter first grade, however, the amount of time devoted to the arts falls precipitously. It is as though the arts are acceptable as long as there is not serious academic work to be done.

Elementary schools tend not to give the arts secure slots in the curriculum. Often the amount of art or music that gets taught may depend on how much interest the teacher has in these subjects. One result of the back-to-basics movement is that the fringe subjects, already on shaky ground, find themselves tottering more than usual. Also, the effort that became so pronounced in the early 1980s to hold down costs, has sometimes meant a hand-to-mouth existence for the arts.

This negative attitude toward the arts by those who

---

set policy is unfortunate, because it would be of benefit to students to have more time for the arts than is usually given from first through sixth grades. A child's development is fostered by the opportunity for self-expression through the creation and appreciation of the arts. Moreover, exposure to the arts during elementary school can lay the groundwork for a lifetime of artistic enjoyment.

It is true that much of what students do in art in kindergarten appears to be play, as they dabble in fingerpaints or draw pictures, but good teachers use these experiences to help children learn about color, texture, and line. Students who look at art that they have made, as well as pictures and slides of professionally created art, gain their first insights into the elements that distinguish art. A good teacher will encourage children who study art to speak of their likes and dislikes, as well as the reasons for their preferences.

Art in the earliest elementary grades is also a vehicle for reinforcing lessons in math about shapes and forms, which lend a basis for geometry. By the first grade, students may knowingly incorporate circles, squares, triangles, rectangles, cones, pyramids, cubes, and cylinders into their art. Similarly, their concept of lines in math is enhanced by a growing awareness of lines in art that are vertical, horizontal, and diagonal.

Among the most important lessons taught through art in the early grades are those having to do with perception. The training that youngsters get in regard to space, dimension, and balance sharpens their budding powers of observation. In the first grade, students develop to the point that the human bodies they draw are more accurate in proportion than the stick figures of earlier years. First grade also is not too soon to begin delving into art history and learning about famous artists and their works.

Ideally, during the second and third grades, the lessons in art should be more complex, as students gain experience in their execution of art in many media and in their perception and understanding of art. Teachers should move quickly in these lower grades to make certain that students realize that art can take free form and does not have to mimic traditional forms. One former elementary school art specialist, Marianne Graham Vecsey, who taught in a district on New York's suburban Long Island, remembers a principal who told her that the only acceptable art in his school was for students to copy other art.

A good school affords students in the lower elementary grades the chance to work in a wide variety of media —clay, papier-mâché, wood, paint, felt pen, paper, and metal. In the third grade, students should be able to speak knowledgeably about the use of color, texture, shape, and form. Art also should be used extensively by this point for children to build on their appreciation of the natural environment. They can borrow ideas from nature and apply their powers of perception to what they see around them. Lessons in art are a convenient entry point by the middle elementary years for instruction in geology, astronomy, and environmental science.

By the third grade, students have the ability to draw objects "the way they look," if they choose. Figures move off the base line of the picture, giving a greater sense of space and distance. Light and dark colors are used more selectively to give contrast. Third-graders can make posters, form designs by bending and cutting heavy paper, make simple costumes and puppets, assemble attractive collages, and glue together small strips of wood to build bridges and houses.

The tests that the National Assessment of Educational Progress used to assess the abilities and knowledge of fourth-graders in art give parents some indication of the attributes they might hope to see cultivated in their children in elementary school. The tests covered five areas: (1) the ability to perceive the elements of a work of art, (2) the extent to which art is personally valued as an important realm of human experience, (3) the ability to produce art, (4) knowledge about art history, and (5) the ability to make and justify judgments about the aesthetic merit of artworks. Parents might thumb through art books at home with their children and initiate discussions that probe some of these same features.

For example, students participating in the National Assessment were asked if they could recognize and describe the subject-matter elements of works of art. A parent, in turn, might—in keeping with the questions on the test—ask a child to identify the objects in specific representational works or to describe how the treatment of objects in two specific works of art is similar or different. Also, children in elementary school can be asked to identify themes of art and events that are depicted, as well as the main idea presented in the art.

In attempting to determine how much fourth-graders valued art as an important realm of human experience, the National Assessment asked questions about how often the students pursued activities that would make them more likely to be oriented toward art. Ideally, students would be openly expectant to enjoy looking at art, respond emotionally to art, and consider it important to see art. Those apt to go in this direction were the youngsters who indicated that they most frequently visited art museums and attended exhibitions, visited school art displays, looked at art in magazines and books, and were aware of aesthetic objects in natural and human-made environments.

Fourth-graders were deemed most advanced in producing works of art, to the degree that they could produce a work that met the demands of space or shape, contained specific subject matter, and had a particular mood, feeling, or expressive character. Their work was assessed according to whether it contained various visual conceptions. They were asked to demonstrate their ability to represent spatial conceptions, which, for example, might mean one person standing in front of another, or a near object and a far object, or a building with a street running in front of it. They were also assessed on the ability to produce works in which the subject-matter conveyed such expressions and emotions as running, walking, laughing, or crying.

A separate area of testing dealt with knowledge about art. Fourth-graders were asked to identify well-known works of art, tell why the works were important or significant, and name the artist who produced the work. Furthermore, they were to select from among several examples those works exemplifying a particular style, and to explain why two or more works of art were similar or different in style.

Another area of knowledge concerned the history of art and an understanding of the relationship of one style or period to other styles or periods. Students were asked to place works of art in the time period in which they were produced. Fourth-graders were also asked to distinguish between factors of a work of art that relate principally to the personal style of the artist and those that relate to a stylistic period. The last area of questioning had to do with the ability to judge art and to justify opinions. This meant evaluating a work as good or bad and giving reasons why the work has or does not have aesthetic merit.

Obviously, some fourth-graders were more adept than others at answering questions about art. However, none were expected to answer the questions with the sophistication of older students, who not only were asked most of the same questions but also were asked more intricate questions. The point here is that the kinds of questions just cited were presented to nine-year-olds, and it is reasonable to expect a good art program to equip students even of that age with the means to cope with such queries, albeit on a rudimentary level.

Art in the fifth and sixth grades should be a matter of becoming more proficient in technique and digging more deeply into the topics introduced by the end of the fourth grade. Some additional topics such as photography are presented in some schools to widen the exposure of students to other art forms, and perhaps a video camera is used to make films in class.

By the end of elementary school, a student who has thrived in a good art program should be able to recognize the style of certain artists who have been studied; know something about art from Asia, Africa, and South America, in addition to that of the United States and Europe; and have an art vocabulary that includes an understanding of such terms as *plane, form, positive and negative space, perspective, rhythm*, and *balance*. They should also have an awareness of analogous and complementary colors and be able to evaluate art on the basis of commonly recognized elements and principles.

Art education is definitely deficient in some elementary schools. A National Assessment report on art education observed: "Most elementary programs give children opportunities to explore different art materials and to make things for themselves or their parents, but formal instruction in art history and criticism is infrequent. Even if there is a special art teacher in an elementary school, children are likely to receive only 15 to 30 hours of instruction per year or about 180 hours during the total elementary period."

Parents who care about the art education of their children must resolve to assume some responsibility for ensuring that it is provided through out-of-school experiences, if possible. Some states do not even require that art be taught in elementary schools. The National Assessment concluded that students are likely to learn more from the art opportunities after school and on weekends than in the classroom. It is clear that schools cannot be counted on when it comes to art.

Music is even less likely than art to be taught in a thorough manner. The day is long gone when there seemed to be a piano in each elementary school classroom and almost every teacher knew how to play the piano so that music could readily be incorporated into the school day. Whether it is a matter of performing vocal or instrumental music or simply listening to music and learning to appreciate it, schools do not give high priority to music.

Children are naturally predisposed toward music and it is shortsighted of any teacher in elementary school not to take advantage of this inclination. Young children hum, they sing, they beat out rhythms. They are ready for music from the time they start school. An astute teacher will cultivate this interest as early as kindergarten to help students recognize upward and downward pitch and to match pitches with voices. Children at this age can get a sense of fast and slow sounds and long and short sounds. Kindergarteners are not likely to be able to harmonize, but they can be made aware of the existence of harmony.

A kindergarten is incomplete without a record player to expose children to a wide variety of music. Teachers may no longer have the ability to play pianos, but it takes no talent to play a stereo. One kindergarten teacher encountered in the preparation of this book made it a practice to play classical music part of the day while children were going about their activities. Singing should be a regular part of the kindergarten program, and children should have ample opportunity to play simple rhythm instruments to accompany songs. Sometimes their bodies become the instruments and they sway to the rhythm. Kindergarten also is not too early to initiate discussions with children—without pressing too deeply—about why they like or dislike certain musical selections.

In a school with a good music program much of the approach used in kindergarten will continue into the first grade. Parents should object if the school more or less abandons music after kindergarten. Also, the first grade is not too soon for school trips to attend musical performances appropriate to the limited attention span of the children. Students should be fully cognizant of the difference between instrumental music and vocal music when listening to a record.

Also, the first grade is a time to expose children to written music by making them aware of the staff, some of the basic notations, and the lines on which notes are enscribed. They can start writing simple rhythm patterns and can develop the ability to sing on pitch within a limited range.

What advances the musical knowledge of some children beyond that of their classmates during the second and third grades is the chance to take lessons on an instrument. Some schools offer lessons, and parents who want their children to study an instrument ought to look into the possibility of private lessons, as well. Reading and math take on such importance in the early elementary grades that the school may very well give little attention to music during this time.

In a school that continues with a full-blown music program, a child by the end of the third grade ought to be able to follow simple written musical notation, recognize from a record the sounds of specific orchestral instruments, and play simple tunes on the xylophone and the recorder.

Fourth-graders were tested in music by the National Assessment of Educational Progress. Ideally, the main objectives at this point in their schooling were for students to value music as an important realm of human experience, perform music, create music, identify the elements and expressive controls of music, and identify and classify music historically and culturally. As with art, many of the most important experiences for students came outside the school.

How are you to know if your child values music? For one thing, according to the National Assessment, the youngster is responsive upon hearing music. This means listening with attention and enjoyment. It won't happen all the time and all kinds of music won't trigger this response. But at least sometimes music will stir such a response and a child of elementary school age, especially by fourth grade, might well be able to discuss the inner mood created by the music, possibly selecting from a given set of descriptions those that most accurately reflect the mood engendered by the music.

Another way a child might show that music is valued is by gaining some acquaintance with the music of different nations, cultures, periods, genres, and ethnic groups. A child who values music will sometimes seek to listen to music for enjoyment and spend some leisure time in musical activities. It is not unreasonable to expect an elementary school–aged student who values music to make and support aesthetic judgments about music. The National Assessment set as an objective for nine-year-olds that they be able to evaluate a musical performance, composition, or arrangement.

There are, of course, many different levels of achievement in performing and creating music. Both vocal and instrumental music should be available to elementary school students, though many youngsters may choose not to learn to play an instrument. But a parent who would like to see a child get the most out of music in elementary school should bear in mind that the National Assessment set as goals that a nine-year-old be able to select and play a short composition on an instrument of choice, be able to read a score, be able to add a melodic or rhythmic accompaniment while listening to a familiar melody, and write a short composition using traditional or nontraditional notation.

As for identifying the elements and expressive controls of music, this could mean—while listening to or playing a rhythm at age nine—showing an understanding of an ongoing pulse, the predominant rhythmic pattern and metrical groupings in two, threes, and combinations thereof. An objective for this age group is that they be able to select from examples of notation the one that most accurately represents the music to which they have listened, identify individual instrumental timbres, and recognize and describe the ways in which structure and form are achieved in music.

If many of these objectives seem beyond the grasp of a child halfway through elementary school, it is not because the goals are inappropriate but because the curriculum may be inadequate for fostering proper musical development in students. Were schools satisfied to accept so rudimentary a level of achievement in students in the basic subjects as they seem readily willing to tolerate in music or art, the education in reading, math, science, and social studies would be deemed inadequate. What is inadequate in many elementary schools is the instruction in music.

These are some of the results when nine-year-olds were asked questions about music on the National Assessment examination:

- Shown a few measures of a staff containing notes and symbols, 29 percent recognized the key signature and 26 percent recognized that a quarter note got one count.

- After listening to a simple tune played on the piano that went first up and then down in pitch, 51 percent selected a line representing the up-and-then-down pattern of the pitch.

- Asked whether music can "change the way you feel," 75 percent of the fourth-graders answered positively.

- Looking at a line of music, 47 percent could identify a half note.

In the fifth and sixth grades, students who have learned in a good music program in the early grades to read musical notation are taught to read increasingly complex scores. They learn as a group to play at a rudimentary level some other instruments such as the guitar or the piano. Musical history introduces them to the lives and times of the great composers. They gain a sense of harmony, melody, tempo, and mood in music.

There should be ample opportunities to perform music in the upper grades of elementary school. Choruses should exist for those interested in vocal music, and the school band or orchestra should be an outlet for instrumental expression. All children are not able or desirous of pursuing music on this more advanced level, but a school that has no chorus or instrumental group is not allowing children to reach their full potential for group participation in musical performance.

A word about the other performing arts. Elementary school should be a place for exposure to dance and drama. Children at this age should gain a sense of these areas both as participants and as audience. Dance should be built into the music program and drama should be an extension of language arts. The children ought to observe performances by professional actors and dancers and create and perform their own dances and plays. The interest in the performing arts cultivated in young children can carry into secondary school and determine whether these forms of expression will be ones that appeal to them either as performers or as audience members.

18

FOREIGN LANGUAGES

An argument for starting the teaching of foreign languages early is that students in elementary school are probably at the best age for picking up another language. Taught properly, a foreign language can interest and stimulate young children and be a fine complement to reading and social studies. Also, an early start in a foreign language can mean that by the time students reach secondary school, they may be ready for advanced work.

"It is simply good common sense that the longer students spend mastering a skill, the more proficient they become at it," said Myriam Met, supervisor of foreign languages for the Montgomery County, Maryland, public schools. "Students who begin foreign language in kindergarten have the thirteen years of their academic career to become fluent in the language."

There are three basic approaches to teaching foreign language in the lower grades—FLEX, FLES, and immersion. The issue is not so much which is best for your child, as what objectives you have in mind.

Foreign Language Experience, FLEX, provides exposure, but does not develop fluency. Students get a taste of a language and the culture of the people who use it. The sessions are relatively brief, maybe no more than once or twice a week for twenty or thirty minutes each time. A very basic vocabulary is introduced and lessons deal with the rudiments of conversation, usually not bothering with reading or writing the language. FLEX is not an exercise in depth, being little more than a supplement to the regular curriculum. It is generally taught by the regular teacher, who does not have to know the language to handle this sort of approach.

Foreign Language in Elementary School, FLES, is an older approach and more comprehensive. Students are expected to acquire some fluency, and reading and writing are a part of the program. Sessions may be daily and are usually held at least three times a week, providing up to five hours a week of instruction. Because the objective is more ambitious, the teacher may be a specialist who meets with the class only for the foreign language instruction.

In the FLES program in one big-city school system, the third-, fourth- and fifth-graders who participate listen on tapes to songs and simple dialogues to gain a sense of the sound of the language they are studying. They respond to the tape by singing the songs, asking and answering the questions, and mimicking the dialogues. Before they start reading the language they grow accustomed to the labels that are placed on every object in the room to give them the name in the foreign language. The first writing they do is to prepare labels of their own and to inscribe the names of objects under pictures.

Immersion, the third approach, is just that, a full-fledged effort in which the foreign language is the medium of instruction for regular subjects. Students do not *study* the foreign language; they study *in* the foreign language. It is what would be likely to happen if a family moved to another country and sent its children to the local schools, where the youngsters would take all their subjects in the local language. Immersion can also occur in an American elementary school where the goal is to give students the sort of exposure to a foreign language that will make them bilingual. After the students gain aptitude in the foreign language, some of the instruction of basic subjects will continue in that language, and English also is used as a medium of instruction.

Experts tend to believe that if the immersion approach is used, it should begin at the elementary school level when children are more flexible and have not yet gotten into the depth of the secondary curriculum. One of the earliest public school immersion programs in the United States was in Culver City, California, where, starting in 1971, kindergarteners and first-graders were taught entirely in Spanish. By the second or third grade students gained fluency in Spanish. An hour of reading in English was introduced in the second grade, and then 40 percent of the curriculum was taught in English in grades four through six. This program and others that were monitored by the Center for Applied Linguistics in Washington, D.C., led to students scoring above the national norms on tests in English and Spanish at the end of the sixth grade.

After examining research on the teaching of foreign

languages, the U.S. Department of Education concluded: "The best way to learn a foreign language in school is to start early and study it intensively over many years." Special praise was given to the immersion approach.

Parents whose children are studying a foreign language in elementary school may want to try some of these approaches to reinforce what is being taught in the school:

- Take them to a restaurant where food native to the culture they are studying is served and let them order and engage in conversation with the serving person.

- Study the same language and share what you are learning with your child.

- Go on a vacation to a country where the language is spoken.

- Get recorded folk music from the country and let your child play it.

- Encourage your child to tune in radio or television programs that are broadcast in the tongue being studied.

- Buy magazines and newspapers from that country.

Two organizations that parents might want to contact with questions about the teaching of foreign language in the elementary school are these:

Advocates for Language Learning
Box 4964
Culver City, Calif. 90231
213-397-2448

National Network for Early Language Learning
c/o Center for Applied Linguistics
1118 22nd Street N.W.
Washington, D.C. 20037
202-429-9292

The Culver City group publishes a newsletter to which parents might wish to subscribe.

Despite the advantages of an early start in foreign languages, there are many school systems that do not offer foreign languages at the elementary level. There are some good reasons for delaying foreign languages until at least junior high school. Some of the most desirable public and private schools in the country do not offer foreign languages at the elementary level. The time factor is the primary reason. Priority should go to reading and math and, given the time limitations of the school day, a foreign language may simply be a luxury.

Also, for students for whom the mastery of English does not come so easily, it is felt that there is some danger of confusion by asking them to cope with Spanish, French, or some other language while they still have problems reading, writing, and speaking in English, their native tongue.

Finally, the teaching of a foreign language at elementary school may fail because the subject is not taught properly, not because the children are not ready for it. The problem may be in the instruction. Teachers who are not themselves fluent in the language have trouble staying ahead of the lessons they are providing for the students. Or a smattering of vocabulary given for a few minutes every few days may be time wasted for students who have no context for the words, no introduction of good pronunciation, and little opportunity for practice.

On balance, though, the case for foreign language instruction in elementary school is compelling, and under most circumstances parents should welcome the programs if they are taught competently.

19

PHYSICAL EDUCATION

Gym class may seem like fluff, but actually it can be an important part of the instructional program. It need not be offered daily, but it should be more frequent than once a week. The difficulty is that in many elementary schools physical education is not taken seriously by teachers. Physical education from fifth through twelfth grades is required in only four states—New York, New Jersey, Illinois, and California.

Some of the objectives of physical education are fulfilled in elementary school through informal, unsupervised activities on the school playground. This may come before or after the school day or during lunch. In addition, many schools have recess breaks when children are allowed to go onto the playground. What is significant to learning during these sessions is the social interaction connected with the rough-and-tumble play. Children quickly devise rules to guide their impromptu games when it is left to them to solve the problems and conflicts that arise. Adults are needed only when things get utterly out of hand.

Much role-playing occurs on the playground, some children evolving into leaders and others into followers. They learn the value of cooperation and, unfortunately, some of the nastier aspects of socialization. All in all, playground activities are a kind of model of life itself and parents should recognize the function that is served by allowing students to spend time on the playground.

The nature of the playground equipment helps determine what students will get out of their informal play. Balance beams, climbing towers, and other apparatus help very young children develop large-muscle strength and coordination. This will become more crucial as they get a little older and engage in sports in which they are not yet likely to participate during the earliest elementary grades. Equipment on good playgrounds is best when it encourages creative play and allows students to get the stimulation they need for muscle development.

Besides informal play, a good elementary school should offer a regular physical education program. This is not to say that physical education is as valuable as academic subjects, but it is sufficiently important to be provided on a regular basis from first grade through sixth grade. These are some of the ways in which students' needs are met through physical education:

- Anyone of any age can sit still just so long. There should be a chance to move around and expend physical energy.

- Exercise is a basic need, and study after study has found that American children are out of shape before they complete elementary school.

- The lessons learned in sports have a carryover effect. Sportsmanship, cooperation, and accepting both victory and defeat with grace are traits for all walks of life.

- Certain athletic skills taught in childhood can be a source of recreational pleasure in adulthood, as for example tennis, bowling, and golf.

- Socialization experiences should be provided for children in many kinds of settings, not just in the academic aura, so that they can become familiar with a wider range of responses.

- Some youngsters who are not able students may find that they are more proficient in physical education, giving them an outlet for building up their self-image.

Yet in many elementary schools few of these outcomes are realized. The physical education program never fulfills its potential. It turns out to be a waste of time. There are several reasons for this failure, and these are a few that you might try to see avoided at your child's elementary school:

- There is no physical education teacher and the class is left in the hands of the classroom teacher, who has neither the knowledge nor the interest to make gym successful.

- There is a physical education teacher, but the person is more like a jail warden, mainly interested in instilling discipline in the students and taking the enjoyment out of what ought to be pleasurable experience.

- Competition is stressed to a degree that some children are afraid to try for fear of failure.

- Gym is more of a recess or a free period with children running wild and no learning taking place.

- So much of the time is devoted to playing games that few skills are directly taught and the students who are less-able athletes are shunted to the sidelines.

- Using the excuse that gym can no longer be a useful class since the law now requires mixed classes for boys and girls, and instructor has abdicated responsibility for running a good program and leaves the students to do what they want.

A major role of physical education in kindergarten and the earliest grades is in helping youngsters develop co-ordination and control over their movements. In the hands of an able teacher, the drills, games, and dances have a purpose. Gradually, children gain confidence in their bodies and learn to perform new feats of physical prowess. During the first and second grades, as these activities continue, the games they play become a basis for learning about sportsmanship and cooperation. They learn to accept winning and losing. Here is an example of what is expected of children in the third grade in one physical education curriculum:

- Throw and bounce large and small balls with one or two hands.

- Bounce a ball while running.

- Catch a ball while running.

- Kick a ball that is resting on the ground.

- Move a ball along the ground with the feet, as is done in soccer.

- Throw and catch hoops and rings.

- Jump rope on one foot, alternating feet as the rope turns forward or backward.

The middle and upper elementary grades is a period during which students should be exposed to unfamiliar games and learn the intricacies of the rules of the various games they play. They should be introduced to gymnastics and calisthenics. They should attain proficiency in the basic running, throwing, and catching movements in softball, and dribbling, blocking, and heading in soccer. A good program presents both team sports and individual sports to children, and by the end of elementary school they will form preferences for athletic pursuits that can add to the fullness of their teenage years.

During the past generation awareness of the need for physical conditioning has increased and parents have come to realize that many children are out of shape by the time they are ten or eleven years old. This is deplorable. An elementary school ought to encourage fitness, along with proper nutrition and good health habits. The physical education program in the upper elementary grades should foster strength and endurance and do so in ways that are not pejorative to children who have difficulty reaching the goals. Children should learn calisthenics that they can do at home and pursue on their own in an effort to maintain fitness.

Presumably, parents today realize that goals in physical education should embrace both girls and boys. Girls are fully able to participate in a program and should in no way be treated as though expectations for them are less than they are for boys. Female students formerly were denied athletic experiences as schoolchildren and did not have a basis upon which to enjoy sports participation as adults. Parents who find that girls are not given equal treatment in elementary school physical education programs should bring such omissions to the attention of teachers. Not only is it wrong for physical education programs to discriminate against girls, it is against federal law.

If you cannot satisfactorily answer your questions about the physical education program in your child's school, then these are some of the organizations to which you might turn for additional information:

The President's Council on Physical Fitness and Sports
450 Fifth Street N.W.
Suite 7103
Washington, D.C. 20001
202-272-3421

Fitnessgram
Institute for Aerobics Research
12330 Preston Road
Dallas, Tex. 75230
214-701-8001

Know Your Body
American Health Foundation
320 East 43rd Street
New York, N.Y. 10017
212-953-1900

National Fitness Foundation
2250 East Imperial Highway
El Segundo, Calif. 90245
213-640-0145

Feelin' Good
Fitness Finders Inc.
133 Teft Road
Spring Arbor, Mich. 49283
517-750-1500

20

THE ROLE OF COMPUTERS

People who continue to believe that fascination with the computer is a fad that will pass like the Hula Hoop or the Pet Rock are dead wrong. The computer is no more likely to disappear from use than the automobile or the telephone. There are occupations that have been transformed by the computer and in which basic operations scarcely resemble those familiar to the practitioners of ten or fifteen years ago. Architecture and engineering, for example, have been radically altered. The preparation of articles from the writing to production has been changed at magazines and newspapers. Wall Street and the legal profession have been able to take shortcuts of a revolutionary nature. Hospitals are run differently and the federal government has a new way of maintaining its bureaucracy.

What all this means to the average elementary school is that if computers are not incorporated into education, students will be denied access to a vital learning resource that is very much a part of the modern age. It is possible for students to get a first-rate education in elementary school without ever seeing a computer, but for a school not to make use of computers is to ignore a resource that can deepen the educational experience of children and enhance their learning.

It is not so much that students must learn how to program computers and understand the technical aspects of the workings of computers. That was the idea in the early 1980s, when computers were introduced in schools and the phrase on everyone's lips was "computer literacy." Now, though, it is clear that there are more important educational uses for computers. Indeed, while some students will grow familiar with the intricacies of computers and become whizzes at programming them, educators now recognize that going in this direction is not necessary for all or even most children.

The emphasis on computer literacy, which included recommendations in more than a dozen states that all students be taught programming and a technical understanding of computers, is giving way to a new realization that what counts most is simply operating the computer, not knowing how it works. It is akin to the idea that to drive a car it is not necessary to know the mechanical principles of internal combustion.

Relatively few jobs require a technical comprehension of the workings of computers. A lawyer who uses a computer to search for case references in preparing a brief does not have to know how a computer works or how to program it. A reporter whose writing is done on a computer does not have to know how a computer works or how to program it. In each instance, what is most important is that the person learn to relay commands to the computer through the keyboard—a sort of advanced form of typing. What the computer can do, though, is far beyond anything of which a typewriter is capable.

What is important is that students use computers to augment their learning, just as they use the library for this purpose. Lessons can be taught on computers and perhaps be more individual than they are in books. Computers can be learning devices to solve simulated problems. They can be research tools, giving students access to mountains of information. Computers can be used for drills and for tutoring, though it is not wise to overuse them for this purpose. Computers are also the basis for word processing, which means that students can hone their writing skills and prepare papers for class. Most of these adaptations fit under what has come to be known as CAI, or computer-assisted instruction.

Computers in the classroom can be a boon to a teaching philosophy in which students become more active learners, taking greater responsibility for their own education. Involved learners who do not merely sit around passively listening to the teacher lecture are apt to be more effective and more motivated learners. "The essence of computer-based education is the direct involvement of the student at the center of the learning process, and the assumption of responsibility by the student for his own learning process," said William C. Norris, founder and chairman emeritus of Control Data Corporation.

Thus, parents should welcome the use of computers in their children's classrooms. But just having computers in classrooms is not enough. They must be used properly. Parents visiting classrooms should try to notice the ways in which the computers are used. These are some of the questions to bear in mind:

- How many students are there for each computer? Only one or two computers in a room is not enough to be a serious part of the educational program.

- Are the computers in a special "computer room" instead of in the regular classroom? This is not ideal. It probably means that the computer is not integral to the educational program and that the children simply are learning *about computers* instead of using the computers to learn *about their subjects*.

- Are the computers used in conjunction with lessons taught by the regular classroom teacher or only with a special "computer teacher"? Putting computers under the direction of a computer teacher means, most likely, that the regular classroom teacher is not conversant with computers and that computers are not integral to the educational program.

A report by the National Assessment in 1988 showed that among third-graders computers were used the most in mathematics. The next most frequent use of computers was in the study of language arts. The least use in the main subjects was in science and social studies. Seventy-eight percent of all the boys in the third grade and 71 percent of all the girls said they had used a computer at some time or other, either in school or outside.

In math, computers can be helpful in presenting students with exercises to apply the basic skills of adding, subtracting, dividing, and multiplying. Then, in turn, students can do drills in these functions and, where necessary, get tutoring through the computer. More importantly, students can be presented with problems to solve on the computer. As matters now stand, students in many elementary schools spend much of their time in the first three or four grades repeatedly doing computational exercises. So much time is devoted to the basic arithmetic of adding, subtracting, dividing, and multiplying that students do not spend enough time thinking about how to apply these skills. Once students have a grasp of the fundamentals, it might be better to let them use calculators and computers to manipulate the numbers so that more attention can be given to problem solving.

When they go on to problem solving with a computer, students—instead of doing drills—can be presented with a narrative on the screen that sets out a situation that, say, requires thinking about what number must be subtracted from another and then deciding, for example, what should be divided by what. If the student heads off in a mistaken direction, the computer can flash a warning, intervening at the point of the error and asking why one number was selected instead of another. The computer can help refocus the student's thinking, continually requiring the student to account for each of the various steps of the solution. Depending on the student's response, the computer can reformulate the problem in a different way.

One cannot overlook the value of the computer as a motivational tool in math, even if it is used for nothing more than drills. Many teachers find that they can get far more out of students when they work at a terminal than when they work with paper and pencil.

A notable contribution of computers in the lower elementary grades has been in teaching about geometric shapes. Students can be asked to draw shapes on the screen and the computer can provide perspectives that add a three-dimensional appearance to the shapes. The computer can respond as the drawing is being executed, giving individual feedback to each pupil more quickly than a teacher who must oversee an entire class. Many students have trouble getting a sense of spatial relationships, and this is an area in which computers can be very helpful. This kind of use of computers can continue through the upper elementary grades and into high school geometry class, as youngsters are called upon to work with increasingly more complex geometric concepts.

In elementary school science, the computer can introduce the possibility of using a spread sheet to learn how to record, organize, and analyze scientific data. Using the matrix form presented on the screen, a student conducting an experiment can insert new information in the appropriate column, quickly compare it with statistics from past observations, and draw conclusions about the progress of the experiment.

Another use of the computer in elementary school involves its role in stimulating students to do more critical thinking. At least one program, Higher-Order Thinking Skills Compensatory Program, has been used with low-achieving students to set up problems that the students must solve with very little help from the teacher. The program was originally funded by the U.S. Department of Education and later got funding from the Ford Foundation, with computers supplied by the Apple Corporation. A similar approach could be used to promote the critical thinking of students at all achievement levels.

This kind of individualization, made easier with computers, can facilitate the ability of the teacher to accommodate the differing needs and ability levels of students. A separate program can be put into each student's computer. Grouping students of different abilities for separate lessons in various parts of the classroom is less necessary this way. Slower students do not have to suffer the embarrassment that so often comes from sitting with the group that the rest of the class knows is the weakest.

Teachers, unfortunately, are slow to adapt computers to some of their most productive instructional uses. In all too many elementary school classrooms, computers are not made integral to the educational program. Another problem in some elementary schools is that there are far too many students per computer, reducing the amount of time that each child gets to spend on the computer. Computers are not distributed evenly among schools and some schools have no computers while others have almost enough to let each pupil have his or her own.

Another reason why computers are not used as extensively as they might be is that educators vary greatly in their understanding and appreciation of computers. Teachers and principals in some schools fail to utilize computers even when they are abundantly available. The average elementary school student used a computer in school only thirty-five minutes a week in 1985, according to a survey by Johns Hopkins University.

Still another limitation on the use of computers has to do with the software that is available. Software makes a computer run, giving it directions that are to be followed when the buttons are pressed. The software consists basically of the disks on which the programs are imprinted. Many of these programs are little more than gimmicks or drills that could be done just as readily in paper and pencil, making them inadequate for good teaching. The only possible advantage of some software is that the student might be more eager to pursue a lesson simply because it allows him or her to use a computer. Not enough good programs have been produced to enable elementary-school-age children to get the most out of their experiences with computers.

Alfred Bork, a professor of computer science and director of the Educational Technology Center at the University of California at Irvine, said that these factors characterize poorly designed educational software:

- Failure to make use of the interactive capabilities of the computer.

- Use of extremely weak forms of interaction, such as multiple-choice questions.

- Failure to use the capabilities of the computer to individualize instruction.

- Heavy reliance on text.

- Heavy reliance on pictures, when the pictures play no important role in helping students learn the material.

- Treatment of the computer screen as though it were a book page.

- Use of material that is entertaining or attractive but only vaguely educational.

- Content that does not fit anywhere in the curriculum.

- Focus on games that have no educational merit.

- Use of long sets of instructions at the beginning of programs that are difficult to follow—even for teachers —and difficult to recall.

- Heavy dependence on auxiliary print materials.

- Use of materials that fail to hold students' attention.

Parents of girls must be especially vigilant to ensure that their daughters do not shy away from computers. Female students, who so often suffer math anxiety, seem now to be afflicted with computer anxiety, as well. More girls than boys tend to avoid computers and, as a group, girls are less confident in using them. Experiments at schools and colleges have shown repeatedly that females, left on their own, do not make as much use of the computers as male students do. It is up to parents to do what they can to counteract this phenomenon, and it is a good idea to expect your child's school to make an extra effort in behalf of the girls with regard to computers.

Perhaps one way to interest girls and probably all children in computers is to encourage them to approach the machine much as they would a typewriter. Forget about the intimidating technology that makes a computer run. It would be far better if people thought of computers as fancy typewriters. A student who learns keyboarding skills can command the computer to perform a host of activities. For some students, the inclination to move on to programming and other technical operations will follow; most others will get what they need from computers merely by becoming proficient at keyboard skills.

Word processing is certainly one of the most valuable functions of a computer. The knowledge required for word processing is not much more complicated than what is needed to operate a typewriter. The ability to write is enhanced by features that allow the user to replace, delete, move, and insert text. This speeds up writing, but more importantly it allows writing and editing to be done simultaneously. Young people using computers for word processing are less likely to submit first drafts. Their work will have the advantage of editing. In the words of one sixth-grader in Jersey City, New Jersey, as quoted in *Principal* magazine: "The computer holds my interest because it can present information in many different ways. I find myself interested in things I was never interested in before. With the word processor I find myself writing more than I ever did before. I can make perfect stories, and worry less about how they look when finished. Not only my grades have improved but I am on a higher reading level now than I was before."

Whether the subject is fiction or nonfiction, a student-writer can let ideas flow into the text as they are imagined, going directly to the spot desired without having to crumple papers and continually start again. A variation of this process is the Writing to Read program developed for IBM by John Henry Martin, which allows kindergarten and first-grade children—using phonemic spelling—to write their ideas on a computer even before they know how to read. There is surely no end to the adaptations possible.

All of the educational uses of computers need not take place in schools, though. There are at least ten times as many computers in homes as there are in schools. It is certainly reasonable to expect that many of these computers at home will be used to help in the education of children, even if they do double duty as video games for entertainment or spread sheets for the family budget. A computer in the home is not a sine qua non to success in school, but it definitely can be helpful.

Parents who decide that having a computer at home is desirable for their children, must realize—as mentioned earlier—that a key to the machine's ability to help their children is the software that is put into it. A computer can be much more than a gimmick, and one way for parents to evaluate software is to see if it is just a lot of bells and whistles or if it truly has substance. In trying to decide whether a particular piece of softwear is suitable for your child, these are some of the questions that Gail A. Caissy, director of curriculum design and development for a software manufacturer, suggests be asked:

- Is the program making full use of the technology of the computer?

- Is the program likely to motivate and interest children?

- Who is in control of the program—the student or the computer?

- Is the ability level suitable to the child?

- Is the instructional design sound?

- Are the instructions in the program clear to the child?

- Is the reinforcement appropriate in its praise and rewards for correct answers?

- Does the program provide a record of student progress?

- Is the program grammatically sound and free of unnecessary computer jargon and spelling errors?

Evanston Educators Inc., an educational consulting group, identified more than 150 software programs for children that it endorsed. In its Family Software Catalogue ($1 from Evanston Educators Inc., 915 Elmwood

Avenue, Evanston, Ill. 60202) it cited these 11 programs for particular distinction:

1. Smart Eyes (Addison-Wesley Publishing)—to raise reading rate and comprehension.
2. Toy Shop (Broderbund)—to print out plans for building twenty working mechanical models.
3. Printmaster (Kyocera-Unison)—to create greeting cards, calendars, and banners.
4. Car Builder (Weekly Reader Family Software)—to design and test automobiles, vans, and trucks on the screen.
5. Polywindows Desk Plus (Polytron)—a memory-resident desktop organizer.
6. Creative Contraptions (Bantam)—to learn mechanical principles by building zany contraptions with pulleys, levers, springs, and magnets on the screen.
7. Homeworker (Davidson and Associates)—a study center for students with a simple word processor, an outliner to help organize papers, a vocabulary builder, a calendar, a grade tracker, and a calculator.
8. Writer Rabbit (The Learning Company)—to let students create and print out their own letters, stories, and award certificates.
9. Homeword Plus (Sierra On-Line)—an easy-to-learn word processor and spelling checker.
10. New World Thesaurus (Simon & Schuster)—has 120,000 synonyms and can be called up with a single keystroke from most leading word processors.
11. Stickybear Math 2 (Weekly Reader Family Software)—does for multiplication and division what Stickybear Math 1, its predecessor, does for addition and subtraction.

Computers offer parents an unusually rich opportunity to make the home a place where the learning imparted at school is reinforced. But parents should not be surprised if their children show more interest in games that allow them to chase computerized asteroids in computerized spaceships than in solving computerized mathematical problems. Human nature is, well, human nature and fun comes first. Perhaps the best approach is for parents not to have unrealistic expectations of how children will use home computers or of what the experience will mean to the schooling of children. If a computer is made available with some decent educational programming that appeals to the child, that is fine. But it could be that the best outcome at home is for children to gain familiarity and a feeling of comfort with a computer so that the computer is more readily used as a learning tool in school.

21

LEARNING HOW TO THINK

t was not until the 1980s that schools started talking explicitly and specifically about teaching students to think. Such pronouncements by the
schools are enough to make parents wonder. What
is it that the schools were doing until the 1980s?
Weren't students being taught to think? What is school
about if it is not about thinking?

These questions are not as easy to answer as it might
seem. The truth of the matter is that schools historically
have not done a good job of teaching students to think.
But it was not until the criticism of education that began
in the 1970s that the omissions became widely noticed.
Schoolwork too frequently has been about memorizing,
not reasoning.

The mounting dissatisfaction with schools that was so
prevalent by the beginning of the 1980s was underscored by test results showing that although students
were more or less holding their own in the acquisition
of basic skills, they were not able to apply those skills

very well. In other words, they had trouble applying their learning at a deeper level so that they could draw inferences and solve problems. This was true whether they were reading or doing mathematics.

Thus, attention is now being given to the teaching of what has come to be known as critical thinking. One difficulty, though, is that despite widespread accord that more ought to be done to teach students to think, there is disagreement over the best way to do this. Some say that separate lessons to teach thinking skills are the best approach; others say it is unrealistic to try to teach thinking in isolation and that the teaching of thinking should be embedded in lessons on subject matter.

Either way, what is important is that students come to understand that being educated means delving into subject matter to draw conclusions, create hypotheses, and figure out the reasons that one step should be taken instead of another. The so-called higher-order thinking skills come into play more frequently in junior high school and high school than in elementary school, but this does not mean that thinking should not get the attention of teachers in elementary schools. There is much evidence to indicate that students who do not begin blossoming as thinkers by the fourth or fifth grade are likely to struggle with the work in secondary school.

Students in elementary school, especially once they are in the upper grades, should be helped to develop strategies for solving problems. Some tactics will be picked up intuitively, but others can be taught. What is involved is a way of regarding knowledge so that a student encountering a problem deals with it systematically. Adults do much the same automatically when faced with familiar problems, usually not bothering to take note of each step of the process. These might be the steps that a child follows in learning a systematic approach:

• *Identify the problem.* Know what questions are to be answered. This is not as obvious as it might seem. Some children can read through a paragraph setting out a problem and still not understand what they are being asked to provide.

• *Know what information is relevant and what information can be discarded.* Usually, a portion of what is given is extraneous to the problem and only some of the facts are needed to find the solution to the problem.

• *Generate possible solutions.* Search the memory for how similar situations were handled in the past, reflect on what was learned that can be applied in this instance, and brainstorm the imagination for fresh ideas.

• *Evaluate possible solutions and select one.* Decide which approach is best by weighing the advantages and disadvantages of each, realizing there may be more than one way to solve a problem. Or, it may only appear there is more than one way.

• *Implement the solution.* The conclusion of problem solving is action. In hypothetical situations—such as deciding how a community health problem would be confronted—students must stop with the previous step, but there should be some experiential learning in which they actually follow through on a decision, as in a complex math problem.

Any list such as this is subject to modification, depending on the goal of thinking. While the term *thinking skills* is used loosely in the schools, there are differences between problem solving and decision making. Furthermore, sometimes a student has to analyze a situation in which there is neither a problem to solve nor a decision to make, though the skills of good thinking are every bit as much demanded for analysis. This is the kind of critical thinking involved in making evaluations. There is still another kind of thinking—the sort of creative thinking that leads to writing a poem or choreographing a dance. In this kind of thinking the main goal is to generate something new.

What is common to all these forms of thinking—which more or less overlap—is that they draw on one's experience in ways that allow the student to open new insights, using what is already known, to discover something new. John Chaffee, author of *Thinking Critically*, speaks of this as a "composing process," which he says is used "to organize our world into meaningful patterns that will help us figure out what is going on and what we ought to do."

A difficulty is that most of the thinking valued in school is heavily dependent on language proficiency and—after second or third grade—the ability to read proficiently. Most situations in which students are asked to think and most problems given to them to be solved depend on an ability to manipulate language and to read. How, for instance, can a child seek the nuances in a story if that child is a poor reader, or how can a child weigh the merits of oral argument if the child's vocabulary is so deficient that many of the words are unfamiliar. This is a problem not easily solved and clearly many students with the potential to be good thinkers are cut off from the process in school because they do not have the language skills that the school requires in order to play the game. Once again, the need for early language devolopment is underscored.

Benjamin Bloom, a professor at the University of Chicago, classified the thinking process according to a hierarchy through which he said that children develop. It begins with the knowledge that is to be considered and then continues with comprehension, application, analysis, synthesis, and evaluation. In this taxonomy, the student must first recall basic information and be sure that he or she understands it. The more challenging part comes when a student must apply what has been learned and go on to the more complicated steps of analyzing the information, drawing out the main ideas, and judging the implications.

Bloom's way of presenting the thinking process is just one version of what occurs. Other experts have their own ideas of the process. What is crucial is that thinking be recognized as a process and not something that just happens by accident. Insects and primitive organisms have the ability to react to stimuli, but that is not thinking. When human beings think, they, in effect, organize their experiences. The response is something far more intricate than a reflex. Schools (and, of course, parents) can do a good deal to help children hone the ability to be careful, efficient, productive thinkers.

Developing these skills is more difficult, though, when students are constantly pursuing studies in which they are asked to take short-answer or multiple-choice tests. Such tests do not cultivate critical-thinking skills the way essay examinations do. Similarly, math problems that are always presented as numbers to be calculated do not compel students to think the way they must upon encountering word problems that call for figuring out what numbers to use, whether they are to be added, subtracted, multiplied, or divided, and which step comes next.

It is beneficial for parents, particularly once children

are in the upper elementary grades, to review tests that youngsters bring home from school—not just to see if the answers are correct, but to find out what questions are being asked. The way questions are posed will reveal much about whether or not the teacher is doing a good job of getting the students to think. Why? Why? Why? The question or some form of it that calls for elaboration should constantly be asked of students in all subjects. Tests that cultivate thinking usually require more than one-word answers.

On the other hand, all dialogues in which teachers ask questions of students are not good ones. Sometimes a teacher manages the task poorly and cuts off the probing by the student, aborting the thinking process. This can happen, according to Selma Wasserman of Simon Fraser University, when the teacher agrees or disagrees with the student; doesn't give the student a chance to think; does the thinking by showing or telling the student what to do or cuts off the student's response. In a classroom in Los Angeles, I observed a teacher who asked a question and then immediately answered it, time and again, not giving students the time to reflect on the question, much less the time to provide the answer.

You also should examine work sheets and workbooks that your child brings home. As has been indicated elsewhere in this book, the use of such materials should not be excessive, because they bore students and, being geared to short answers, usually do not promote higher-order thinking. Such materials are used more frequently in the first, second, and third grades than in the fourth, fifth, and sixth grades, because the younger children are still practicing basic skills.

A notion of the goals that parents ought to set for the elementary school program so far as thinking is concerned comes from the College Board, which has identified five reasoning skills that experts consider essential for success in higher education. Though few students would master these areas while still in elementary school, it is worth keeping them in mind because the foundation ought to be provided during the elementary school years. These are the five skills:

1. The ability to identify and formulate problems, as well as the ability to propose and evaluate ways to solve them.

2. The ability to recognize and use inductive and deductive reasoning and to recognize fallacies in reasoning.

3. The ability to draw reasonable conclusions from information found in various sources, whether written, spoken, or displayed in tables and graphs, and to defend one's conclusions rationally.

4. The ability to comprehend, develop, and use concepts and generalizations.

5. The ability to distinguish between fact and opinion.

Most programs for teaching thinking skills are aimed at students in secondary schools and colleges. Some programs, though, are designed specifically for the elementary grades. One such program, Philosophy for Children, operated by Matthew Lipman of Montclair (New Jersey) State College, is based on the teaching of short novels written for the program. The novels set up situations that can lead to discussions in which the desired thinking skills are teased forth. The goal is to teach youngsters how to think, not what to think. These are some of the skills taught in Philosophy for Children:

- Recognizing improper questions.

- Avoiding jumping to conclusions.

- Analogical reasoning.

- Syllogistic reasoning.

- Finding underlying assumptions.

- Sorting out statements of inclusion and exclusion.

- Detecting ambiguities.

- Identifying good reasons.

- Recognizing dubious authority.

- Recognizing contradictory statements.

- Discerning causal relationships.

These are samples of questions used to test the understanding of fifth-graders and sixth-graders on the sort of thinking skills taught in Philosophy for Children:

1. If it's true that only animals are cats, then it's also
   true that:
   (a) all cats are animals
   (b) all animals are cats
   (c) neither of the above

(The correct answer, "a," tests the ability to sort out
   statements of inclusion and exclusion.)

2. Glenn said, "Here comes a police car racing down
   the highway. There must be an accident." Glenn
   is assuming that:

(a) when police cars speed along the highway, it's usually to chase criminals

(b) when police cars speed along the highway, it's to get to an accident

(c) when there's been an accident, police cars speed along the highway

(The correct answer, "b," tests the ability to find underlying assumptions.)

3. All cats that cry are cats in pain. All cats in pain are suffering creatures. Therefore:

(a) all suffering creatures are cats that cry

(b) all cats in pain are cats that cry

(c) all cats that cry are suffering creatures

(The correct answer, "c," tests the ability to engage in syllogistic reasoning.)

Another program used with elementary-age children is Instrumental Enrichment, which has been especially successful with low-functioning children. Through a series of fifteen lessons consisting of paper-and-pencil exercises, the students are provided with "mediated learning experiences" intended to give them an appreciation for accuracy and to make them less passive as thinkers. Encouraging students to be "active" rather than "passive" thinkers is a major feature of most good efforts to teach thinking, because active thinkers are alert to facts and details that are frequently ignored by passive or lazy thinkers. The "mediation" of Instrumental Enrichment involves pointing out details to the student and going beyond the provision of information to offer explanations and reasons for what is occurring.

Instrumental Enrichment and Philosophy for Children are two approaches among many that have bubbled to the top and won wide acceptance. Some advocates would have educators and parents believe that one or another of the various formal approaches used to teach critical thinking is a panacea. This is unlikely and it is not even necessary that a teacher use one of the formal approaches, almost all of which require some training on the teacher's part.

Some teachers can get students to think critically without employing any special program. These are people who are simply what all adults working in classrooms ought to be: good teachers. They make thinking an integral part of most of what happens in their classes. The problem is that many teachers either do not possess these skills or find that the demands of dealing with large classes cause them to compromise their goals.

Parents should do what they can to get their children assigned to the classes of teachers who are strong in the teaching of thinking skills. This means not only the possibility of a specific program to teach thinking, but—more importantly—a teacher who incorporates the approach into all that /he or she does. These are some of the signs of such teachers:

• *The use of questioning.* Good teachers since the days of Socrates have followed his example of teaching through questioning. Teachers should use questions like mines planted in the minds of their students, detonated to explode in ways that provoke deep thinking.

• *Student-centered learning.* Students should be given some responsibility for their own learning by teachers who create situations in which the students pursue knowledge on their own and do not sit back waiting for the teacher to lecture and pour information into them, as though they were empty vessels.

• *Assignments and tests that demand more than short answers.* The work given to students must be structured so that they have to dwell on deeper meaning and hidden significance.

• *A great deal of writing.* One of the best ways to get students to think is to have them write. It forces them to reflect on information obtained from the teacher, their books, and their observations. Students must organize those experiences in their minds and draw on them. A good writing assignment will, by necessity, require critical thinking.

• *Discussions of strategies for problem solving.* Young students must be helped to see the methods they should use in dealing with problems. It is good to have students of all ages think about the way they think. Strategies should not be forced upon them, but students should be made aware of thinking strategies by their teachers.

• *Modeling of the problem-solving approach by the teacher.* The teacher should provide an example, describing aloud his or her approach as he or she goes through problems for the class.

Cathy Skowron, a first-grade teacher in Provincetown, Massachusetts, exemplifies the sort of teacher who ensures that her students will have to think. She typically will close a reading of a story like *Chicken Little,* the tale about the sky falling, with the question: "What are some of the mistakes the animals made in believing Chicken Little?" And so it goes, as she has the children examine the classic tale in ways that make it more than idle entertainment for them.

Some teachers are able to build such an approach into

almost every lesson they teach on each subject. Other teachers use formal thinking programs in an attempt to achieve the same results. If a teacher uses a specific program to teach thinking skills, she or he should recognize that the program is not like a pill that children swallow to convert them into full-blown thinkers. The process is much more sophisticated than that.

There are some very good programs, but trained educators must sort out one program from another and understand that not all the programs are equal. "The cornucopia of options almost paralyzes," observed D. N. Perkins, co-director of Harvard Project Zero. "We must be wary of a misguided effort to oversimplify. Human thinking is complex and many-faceted."

The National Association of Secondary School Principals, approving in general of the idea of using a program to teach thinking, warned of some pitfalls. The message of the warning seems to apply to elementary schools as well as secondary schools. Here are the pitfalls that the association said should be avoided by teachers in teaching students to think systematically:

• *Moving too fast.* Teachers should not jump into programs without the prerequisite training and until there are ways set up by the school or school district to support their efforts.

• *Attempting to do too much.* Setting up long lists of goals for students to accomplish runs the risk that the approach will be scattered and the students will be demoralized.

• *Expecting too much.* Eventually, standardized test scores may rise for students who have gone through thinking programs, but that is not what the programs are all about.

• *Taking the short view.* Becoming a thinker takes a long time.

• *Neglecting evaluation.* There should be some way of ascertaining what the program is accomplishing for students.

• *Neglecting the home environment.* Programs that involve parents are more fruitful than those that don't.

• *Neglecting traditional course content.* Thinking should not be taught to the neglect of subject matter itself.

• *Capitulating to early failures.* If the program does not work well at first, the teacher should make appropriate modifications and continue until it has had a full trial.

Whether a teacher uses a formal program to teach thinking or just does it in the course of normal teaching, there should be attention to strategies and tactics. Students should be trained to be good observers so that they will be more apt to absorb the information they will need. This means working with students to help them recognize main ideas in sentences and paragraphs and to recognize words and phrases that signal "cause and effect." Students must learn to classify and sort information so that it can be more systematically organized in their minds for problem solving. They should be inclined to compare and contrast new knowledge with previously learned knowledge. They should have the mental tools to evaluate the logic of an argument and to marshal arguments to defend their conclusions.

The bottom line is that students can and should be taught to think and that elementary school is not too soon to start. Thinking is what is sometimes called "reading between the lines." It is logic. It is common sense. The goals of good programs to teach thinking should be the same. Students should be encouraged to search for deeper meanings. They should be able to read a passage and answer questions about why certain events occurred. They should be able to evaluate and judge outcomes.

If you or your child's teacher wants to obtain information on the teaching of thinking skills the following materials are available from the National Education Association Professional Library, P.O. Box 509, West Haven, Conn. 06516 (203-934-2669).

Books

Cooperative Learning: Student Teams
Critical Thinking Skills
Listening Processes: Attention, Understanding, Evaluation
Measuring Thinking Skills in the Classroom
Questioning Skills for Teachers
Thinking Skills: Research and Practice

Filmstrips

Applying Student Thinking Skills
Identifying Student Thinking Skills
Evaluating Student Thinking Skills

Videotape

Looking at Thinking

22

BUILDING CHARACTER

Forget it when someone tells you that the teaching of values has no place in school. This is nonsense. Almost nothing that happens in school is value-neutral. Teachers certainly are not. Everything a teacher says and does affects what students think and feel. There is no way to prevent this, and so the best approach is for the school to come to terms with its role in influencing values.

The authors of two articles in the *Phi Delta Kappan,* a leading educational journal, amplified this point. Kevin Ryan, a professor at Boston University, said: "The education profession must make moral education and character development high priorities—part of the profession's core responsibilities. Schools need to shed the notion that they can remain value-neutral for the sake of pluralism or that they can treat values as relative." Perry London, a professor at Harvard University, said: "What was once the secondary responsibility of schools for character education—reinforcing cultural norms that were inculcated elsewhere (especially in the home) and reinforced everywhere in society—has become a burden that other social institutions no longer carry. Schools must now lead the battle."

Because there is growing recognition of the need for this involvement by schools, educators are increasingly setting out deliberately to teach values. There is nothing wrong with this objective. The problem, though, is that it can be done well or poorly. A parent should not hesitate to discuss with teachers and with the principal what posture the school is assuming in connection with the teaching of values. A way to get a sense of a teacher's approach to values is to observe some social studies lessons. It is not that social studies is the only subject through which values are transmitted, but sometimes the message is more overt in social studies.

Also important in influencing students is the manner in which the teacher runs the classroom and interacts with students. The values of punctuality and reliability, for example, are taught best not through lectures, but by expecting students to be in class on time and to turn in homework when it is due, perhaps even rewarding them for such behavior. The message is tacitly reinforced by a teacher who exhibits punctuality and follows through in a reliable fashion on promises that are made to students.

One reason to try to be sure that your child gets a good teacher is that the teacher and the way the teacher runs the classroom have so great an impact on the values formation of the children in that classroom. Students learn much besides academics from a teacher who is caring and sensitive to their needs. Also, teachers who are able to organize their classes in ways that play down the competitiveness that is so often a part of schooling do students a favor and help them learn the value of cooperation. There are specific teaching methods that promote cooperative learning when students work together. Similarly, a teacher who does not make a virtue of conformity can help students learn to respect others and be comfortable with individual differences.

It is important to remember that the teacher bears a responsibility to help students feel good about themselves. Developing solid values has much to do with how one feels about one's self. Young people who behave in antisocial ways almost always are lacking a positive self-image. It is up to the teacher to be sure that almost everything that happens in the classroom allows children to grow in confidence and to enlarge their sense of worthiness. Otherwise, the teaching of values is not likely to be successful.

It is important to recognize the impact on a student of the time spent in the company of the teacher, who almost certainly sees more of the child during the waking hours than a parent does. "A teacher affects eternity," said Henry Adams. "He can never tell where his influence stops." We are products of our schooling just as we are of our home life, and so the values implanted in the classroom cannot be taken lightly.

But parents should never lose sight of the fact that they are the primary teachers of values to their children. Parents should first examine their own behavior if they have questions about the values of their children. The most powerful lessons that parents teach children are those that are totally unintentional, those that come out of everyday life. Parents who smoke pot and drink alcohol, for instance, can forget about all the lectures they deliver to their children about drug and alcohol abuse. This is not to say that exemplary behavior by parents guarantees that wholesome values will be instilled in their offspring. There are no guarantees in child-rearing, but there are measures that improve the odds in terms of achieving desired results.

The pressure on schools to take responsibility for shaping children has grown because of societal changes. American families are fractured by 1 million divorces a year and one of every five children lives with only one parent. Having only one parent on the scene—whether the family is affluent or poor—increases the burden of child-rearing on the remaining resident parent. It diminishes the likelihood of a youngster getting as much positive input as when both parents are present. These various changes in family structure make it less likely that children will get moral instruction at home, increasing the need for the school to fill the gap.

Underscoring the urgency of the situation is a climate in which the public is treated to repeated breaches of ethical behavior. In the late 1980s there was the specter of an ethical collapse in society. Wall Street financiers cashed in on inside information; federal officials lied and concealed the truth about activities in Central America and the Mideast; a major political candidate got involved with "another" woman; and television evangelists bickered over sex and money. The lessons were assuredly not lost on the young.

The lives of children today are afflicted as never before by drugs, suicides, and out-of-wedlock pregnancies. Somehow an anchor must be set in place so that young people have something on which to take solid hold. The problem of early drug addiction—crack has become a pernicious substance used by children as early as the third and fourth grades—attests to the difficulty. It should be apparent by now that the United States is not going to be able to halt the importation and sale of drugs any more than it was able to do so with alcoholic beverages during Prohibition. Unless the values of children are oriented toward rejecting drug use, there is probably no way that this addiction will be halted.

Yet, the teaching of values is fraught with controversy. Not only do people disagree on what ought to be taught, but they dispute how to teach it even when they coalesce around goals. The teacher often is caught in the middle, told that she or he bears some of the blame if young people are not growing into responsible adults, but at the same time teachers are cautioned against expressing opinions and taking sides. "Teachers are told in one breath to socialize the rising generation and in the next to check personal values at the door," said the *Education Letter* of the Harvard Graduate School of Education.

A starting point in most schools is likely to be the teaching of responsible citizenship. Students in the lowest grades are not too young to discuss civic behavior—what people can do to make life more pleasant for one another and to keep democratic government operating efficiently. In some places this is known as citizenship education, not quite the stuff of deep moral dilemma, but certainly meaty enough to matter.

There is a long and honored tradition in the United States for using the public schools to promulgate the message of citizenship. Alexis de Tocqueville noted this in his famous *Democracy in America,* a book that was the result of his travels across the country in 1831 and 1832. Wrote de Tocqueville: "It cannot be doubted that in the United States the instruction of the people powerfully contributes to the support of the democratic republic; and such must always be the case, I believe, where the instruction which enlightens the understanding is not separated from the moral education which amends the heart."

Some teachers, in imparting the lessons of citizenship, start with the class itself, portraying the class as a microcosm of the community, a place where careless or unthinking actions by one person can penalize others. It is in this context that students might learn about the evils of littering and graffiti, the need to wait in line and obey laws, the philosophy of majority rule, and respect for dissenting opinions.

A complaint of some observers is that the schools are not doing enough to teach specifically about democracy. Citizenship education, they say, does not go far enough. In fact, the American Federation of Teachers in 1987 spearheaded the drafting of a lengthy statement of concern, "Education for Democracy," that worried over whether the principles of democracy are being adequately conveyed to students. "There appears a certain lack of confidence in our own liberal, democratic values, an unwillingness to draw normative distinctions between them and the ideas of nondemocratic regimes," the statement observed.

Good citizenship in the classroom starts with students taking responsibility for their actions in dealing with fellow students and for their behavior toward the teacher. It is certainly desirable that students acquire the sort of self-discipline that makes it unnecessary for the teacher to impose discipline externally. There can be neither teaching nor learning in a class in which students are unruly and rights are ignored. This is less of a problem in elementary school than in high school, but more than one elementary school teacher has been so distracted by the misconduct of a handful of pupils that the instruction of the remainder of the class suffered. It is worth noting, though, that some teachers bring the behavior problems on themselves, as is illustrated by the very different behavior that may be exhibited by the same class when led by two different teachers.

On the other hand, the lessons of democracy are undermined when a teacher—in the name of discipline— runs a classroom in autocratic fashion. This is not to say that to be democratic a teacher must cede authority to the students, but there is something downright hypocritical about a teacher extolling democracy one moment and giving students absolutely no leeway for decision making the next. A good class, in any grade, is one in which students are not simply bossed by the teacher, but allowed to express their opinions and to exert some influence on the events that transpire.

Thus, whenever possible, discipline should be meted out in a democratic manner. There are notable exceptions, egregious cases in which students threaten the safety of others and must be dealt with swiftly and firmly. So far as punishment generally is concerned, however, the U.S. Supreme Court declared that students are entitled to due process; parents should see that it is provided.

Self-discipline is only one of many traits that a school interested in developing values hopes to inculcate in students. More and more there is the idea that schools ought to be more deeply involved in cultivating the character of students. Usually, this means trying to encourage desirable traits that are essentially uncontroversial such as honesty, fairness, loyalty, dependability. Once it was taken for granted that such character traits would automatically develop in favorable ways as the schools went about their normal business. Now, it is not taken for granted and there is increasing attention to the explicit teaching of values.

Debbie McNamara, a third-grade teacher in Schellsburg (Pennsylvania) Elementary School, told how she set out to teach her class about pride, an especially valuable trait when children have low self-esteem. Each week of Pride Month dealt with pride on a different level, starting with self-pride and going on to pride in school, pride in community, and pride in country. At the heart of the program were the activities pursued by the students. Children described their hobbies and invited family members to school for lunch. Teachers were interviewed by the students and posters were designed to boost school spirit. Community officials spoke at the school and local history was studied. There was an American songfest and a discussion of the meaning of the Nobel Prizes (more of which have been won by Americans than by citizens of any other country).

One view of the character traits desirable for students to develop comes from teachers at St. Paul's School in Concord, New Hampshire, a leading boarding school, who were interviewed by Robert Coles. They proposed, among other attributes, that students acquire self-discipline, the ability to respond to setbacks, the ability to form attachments to the ideals of the larger community, a sense of humor, the ability to be an individual in a crowd, and the ability to disagree without condemning or losing respect for others.

Reo Christenson, a professor at Miami University in Ohio, drafted a list of values and attitudes to be taught by the schools, which dovetails somewhat with the findings at St. Paul's. The Christenson list probably could win wide support among parents and might be good for teachers and principals in elementary schools to consider. It consists of the following:

1. Acknowledging the importance of self-discipline.
2. Being trustworthy.
3. Telling the truth.
4. Being honest in all aspects of life.
5. Having the courage to resist group pressures to do what we would refuse to do if alone.
6. Being ourselves, but being our best selves.
7. Using honorable means, those that respect the rights of others.
8. Conducting ourselves, where significant moral behavior is concerned, in a manner that does not fear exposure.
9. Having the courage to say, "I am sorry. I was wrong."
10. Practicing good sportsmanship.
11. Maintaining courtesy in human relations.
12. Treating others as we would wish to be treated.
13. Recognizing that no person is an island, that behavior that may seem to be of purely private concern often affects others.
14. Bearing in mind that how we conduct ourselves in times of adversity is the best test of our maturity and our mettle.
15. Doing work well, whatever that work may be.
16. Showing respect for the property of others.
17. Giving obedience to the law except where religious convictions or deeply held moral principles forbid it.
18. Respecting the democratic values of free speech, a free press, freedom of assembly, freedom of religion, and due process of law.

19. Developing habits that promote physical and emotional health and refraining from activities destructive of those ends.

20. Abstaining from premature sexual experience and developing sexual attitudes compatible with the values of family life.

21. Recognizing that the most important thing in life is the kind of persons we are becoming, the quality of character and moral behavior we are developing.

An inherent problem in elementary school has to do with the ease with which the teaching of values can turn into indoctrination. This drawback is perhaps best illustrated by the effort of some people to censor textbooks that they think transmit the wrong values to children. Proceeding on the assumption that some books do not reinforce desirable traits, certain teachers, parents, school board members, and elected officials propose to outlaw books they find offensive. According to Robert P. Doyle, officials of the American Library Association say this has meant bans on *Death of a Salesman* in French Lick, Indiana, because it contained such words as *goddam, son of a bitch,* and *bastard; Flowers for Algernon* in Glen Rose, Arkansas, because the book allegedly contains sex scenes; *Ms.* magazine in Contra Costa, California, because it was allegedly pornographic; *The Adventures of Huckleberry Finn* in Warrington, Pennsylvania, because it allegedly fostered racial tension.

This is not to say that everything in print or on film or tape is appropriate for elementary school students. Choices have to be made, and just because material was published or taped does not mean it is for everyone or even that it is good. Responsible educators and librarians, sensitive to the concerns and values of parents, ought to make such decisions. The problem comes when individual citizens and parents and small groups set themselves up as arbiters.

Where are schools to draw the line in their role as transmitters of values? This is a difficult decision when schools try to go beyond the teaching of specific values and provide instruction in applied ethics or moral reasoning. Teaching a student to be honest is one thing, but getting into moral thinking is another. What happens when money is found on the street and no one is in sight? What obligation does the finder bear in trying to find the owner? What happens when the only way to get expensive medicine that will save a life seems to be to steal it? This type of teaching is fraught with dynamite, and unless it is handled with care it can explode. Thus, many parents prefer to see the schools stop with character education and not enter into the area of moral reasoning.

Reflective of the controversy is the dispute surrounding a movement that swept through the schools, particularly in the Northeast, during the late 1960s and the 1970s to teach values clarification. This approach, which boasts of its neutrality, is aimed at getting students to clarify their own beliefs and values, implying that value judgments are essentially equal and that none is more worthy of acceptance than another.

But there has been growing criticism of this relativistic method of getting students to think about values. There are rights and wrongs. Some absolutes provide an underpinning to our civilization and should be inculcated.

It can readily be seen that once schools go beyond the simpler area of character traits and into moral reasoning there is apt to be controversy. Perhaps a more acceptable route into moral reasoning is to let it flow naturally from the regular subject matter in reading, social studies, and science instead of setting out to pursue it through a specific program. After all, literature is full of moral dilemmas and they are sure to be discussed and written about by the students within the context of the curriculum.

Some maintain that there is yet another way to teach moral reasoning: to have children seek divine guidance in school. According to this body of thinking, prayer helps lead students to God, and that in itself is the road to morality and good values. A problem with this idea is that having prayers pronounced in school is illegal. There is no such thing as a neutral prayer; the mere existence of a prayer indicates a belief in a supreme being to whom the prayer is directed. For a school to endorse or mandate a prayer is to put an official imprimatur on the prayer.

This need not mean, though, that students cannot study religion as a historical and literary force. There were ancient Hebrews and they did develop a monotheistic religion. Christianity was founded on the teachings ascribed to Jesus of Nazareth. Mohammed did inspire a religion called Islam. Martin Luther was a priest whose dissatisfaction with what he saw in his church contributed greatly to the Protestant Reformation.

These historic developments and the literature they spawned should be studied in public elementary and secondary schools. To ignore religion, as is usually done in schools, is to give an incomplete picture of the unfolding of civilization. The Association for Supervision and Curriculum Development, a leading organization of specialists in creating curriculum, issued a report urging that public schools "end the current curricular silence on religion."

Usually, religion is not studied because educators in public schools are frightened to death that they will be accused of bridging the wall between church and state. What they and their potential critics fail to understand is that it is perfectly within the bounds of the Constitution to teach *about* religion. What is illegal is devotional exercises. It is time that students learned more about religion in public schools. Parents should not object to thoughtful, well-planned curriculums that include such material. For those who want prayer and the fostering of specific religious values and dogma in school, there are parochial schools.

Finally, on the subject of values, there is sex education. In an ideal world, parents would present to their children all that should be known about the sexual and reproductive sides of life. But did your parents share these facts of life with you? Few parents do.

The gap between what students know about sex and what they ought to know is enormous. The United States had the highest rate of teenage pregnancy of any of the thirty-seven industrialized countries studied by the Alan Guttmacher Institute. A total of 10,000 babies are born across the country each year to mothers of the age of fifteen or younger. It is estimated that from 25 to 40 percent of the females who drop out of school are pregnant or already mothers. And now AIDS looms as the potentially fatal ultimate outcome of promiscuous sexual activity. And yet there are people who say sex education does not belong in the schools.

Sol Gordon, professor emeritus at Syracuse University

and an expert on sex education, worries that there is much too little sex education in the schools and that "where it exists at all [it] is usually a course in plumbing —a relentless pursuit of the fallopian tubes." He believes that sex education, to be in a proper framework, should begin with a discussion of the most important aspects of a mature relationship between two people, such qualities as love and commitment, a sense of humor, and meaningful communication.

Elementary school is the right place for a tasteful, low-key, restrained approach to sex and family education. Much of what might be acceptable for teenagers is still out of place in elementary school. But elementary school is assuredly the place for sex and family education to begin. Parents who wonder about what is being taught ought to request a copy of the grade-by-grade curriculum plan for sex education in elementary school. A good school system should readily share such information with parents, and perhaps even teach model lessons for the parents so that they will better know what is being presented to their children.

If your school has no program of sex education or if it seems to be poorly conceived, one direction in which to turn for guidance is toward New Jersey. This state has been a pioneer in the creation of a solid, statewide required curriculum of sex education. Information is available from the New Jersey State Education Department in Trenton. Also, there is a study of New Jersey's sex education curriculum that is worth reading. It is entitled "Creating and Implementing Family Life Education in New Jersey" and is available from the National Association of State Boards of Education, 701 N. Fairfax Street, Suite 340, Alexandria, Va. 22314. The cost is $10.

In summary, your child is going to come out of elementary school with much of his or her value structure in place. There will still be room for adjustments, but the overall outlines will be there, and since there is only one time around for character formation every parent ought to do all that is possible to assure that it is done properly.

23

READING IN THE
UPPER GRADES

Much of the time that students spend with books until the fourth grade is devoted to learning how to read. In the upper elementary grades, they read to learn. Students should have enough reading experience by the fourth grade to figure out the meaning of many unfamiliar words from the context in which they are used or from the positions of the words in sentences.

Reading transforms itself into a device to study other subjects once students have mastered the rudiments. Also, students read well enough at this point to do so solely for the purpose of pleasure. Fourth-grade children can enjoy full-blown novels. They are starting to look for developed characters and are ready to relish biographies, as well as historical fiction. Students who have progressed along with the class can read well enough in fourth grade to delve more deeply into social studies, science, and other subjects. Reading should no longer be an obstacle to solving word problems in mathematics, though the math itself might prove to be a barrier.

Yet, though they have supposedly been presented with all the basics of reading, fourth-graders continue to be taught reading as a separate subject, along with math, science, and social studies. This makes it more likely that reading will be emphasized. Students must encounter and reencounter words to reinforce the lessons learned during the first three grades. Those who have kept up with their classmates are fairly adept readers by the fourth grade, but the experience of learning to read is sufficiently recent to make it useful to brush up. In the fourth grade, for instance, students very likely will still be strengthening their knowledge of synonyms and antonyms and prefixes and suffixes.

Most elementary schools continue to use a basal reading series in the fourth, fifth, and sixth grades, just as in the lower grades. The basal reader and accompanying materials are intended to expose students to various skills that are to be reinforced. A regular part of the day is set aside for formal instruction in reading with the basal reader. It is used by students individually, in small groups—usually organized by achievement levels—and in whole-class sessions.

Students at this point are exposed to more and more expository reading, that is, content of a straightforward informational nature instead of the fictional stories that make up so much of their reading in earlier grades. This nonfictional content also ties in with the reading that they do in the fourth grade in other subjects for which reading is now so important as a tool for extracting information.

What especially distinguishes reading instruction be-

ginning in the fourth grade is the emphasis on inferential comprehension. After the rudiments have been
absorbed by students, teachers can more fully turn attention to the content itself. Students are freer to read
for deeper meaning, no longer having to worry so much
about the attack skills for decoding words, which now
are supposed to come more naturally.

By the fourth grade, it is not simply that the student
reads a story and recognizes that the character had long
brown hair and was wearing a blue coat, but that the
student increasingly understands why the character be-
haved as she did. Inferences are drawn. Reasoning leads
to deeper meaning. This ability is essential if a student
is to use reading for higher-level learning. The stress on
inferential reasoning is reflected in the upper elementary grades by the reading tests, a greater portion of the
questions having to do with comprehension.

These are some of the ways in which students in the
fourth grade are expected to show reading comprehension:

- After reading a selection consisting of several paragraphs the student will be able to distinguish between
  the main idea and the subordinate ideas.

- The student can recognize the statement that is the
  climax in a short selection.

- Given a main-idea sentence, the student will be able
  to pick out details in the sentence that support the
  main idea.

- The student will be able to determine the main idea
  that is implied in a selection a paragraph in length,
  even if that main idea is not explicitly stated.

- A character's feelings or thoughts can be determined by the student.

Another way that fourth-graders increasingly evince comprehension of ever more complex material is in the ability to sort out fact from opinion. They learn to recognize such clues as "I believe . . . " or "In my opinion . . . " This ability is particularly important as they use reading to dig more deeply into topics.

The continued expansion of vocabulary is vital through the upper elementary grades. Experiences in the home can play a large part in this development. No less than in earlier grades, what students bring to the reading assignment will largely determine what they get out of it. Those who have their experiences augmented at home derive an advantage. Despite the more sophisticated approach to reading in the fourth grade, reading aloud by parents at home should not end. It remains important to keep children hooked on books and for them to see that parents still value reading books to them. Of course, students are sufficiently proficient as readers by the fourth grade to read to their parents, too.

In these middle elementary grades, as students are poised on the brink of challenging academic work, parents should do all they can to fortify and enlarge the vocabularies of their children to strengthen their ability to derive meaning from what they read. These are some activities to consider at home:

- Play Scrabble and other word games regularly and try to make sure that every word that gets spelled out on the board is defined.

- Encourage the use of crossword puzzles.

- Have sessions around the dinner table in which family members take turns each evening introducing new vocabulary words and defining them for the rest of the family.

- Propose that your child jot down unfamiliar words encountered in reading and put them on index file cards with definitions written out on the back so that they can be reviewed periodically as refreshers.

Writing plays a growing role in the language arts. By the fourth grade, the greater language sophistication of students means they can take on some rather complex writing assignments. One side of progress is that students are more likely than they were in earlier grades to be able to do persuasive writing, that is trying to use reason and logical arguments to convince a reader of a point. The aim of this kind of writing is to produce some action or change in the reader. Newspaper editorials frequently typify persuasive writing. Students do not have sufficient skills and a thorough enough grounding in language to delve very deeply into persuasive writing in the early grades.

Two other kinds of writing that began in the earlier grades will now get greater emphasis. One of these is expressive or imaginative writing, in which students deal with feelings, perhaps writing some poetry and fiction. The other is explanatory or informative writing, a factual narrative approach telling about, say, an event that happened or describing how something is done. A goal in explanatory writing is to present information and share ideas. The student reports and describes. Explanatory writing is the type that students are asked to do most frequently in school. The accent is on encouraging expression. By about the fourth grade, teachers have expectations for the structure of written work that were overlooked earlier. Fourth-graders are not accomplished writers, but they have learned enough about language to start showing signs of craftsmanship.

In explanatory writing, fourth-graders should be able to link ideas in a way that provides a genuine narrative flow. The product of their efforts should no longer be the jerky, stop-and-start writing that interrupts the flow so often in pieces written by younger students. In other words, the piece should be cohesive. The maturity of the students shows in the syntax of the sentences. There is variety in the length and construction of sentences. The work is a mixture of shorter and longer sentences to make it more interesting. Sentences are more than just simple declarative statements with subjects and predicates. There are clauses and phrases to enrich the writing.

Here are the traits that scorers of writing samples were told to keep in mind in rating students in the middle elementary grades who were taking a statewide examination:

- A consistent point of view.

- Consistency in dealing with the past and present tenses.

- A sense of the audience for whom the piece is written.

- A general plan of organization and logical sequencing.

- Coherence within paragraphs.

- Appropriate transitions.

- Appropriate level of generalization.

- Exclusion of irrelevant details.

- No basic problems with syntax, vocabulary, and mechanics.

In many schools, writing is apt to be taught at this point by having students think more about the process itself. There has been a revolution during the last fifteen years in the way writing is taught at all levels of education. Students are encouraged to spend more time considering a prospective topic and the way it is to be handled. Teachers have learned to stop expecting students to take a blank paper and write a page or two without some planning. It is now generally recognized that part of writing is the period during which nothing is written. This "rehearsal," as it is sometimes called, is when the author mulls over ideas and may even bounce ideas off others.

Then there is the drafting and revising that is a part of the process, if writing is taught properly. A student should come to realize that writing means editing, editing, and more editing. The final product may differ considerably from the first draft and that is the way it should be. Such extensive changes are made no less by professional writers, who view the editing process as a basic part of the writing itself. Students learn that it is in no way a weakness to concede that what was written on the first try can be improved. Revision is the essence of good writing. During the process students learn to read their work to others and to get feedback that they might want to consider in revising the work.

There is some difference of opinion among educators as to how much emphasis to put on matters of grammar and punctuation during this process when students are still in elementary school. Those favoring a looser approach maintain that a student's effort to be creative and produce ideas should not be inhibited by having to worry unduly about formalities. There is merit to this approach because literary expression is the essence of good writing. Some students in past years never got beyond the formalities and into the real writing, because teachers so burdened them with having to deal with the mechanical, nonliterary aspects of writing.

On the other hand, parents should expect that students will eventually be taught the elements of grammar and punctuation. While teachers, out of a concern about literary expression, may be somewhat lenient in marking compositions, the teaching of grammar should nonetheless take place in other ways. Diagramming sentences is not a substitute for writing, but in one way or another students should get a firm foundation in syntax and mechanics. The manner in which sentences are constructed is basic to the power and majesty of writing. Creativity is enhanced, not diminished, by a writer's command of form.

Spelling, too, must eventually get attention. As it happens, teachers are less likely than in former years to stress spelling. Fewer of them assign lists of words that are to be memorized each week for spelling and meaning. Lapses in spelling may be overlooked in hopes that spelling will be picked up more informally. The argument is that rote memorization is not effective, though some middle-aged adults who became good spellers and enlarged their vocabularies because of regular tests on word lists would take exception to this point of view.

A word about spelling. At least 20 percent of the words in English do not follow regular spelling patterns because English borrowed its words from several languages. Moreover, the spellings of some words were altered in strange ways over the years. Thus, children must learn to spell such words as *knight* and *night*; *gnu*, *knew*, and *new*, and *draught* and *draft*. Such inconsistencies defy the orderliness that young minds may seek. Yet, there is a certain pattern to many of the irregularities and spelling, properly taught, can provide a glimpse of consistency where there appears to be only inconsistency. The point is that parents should expect spelling to be taught, but not to the detriment of the teaching of composition.

How much writing should be expected of fourth-graders? One yardstick against which to make a judgment is provided by the National Assessment of Educational Progress. Asked how many reports and essays they had written in all subjects during the past six weeks, one out of five fourth-graders said none and, at the other end of the spectrum, one out of five said more than ten. Twenty-six percent did one or two, 15 percent did three or four, and 20 percent did five to ten. Since at least 40 percent of the students wrote five or more reports or essays over a six-week period, it would not be unreasonable for parents to have at least the same expectation, at a minimum, for their children. Clearly, most students in the upper elementary grades are not being asked to write enough papers. Just as students learn to read by reading, they learn to write by writing.

The survey did not find out whether students were asked to write short pieces or long pieces and observed that students "need experience in writing extended, elaborated pieces." What is important is the general understanding that writing means self-generated work, reflecting the author's point of view. This is vastly different from what passed for writing in the schools of nineteenth-century America, when writing meant copying passages verbatim from the Bible and literary classics—and doing it with an accomplished hand.

Language arts are taught in the fifth grade very much as they were taught in the fourth grade except that, with each grade level, teachers may make less use of the basal reading series and rely increasingly on real books. Whatever reading materials are used, it is the responsibility of the teacher to ensure that the needed review of the basics is provided for all who require it.

There are not sharp differences in the upper three elementary grades in terms of what is taught, grade by grade, in the language arts. The increasing sophistication and complexity of the work is what characterizes it most. One aspect that the three upper elementary grades have in common is the finding, well-documented by tests used across the country, that improvements in reading scores in the lower elementary grades are not sustained in the upper levels of elementary school. This lapse manifests itself in the failure of students to do well in inferential comprehension, which is the basis for strong reading.

Students in the fourth, fifth, and sixth grades should read well enough to pick up clues that give them insight into the feelings and thoughts of characters; they must recognize which sentences contain the most vital information; they must be able to pick out details that support ideas that are only implied, and they must understand cause-and-effect relationships.

The upper elementary grades can be a frustration for parents because it is not as readily apparent when students are not reading as well as they should be. A parent knows quickly when a child cannot sound out a word in the earlier grades because such a failure is more readily recognized. But how is a parent to know if a student in the upper grades is having trouble reading for meaning, a more subtle kind of failing? The best guide for parents should be common sense. Ask your child to read for you.

Parents should read the same selections as are assigned to their children and then talk to them about what is written and what it means. After all, in just a very few years these same students will be in junior high school, where subjects are compartmentalized into such departments as science and social studies and taught by specialists who expect the students to read well enough to understand all that is assigned to them. Teachers in junior high are not likely to provide specific instruction in reading.

To prepare students for the expectations of junior high, teachers in elementary school should be conscientious about stressing comprehension. One way to do this is for them to have discussions with students before an assignment is read. The conversations revolve around some of the aspects to which the students ought to be alert. If, for instance, they are to read an account of an unsuccessful mountain-climbing expedition, the teacher might suggest that students be sure to notice the descriptions of how the gear is used and the discussions of the weather. The teacher may also recommend that students carefully note what the narrator says about the differences of opinion among the climbers concerning the amount of cooperation needed during the climb. After the selection is read, the class will have another discussion, a sort of debriefing, in which pertinent inferences from the selection are analyzed for their meaning.

A teacher who does not regularly have such prereading and post-reading discussions with the class is not doing all that might be done to help students develop their powers of inferential comprehension. Young readers should be guided to approach assignments from a certain mindset that is apt to lead them to draw forth the writer's deepest insights.

In these upper elementary grades students grow more familiar with the ways in which authors of fiction use protagonists, how the strengths and weaknesses of character traits figure into plot and action, the way that setting takes on importance in a story, and how environment, personality, and societal forces affect the motivations of characters. Similar insights are brought with growing frequency to their reading of plays, biographies, poetry, and essays.

In the upper grades of elementary school, most students still have the same teacher for all subjects and that teacher should be incorporating reading and writing instruction into social studies, science, math, and every other subject. Fourth-, fifth-, and sixth-graders should not have to wait for language arts to get such specific instruction. Concern about reading and writing should flow through all parts of the curriculum.

This concept of infusing every subject with instruction in reading and writing is known as Language Across the Curriculum. Educators have learned that it is foolish and unnatural to concentrate the teaching of reading and writing in one part of the school day. A good teacher in the upper elementary grades will pay as much attention to the quality of a student's writing on a paper or a test in science or social studies, as in a specific lesson in the language arts. The principles of good writing and the ability to read well are traits a student should exhibit in every subject.

An elementary school teacher, handling all the subjects as she or he does, has a special opportunity to ensure that language skills figure into all subjects. If a parent sees that a teacher is not taking writing seriously in science or social studies, then it would be good to have a conversation with the teacher about the philosophy that is guiding his or her instruction.

What becomes more and more apparent in the fifth and sixth grades is that reading has a direct tie to cultural literacy. Success in secondary school and, eventually, in college is very much related to the degree of familiarity that a student gains with literature, arts, historical events, and lives of famous people from many walks of life. Students who become conversant on these topics bring more to each reading experience.

Many of the textbooks in basal reading series contain made-up stories rather than pieces of literature. Thus, parents cannot always count on the school curriculum to provide the cultural literacy that it ought to be imparting, though this is less and less true of the better new basal series, which tend increasingly to be steeped in real literature.

Diane Ravitch, a historian of education, pointed out what children miss when basal readers take an insipid nonliterary approach:

The greatest literary rewards were stored up for those youngsters who reached the fifth and sixth McGuffey readers. There were few public high schools, so these students were probably no more than 12 to 14 years old. They encountered not only Alcott and Hawthorne, but Shakespeare, Tennyson, Longfellow, Washington Irving, Oliver Goldsmith, Daniel Webster, Byron, Keats, Thoreau, Audubon, Thackeray and James Fenimore Cooper. In the fifth reader, they were treated to the historian George Bancroft's account of the Boston Massacre; to Dickens's description of the schoolmaster Squeers in *Nicholas Nickleby*; to Robert Southey's antiwar poem, "The Battle of Blenheim."

Parents may want to consult with neighborhood librarians and booksellers to make certain that their children are provided with the books they ought to have for pleasure reading. A report by the U.S. Department of Education stressed this need. "One point cannot be repeated too emphatically," it stated. "Children must have access to books. Every elementary school should have a library. Every classroom should have its own mini-library or reading corner. And parents and schools should make sure children know how to use the public library." By the time they are in about the fifth or sixth grades the more precocious students will probably enjoy these books published in 1987 that the American Library Association put on its list of Notable Children's Books:

Into a Strange Land: Unaccompanied Refugee Youth in America by Bret Ashabranner and Melissa Ashabranner. Dodd. Heartbreak, courage, and resilience mark the stories of youngsters separated from home and family as they make a new life in America.

The Incredible Journey of Lewis and Clark by Rhoda Blumberg. Lothrop. A spirited account of the exploration of the Louisiana Purchase with well-chosen maps and photographs.

M.E. and Morton by Sylvia Cassidy. Harper/Crowell. Lonely, imaginative M.E. sees her learning-disabled brother through new eyes when Polly becomes friends with both of them.

A Nightmare in History: The Holocaust, 1933–1945 by Miriam Chaikin. Clarion Books. A clear, well-organized, and moving description of individuals and governments involved in the Holocaust.

African Journey by John Chiasson. Macmillan/Bradbury. This spectacular photo journey across middle Africa describes how six different communities are affected by nature and modern development.

The Goats by Brock Cole. Farrar. Targets of a cruel joke, a boy and girl escape from an island and struggle for survival.

Roscoe's Leap by Gillian Cross. Holiday. In a suspenseful tale, old memories and secrets mysteriously divide a family who live in an eccentric man's equally eccentric house.

British Folk Tales: New Versions by Kevin Crossley-Holland. Watts/Orchard. A large collection of familiar tales is given new life and flavor.

The House on the Hill by Eileen Dunlop. Holiday. A gloomy house, an empty room, and ghostly presences alter Phillip's stay with his Great-Aunt Jane.

Indian Chiefs by Russell Freedman. Holiday. In portraying the life histories of six famous chiefs, Freedman provides a different, historical perspective of the conflict for land expansion in the West.

Lincoln: A Photobiography by Russell Freedman. Clarion Books. Cogent narrative and well-chosen photographs document and bring to life Abraham Lincoln and his times. The 1988 Newbery Medal Book.

Wise Child by Monica Furlong. Knopf. An evocative fantasy set on a Celtic island involves the growth of a spoiled girl sent to live with a reputed witch in the early days of Christianity.

Waiting for the Rain: A Novel of South Africa by Sheila Gordon. Watts/Orchard/Richard Jackson. Childhood playmates Tengo and Frikkie, one black, the other white, know few differences, but the effects of apartheid become clear as they choose different roads to adulthood.

"A Convention of Delegates": The Creation of the Constitution by Denis Haupty. Atheneum. As the drama of the Constitutional Convention unfolds, the important actors emerge as fallible but impressive figures.

The Return by Sonia Levitin. Atheneum. An adolescent Ethiopian Jewish girl escapes to Israel with her older brother and younger sister in a harrowing journey of hardship and hope.

After the Rain by Norma Fox Mazer. Morrow. Sensitive, journal-writing Rachel and her irascible grandfather develop a special relationship during the last months of his life. A 1988 Newbery Honor Book.

Hatchet by Gary Paulsen. Macmillan/Bradbury. Brian's amazing 54-day survival in the Canadian wilderness following a single-engine plane crash is chronicled in fascinating detail. A 1988 Newbery Honor Book.

The experience students have gained in poetry by the sixth grade should allow them to bring more to both their reading and writing of poetry. They should be familiar with both regular and irregular forms. They should understand and use in their writing both simile and metaphor. Some students should be blossoming as able and expressive poets at this point.

In some school systems a basal reader continues to be used even into seventh and eighth grades in a final effort to impart the basics of reading and give students what for most may well be the last review of the reading basics they will get in their schooling. Comprehension skills receive the major emphasis at this point and students are asked to draw inferences of all sorts—the main idea, the unstated era, and the unstated place or setting of a story, the reasons for a character's action. They are also expected to identify the antecedents of pronouns.

By the end of sixth grade, reading instruction is supposed to equip a student for junior high school, with the teaching of what are called information skills. These are the skills that allow a student to become an independent learner. Youngsters should be accomplished by the end of the sixth grade in how to ferret out information from encyclopedias and other reference volumes, how to use the library index (increasingly computerized), how to derive facts from graphs, diagrams, and schedules. These are skills that are taught and reinforced throughout early grades and they should be firmly in place as a student goes off to junior high school.

Above all, students who have been properly taught understand the roles of speaking and listening as tools for gathering information. They appreciate that asking the right questions yields valuable information, and that listening carefully to what is said may be a key to gathering needed knowledge. More than that, information skills include what are otherwise known as study skills.

This means students learn how to take notes from a book or a lecture, how to organize information in their minds so that it lends itself to more ready recall.

Meanwhile, students should be enriching their writing with details and examples. Synonyms, antonyms, and action words should appear in their work in ways that exhibit understanding. Words should be chosen carefully for precise meaning, and when writing is spare it should be because of the effectiveness of economy of words, not out of impoverishment of vocabulary. The ablest sixth-graders employ words in ways that convey sounds, feels, smells, and sights to the reader. Personal writing flows more easily now because transitions are used more effectively and such subordinative linking words as *when, since,* and *although* tie together thoughts.

By the end of sixth grade, parents should want their children to be competent communicators who express themselves proficiently in writing and speaking and who can read and listen well enough to learn whatever is presented to them in junior high school. In sum, the skills that come under the rubric of the language arts should be the most important tools in the intellectual kit that they carry with them through the remainder of their career as students and into the life that awaits them after formal learning is completed.

24

MATHEMATICS IN THE UPPER GRADES

Mathematics in the upper grades of elementary school builds on what was taught during the early years. The computational emphasis that usually marks early instruction should increasingly give way to problem solving—though this does not mean that problem solving should not have an important place in the curriculum up to fourth grade. It is just that children in the upper elementary grades have the capacity to think more abstractly. Parents should be vigilant to the tendency in some schools to spend too much time in the upper grades merely reviewing the computational techniques imparted in the lower grades. Review has its place, but it is excessive when it leads to monotony and thwarts further growth.

Just what is meant by problem solving? A good explanation was provided by the National Assessment of Educational Progress, which said that the steps to solve a problem should involve preanalysis, analysis, selection of strategy, and the ability to interpret the solution. The sophistication of the approach depends on a child's age, but the steps are about the same. Thus, for a student confronted by a problem in math, the procedures might be as follows:

Preanalysis

• Formulation of reasonable mathematical hypotheses from the information given in the problem.

Analysis

• Identification of known facts, unknowns, or questions in the problem.

• Identification of which information that is given is needed for the solution and which is extraneous, as well as an understanding of the technical terms.

• Recognition of problems in which the underlying mathematical processes are the same as those in a given problem, but the context is different.

Selection of Strategy

• Identification of general strategies that may help solve the problem—as, for example, making graphs or tables, working a simpler version of the problem, or working backward.

• Identification of the sequence of steps and operations that will lead to a solution.

• Use of estimation to predict a reasonable solution.

Interpretation of the Solution

- Recognition and/or verification of a sensible solution for a given problem.

- Identification of new relationships or prediction of possible consequences based upon the solution.

Good teachers help students realize that there is much more to mathematics than getting answers correct. Such teachers worry that students, caught in the competitive atmosphere of school, fail to see that a correct answer based on faulty comprehension of a concept is less valuable than a wrong answer based on an understanding of the concept.

More than perhaps in their parents' school days, students today are presented mathematics in the form of word problems. This form encourages more problem solving because the student must determine what steps to take. It requires a great deal more thinking than is involved when a youngster is given a work sheet with lots of numbers on it and asked to compute them. The situation is more lifelike when a youngster must read a story, figure out which information is relevant to the problem, decide which numbers are to be added, subtracted, multiplied, and divided, and reconize and verify a solution.

There is a difficulty, though, in this sort of approach for children who are still struggling with reading. Their shortcomings in reading may very well handicap them in dealing with word problems. Setting up the problems for them and having them do only the computing may give them practice in computing, but in the long run it will neither help their reading nor help their problem solving. There is no easy answer for such students and their difficulties underscore the need to ensure that they get lots of assistance in reading.

The basics of addition, subtraction, multiplication, and division should be introduced by the end of the third or fourth grade. Students thereafter can be expected to perfect their skills in these operations and apply the principles to solve problems with increasingly larger numbers.

Numbers, being the language of mathematics, remain at the heart of the curriculum in the upper elementary grades. The numbers are applied to measurement, statistics, probability, and the fundamentals of geometry and algebra. The instruction should be permeated by problem solving and reasoning.

As far as basic operations are concerned in the fourth grade, students still work on memorizing the multiplication tables through 12 × 12. A student familiar with the mutiplication tables is much more likely to tell at a glance whether or not the product of mutiplying two numbers is likely to be correct. This is important for estimation, a skill closely allied to computation as it is taught in the upper grades.

Students in the fourth grade multiply two-digit, three-digit, and four-digit numbers by one-digit and two-digit multipliers. They multiply three-digit numbers by three-digit numbers. They learn to work with 0's in the multiplier and learn to multiply by multiples of 10. They learn that the position of the numbers being multiplied can be switched, as they can in addition, without affecting the answer.

In division, they do computations in which they are asked to divide one-digit and two-digit numbers into three- and four-digit numbers, an application of the basics they probably learned in third grade. They estimate quotients, as they do with the products of mutiplication, and they get experience working problems in which there is a remainder. The goal, as it was at the outset, is to get students to regard division as an inverse operation of multiplication.

Starting with long division in which the dividend is divided by a single-digit divisor, they do the computation in long form, multiplying the divisor by the quotient and subtracting the product from the dividend. But soon the teacher moves the students into short division, in which they calculate in their heads instead of writing out the numbers and subtracting underneath the divisor. This may be a difficult transition for some children.

Fractions and decimals get a significant emphasis in fourth grade. The teacher tries to get students to think about fractions as parts of whole numbers, building on an approach that was used in the lower grades. A child may be asked to hand out half the pencils to classmates. Another child may be asked to take one-third of a pie. As they come to realize that fractions are simply representations of parts of whole numbers, students learn to add and subtract fractions. In some problems, fractions will be combined with whole numbers. Students go back and forth, converting whole numbers into fractions and fractions into whole numbers.

Money is often used to help familiarize students with the decimal system. Then, decimals are presented in table form and in word form. Students will add and subtract decimals and order and compare them.

Enlarging on what was taught in the third grade, geometry continues to be presented to students, even though it may not be called by that name until the subject is encountered in high school. Students are taught about the sides and vertices of plane figures and about lines that are parallel and those that intersect. They begin coordinate graphing and see lots of circles so that the concepts of center, radius, and diameter grow familiar.

The National Assessment tests fourth-graders, looking for their strengths and weaknesses. The results are an indication of what students are and are not learning in mathematics during the first four grades of elementary school. The National Assessment found that fourth-graders were strongest on basic facts in addition, slightly weaker on subtraction basic facts, and weakest on multiplication basic facts. Division was still fairly new to many of them. Difficulty with problem solving was demonstrated by the fact that only 35 percent could correctly answer the following question: "Jason bought 3 boxes of pencils. What else do you need to know to find out how many pencils he bought?"

The correct answer, of course is: How many pencils were in each box. This was a failure not of computational skill, but of reasoning ability.

It was also revealed by the National Assessment that fourth-graders had trouble with place value. When called upon to consider place value (as, for instance, 38 being 3 tens and 8 ones), they were weak.

Students were tested on their ability to perform a one-step multiplication problem when presented with extraneous information. The question: "One rabbit eats 2 pounds of food each week. There are 52 weeks in a year. How much food will 5 rabbits each in one week?" The correct answer of 10 pounds was given by 47 percent of the students. Some were confused by what to do with the 52 that they were supposed to ignore.

On another question they were tested on their ability to apply information from a word problem involving measurement. The question: "Mr. Jones put a wire fence all the way around his rectangular garden. The garden is 10 feet long and 6 feet wide. How many feet of fencing did he use?" The correct answer of 32 feet was given by 9 percent of the students. One possible strategy for solving the problem might have involved drawing a sketch so each side of the garden could be visualized.

The following is what it is desirable for children to accomplish by the end of the fourth grade, though some of the goals may not be realized until later because the curriculum is covered at different rates in each school and children's mathematical ability develops at different rates. Even when exposed to the following in the fourth grade, some students may take until the fifth or sixth grade to master it:

- Identify place value for four-digit numbers.

- Add four-digit numbers.

- Add and subtract decimals.

- Multiply a four-digit number by a one-digit number with regrouping.

- Multiply a three-digit number by a two-digit number.

- Divide a three-digit number by a one-digit number with regrouping and a remainder.

- Solve a word problem involving division.

- Determine simple fractions of whole numbers from word problems.

- Reduce to lowest terms a proper fraction in which neither the numerator nor the denominator exceeds 81.

- Compute sums and differences of fractions with like denominators.

- Recognize improper fractions in which the numerator is larger than the denominator.

- Be introduced to calculations involving mixed numbers and fractions.

- Approximate and measure, using both American and metric systems, length, weight, capacity, and temperature.

- Gain some familiarity with the concept of volume.

- Describe and compute the perimeter of squares and rectangles, though this is an area of difficulty, according to the National Assessment.

- Be introduced to problems involving the properties of the circle—center, radius, and diameter.

- Write an appropriate sentence, including numbers, for presenting a word problem.

- Sort out the relevant information from a word problem that includes extraneous information and solve the problem.

- Make inferences from statistical data.

- Given a picture of a clock, solve an addition problem involving lapsed time.

Moving on to the fifth grade, pupils should do more than simply review what was taught in earlier grades, as tends to be the practice in many fifth-grade classrooms. Students should be taken deeper into topics already learned, pursuing the work, as much as possible, in the context of solving problems rather than merely computing numbers that are given to them. Also, they should delve further into the rudiments of geometry and algebra.

There is a dilemma in the upper elementary grades as teachers try to find a balance between review of old work and presentation of new work. Without sufficient review, students are in danger of not retaining a firm grasp of the basics. But too much review can mean stagnation at a time when students should be pushing forward. The sequential nature of math demands that students understand previous lessons so that new lessons can enlarge on what was taught earlier.

A parent should be concerned about a child who is struggling with math at this point, because the problems hold promise of persisting for the length of the student's schooling. The child may be in need of new teaching approaches. Clearly, earlier methods did not work for that particular student and more of the same may be no better. A teacher who can get the student to look at numbers and computation from a fresh standpoint may be needed.

What is distinctive about computation in the upper grades is that besides working with whole numbers students spend much of their time adding, subtracting, multiplying, and dividing fractions and decimals. A student who understands the principles of the operations should be permitted to make extensive use of a calculator and, where appropriate, a computer. A minimum amount of time should be spent on drills and paper-and-pencil calculations once a student grasps a concept.

In their study of numbers and number systems in the fifth grade, youngsters further explore the meaning and representation of numbers and number relationships in fractions, decimals, percents, ratios, and proportions. They grow more comfortable with expressing the same number in different ways in fractions, decimals, and percents.

Students by fifth grade must come to understand that 10 is the basis of the number system. This is stressed with more study of monetary units and the metric system and by discovering patterns in sequences of numbers.

In multiplication, the 10 theme continues with students getting lots of practice mentally multiplying by powers of 10—for instance, 10×8, 200×150, $1,000 \times 30$. In division, they divide decimals and whole numbers by powers of 10. In general, ever-larger numbers are used in multiplication and division. Students are introduced to prime numbers, if they have not already encountered that concept.

Students continue to expand their base for algebra by getting more work with fractions. They practice looking for the least common denominator and changing whole numbers and mixed numbers to fractions. They look for missing numerators or missing denominators. There are fractions to be multiplied and divided.

Often students use calculators for lessons that stress the inverse relationships between multiplication and division and between addition and subtraction. This is the foundation for algebra, as they come to see the role of the function number written as x in the equation.

The work with decimals continues with the multiplying and dividing of decimals, and many teachers have students practice rounding off decimals, though sometimes too much time is spent on these exercises.

In geometry, the shapes and figures of earlier years appear and reappear. Besides reviewing what was taught earlier, fifth-graders will learn to use the protractor if they did not do so in the fourth grade. There will be lines, lines, and more lines, and wherever they converge there will be angles. Fifth-graders learn to classify angles as acute, right, and obtuse. Students in the fifth grade are also introduced to such polygons as the rhombus, the parallelogram, the trapezoid, and the quadrilateral. Angles and lines will form new triangles—namely, isosceles, equilateral, and scalene. Students will gain some familiarity with formulas for determining area and volume.

This is what it is good for a student to be able to do by the end of the fifth grade, though some may not do so until a later grade because of developmental differences and variations in the curriculum from school system to school system:

- Identify place values for five-digit numbers.

- Recognize Roman numerals through thousands.

- Add four five-digit numbers.

- Subtract two four-digit numbers with regrouping.

- Multiply two three-digit numbers.

- Divide up to a three-digit number by a two-digit number.

- List four equivalent fractions, such as $\frac{1}{2}$, $\frac{2}{4}$, $\frac{4}{8}$, and $\frac{5}{10}$.

- Change an improper fraction to a mixed number and a mixed number to an improper fraction.

- Determine the greatest common factor of a set of two-digit numbers.

- Subtract a whole number from a mixed number.

- Multiply two proper fractions and change the answer to simplest form.

- Divide two proper fractions and express the quotient in simplest form.

- Add and subtract decimals with different place values.

- Multiply a two-place decimal by a one-place decimal.

- Be able to make relationships of weights and lengths between the American and metric systems.

- Solve word problems involving averages.

- Compute the mean of a group of numbers.

- Have some proficiency in estimating answers to basic addition, subtraction, and multiplication before performing the actual calculations.

- Be familiar with the properties of a circle: center, radius, and diameter.

- Use a calculator to solve problems requiring several steps.

The sixth grade is a point at which review usually outweighs the introduction of new material as teachers try to get students ready for junior high school. The goal is to be sure they have been exposed to all of the math that is supposed to pass in front of them in elementary school and that they have the base from which to tackle any problems in junior high school that depend on mastery of elementary school math.

A problem with this is that the majority of mathematics in the seventh and eighth grades in most schools is also a review of the earlier grades, so for the three years after the fifth grade students end up mostly reviewing what was taught in the first five grades. Enough is enough.

In a sixth-grade classroom, where problem solving is emphasized, students will be encouraged to go beyond what they have already learned to develop and apply stategies to solve one-step, multi-step, and nonroutine problems. With the skills that have been acquired by the sixth grade, students should be able to wrestle with more complex problems involving probability, statistics, geometry, and rational numbers.

Problems should be fun and challenging, not frightening or boring. If math is frightening, the student has not been properly taught and gained confidence; if it is boring, the work is too easy and, perhaps, too repetitive. A good teacher will let students work in teams to solve some problems so that they can collaborate as people do in the real world and be stimulated by each other.

The new work in the sixth grade includes prime numbers and prime factorization. Skills of estimation are honed so that students can tell at a glance the approximate range of answers to a problem.

The study of fractions is augmented to include reciprocals. Students will also be exposed to word problems that contain both fractions and decimals. If they have not previously done much computing with percentages, they certainly will do so before the end of the sixth grade. There is much work on conversion problems of all sorts—converting between uneven fractions and mixed numbers, converting between decimals and fractions, converting between decimals and percents.

A new area of exposure in some sixth grades is that of positive and negative numbers, which students will have to add and subtract to solve some of the problems they encounter. This is a prealgebra skill that is still too abstract for some students this age.

The preparation for geometry continues as students confront again the whole range of shapes they have learned about in earlier grades. They are asked to do more work on finding the areas and other attributes of these different figures. There are still angles to be studied, as well as parallel, perpendicular, and skewed lines. It is the triangle that may be studied most because of the learning possibilities. Measuring and comparing the sides of similar triangles helps students grasp the concept of similar figures and discover the relationship between the angles and sides of similar triangles. This is the stepping stone into trigonometry.

The compass, the ruler, and the protractor become familiar tools. Students study pi, the hypotenuse, and the Pythagorean theory, which they may visualize by cutting small squares into pieces that can be rearranged into one larger square.

Sixth-graders can make good use of the computer to explore the properties of figures, to make conjectures and to test them. There is some excellent software that permits this kind of work and the computer is a powerful learning tool at this point. It allows the construction on the screen of two-dimensional and three-dimensional figures that can be flipped and turned to be seen from various perspectives.

Related studies are devoted to measurements of all

kinds. Length and weight are measured in both American standard units and metric units. A great deal of the measurement occurs in the context of geometry, where angles are measured and areas of figures of different shapes are compared. The idea here is not just to get students to perform accurate calculations, but to reason deductively and to recognize relationships. Problems calling for the calculation of time and temperature also appear with greater regularity in the sixth grade.

During the sixth grade and continuing into the seventh and eighth grades, students build a mental bridge from the concrete approach of the early grades to the abstract approach that will be expected of them increasingly in high school. The bridge must be strong enough that they are able to cross it and enter the world of algebra and calculus. The National Council of Teachers of Mathematics, in a draft of a proposed curriculum, recommended that during these transition years in the upper elementary grades and into junior high school students should explore algebraic concepts and processes so that they can:

- Understand the concepts of variable, expression, and equation.

- Represent situations and number patterns with tables, graphs, verbal rules, and equations, and explore the interrelationships of these representations.

- Analyze tables and graphs to identify properties and relationships.

- Develop confidence in solving linear equations using concrete, informal, and formal methods.

- Investigate inequalities and nonlinear equations informally.

- Apply algebraic methods to solve a variety of real-world and mathematical problems.

This is what a student may be expected to do at the end of sixth grade, and those who are unable to do so are the ones most likely to encounter problems in mathematics in secondary school:

- Work with numbers up to 1,000,000.

- Read and interpret decimals and compare them with numbers expressed in other forms.

- Recognize, read, and analyze place value.

- Multiply by tens, hundreds, and thousands.

- Multiply and divide multidigit numbers with regrouping.

- Divide by a decimal.

- Add and subtract mixed numbers and fractions with unlike denominators.

- Determine the number a percent represents.

- Choose the proper operations to solve a challenging word problem.

It is difficult to say precisely what each student will confront in math in each grade, because the sequence of topics and skills taught varies throughout the country. But parents can reasonably expect that much of what is discussed here will appear in one or another of the elementary grades. Because the study of math in the seventh and eighth grades is so heavily a review of the elementary years, those two years are available for elaborating on basic concepts and introducing them if somehow they have not been presented by the end of the sixth grade. Ideally, though, the beginning of junior high school will not be a time when students are getting their first taste of what should have been presented in elementary school.

Parents find it increasingly difficult to help their children in math in the upper elementary grades. This is understandable since many adults make little use of what they learned about math in school and therefore forget much of it. In addition, some adults may not have learned the material very well in the first place. If parents are persistent, though, there are ways to assist their children.

One of the better ways is to use the Family Math Program sponsored by Lawrence Hall of Science at the University of California at Berkeley and available anywhere in the country. A group of interested parents, perhaps through a PTA, can write to Lawrence Hall and get information on setting up a workshop for parents.

Usually, the workshops are organized by grade levels —one, for instance, for parents of students in the second and third grades; another for parents of students in the fourth, fifth, and sixth grades. Workshops typically meet for an hour or two once a week for at least a month. The heart of the program, once parents have attended the workshops, is a thick volume of math problems that parents can do with their children at home.

Information is available from the EQUALS Program, Lawrence Hall of Science, University of California, Berkeley, Calif. 94720.

25

REINFORCING SCHOOLING
IN THE HOME

There are two main ways by which the work of the school is extended beyond the confines of the classroom: through homework and through tutoring. In either case, the goal is to reinforce what has been taught and to strengthen a student's base for further learning. But because children tend to believe that schoolwork is supposed to stop at the schoolhouse door, there is a natural inclination on their part to object to any exercise outside of school that has an academic aura.

Thus, there is the homework battle, as regular a part of child-rearing as having youngsters refuse to eat vegetables. Few are the parents who have not had to fight to get their children to do homework.

If your child's elementary school does not assign homework it is in a tiny minority. Though experts are mixed in their opinions about the value of homework in elementary school, most teachers accept as an article of faith the idea that doing out-of-school assignments is good for children. Supposedly, it builds character. And, if for no other reason, homework is assigned because parents expect it. The assumption is that the homework load ought to grow heavier as students progress through school. In first grade this might mean fifteen or twenty minutes of homework, and by the upper elementary grades there may be an hour to an hour and a half of homework each night.

Of course, a teacher can only estimate how much time homework will take because not all children take as long to complete an identical assignment. One will struggle over a piece of work that another will whiz through. An assignment in a second-grade class, for instance, could take ten minutes for one child and a half hour for another. However long children devote to homework, these are its main purposes:

- *Reinforcing classroom lessons.* Most of us find that going back over something we have been taught and reviewing it makes it stick in our minds more firmly.
- *Expanding on the lessons.* A teacher has just so much time in class and must attend to the needs of many students. The lesson in the schoolroom may be limited to the bare bones. A good homework assignment can help a student learn a great deal more about the subject than the teacher imparted in class.
- *Being prepared for an upcoming lesson.* If students gain an introduction to material to be presented the next day, it will be unnecessary for the teacher to have to dwell on minor matters and the lesson can be more interesting and more easily comprehended.
- *Studying for a test.* It is usually important to review work before a test, and it may be especially crucial when a test covers work taught over a fairly long period.

• *Learning to do research.* There is often not enough time in class to study related material and take notes, a process that a student might do more easily on his or her own at home or at the library.

• *Working independently.* Ultimately, an aim of formal schooling is to equip each person to continue as a self-motivated learner working on his or her own. As adults know, there is not always someone to help with each task that must be learned; learning how to learn is vital.

• *Acquiring habits of organization and time budgeting.* Study habits are built over the years and students who master those habits have an easier time in school.

Homework is a source of anxiety for many children. They fear that without anyone to lead them through the work they will not be able to do it. Ideally, a teacher will put students at ease by letting them know that there is not so much at stake that they have to feel trepidation. Easier said than done, though. We all have our own ways of building up dread in situations when we ought to realize that there is no rational reason to be so worried.

The uneasiness of students is not without foundation. There are some important considerations involved. Often homework is graded and students have more at stake than if they were merely performing practice exercises. Furthermore, homework assignments usually call for meeting deadlines, a prospect that can be unnerving to anyone. Some teachers make matters worse by not carefully planning the assignments they make. Homework should contain a minimum of meaningless memorization and boring practice drills. This is difficult for some teachers to appreciate, because of a misguided notion that homework best disciplines the mind by being somewhat tedious and onerous.

An effect of the school reform movement of recent years has been to put pressure on teachers to assign more homework. In Chicago, for example, a policy was adopted that mandated that all teachers assign a specific amount of homework each night. The mandate called for fifteen minutes of homework in kindergarten, thirty minutes in grades 1 through 3, and forty-five minutes in grades 4 through 6. Students were required to keep notebooks listing assignments, due dates, and time spent on the work.

Such directives have come forth more frequently in schools during the last few years. Yet, as homework assignments have increased, there has been little commensurate attempt by educators to establish, once and for all, that homework is beneficial. The research is not conclusive one way or the other. Furthermore, homework assignments frequently violate a tenet of good teaching in that they fail to differentiate among the varying developmental needs of individual students. Usually, the same homework assignment is given to everyone in the class, instead of an individualized assignment for each student.

Some teachers, however, are more careful than others in making homework assignments; they devise them in ways that consider individual needs. A review of the research on the effects of homework by Joe Dan Austin led him to offer suggestions that teachers should take to heart, especially in connection with mathematics, in making home assignments. Parents should look at their children's homework assignments with these recommendations in mind:

• Homework consisting of routine drills is probably of limited value.

- Homework in math seems to improve computational skills, but the findings with regard to problem-solving skills are mixed.

- Long homework assignments are not clearly more effective than shorter assignments.

- Teachers should grade at least some of the problems assigned as homework.

- Teachers' comments on homework that students turn in can help boost achievement.

- Early feedback by teachers to students on homework assignments is preferable to delayed feedback.

The point is that a teacher can take steps to make homework more useful as a learning device, as well as more satisfying to students. Giving students feedback is one of the most important parts of homework. Students should know that the teacher is reading the homework and they should get some response, so that homework can be enhanced as a learning experience. Students should not be blamed if they get cynical about homework when, after submitting it in on time, they do not get it marked and returned to them by the teacher in timely fashion.

When parents see problems developing in the way that their children handle homework, it might be good to ask the teacher for advice on how to cope with the difficulties. These are some of the problems of which parents should be aware:

- Taking an inordinately long time to do homework.

- Not being able to work independently.

- Always waiting until the last minute to do an assignment.

- Telling parents there is no homework when in fact there is.

- Being consistently late in turning in assignments.

On the other hand, parents should not expect children to enjoy homework any more than parents like having to perform extra chores around the house after coming home from work. Students don't like homework because it infringes on time they believe is supposed to belong to them to spend as they please. It is unlikely parents are going to be able to talk children into adoring homework, but they can try to make youngsters understand that not all of schoolwork is done in school and that it is no less important just because it is done at home. A parent whose job involves bringing home work to do at night might be able to make this point more easily to a child by pointing out the similarity in their situations.

It also helps to have a designated place and time for homework. Making it more businesslike annd less haphazard helps impress on a child that homework has official standing. This approach will probably make it easier to get the homework done. Perhaps a corner of the child's bedroom could be the place for doing homework. A small table and chair could be moved to the spot or maybe, if it can be afforded, there might be a shopping expedition to let the youngster select a desk. Then there might be some enjoyment found in a trip to a stationery store to buy supplies for the desk.

The child should have a role in deciding the best time for doing homework. Maybe it is immediately after school or perhaps right after dinner. Whatever the decision, it will probably work best if the schedule is followed—without getting altogether rigid about it—and there is an understanding that nothing else is to be scheduled during that period.

Parents have an obligation to keep the home somewhat quiet during homework period and to respect the needs of the child. If a bedroom is the place for homework and it is shared with a sibling, then the other child ought to stay out of the room during that time. It is probably best to let children in the same family have separate homework periods—or separate places to do homework—because there is a good chance that not much homework will get done if they are in the room together, sharing a homework period.

There is pressure on the rest of the family in a home that is less roomy, because it may mean that homework has to be done in the living room or at the kitchen table. In any event, if the family doesn't show respect for the child's needs during this period, the unspoken message is that homework is not very important.

If a child wants to listen to music while doing homework parents should probably try to talk the child out of it, pointing out that music might interfere with the ability to concentrate. But if the child is insistent and the music does not seem to undermine the homework, it might be best to let the child have the music.

Homework should be done in a comfortable setting so that having to do it is less objectionable. A child should no more have to sit upright in a stiff-backed chair to do homework than an adult should have to sit in such a way to read a magazine. Homework is a time when a child should be able to lie on a couch or sprawl on the floor if that is the preferred position. Food should be permitted, if desired, and breaks should be allowed. Adults drink coffee at their desks at work and frequently get up and walk around. Why should students not be permitted the same freedom? Homework routines should be adapted to the learning style that feels best to a student.

A problem in America today is that too many students fail to do homework regardless of what provisions are made for the task. Furthermore, some parents do not try or are unable to get their children to do the assignments. Teachers in some of the more troubled schools have even stopped asking for homework because of the futility of the request. Unfortunately, the students least likely to do homework tend to be the lowest achievers, who most need the additional work. Boston attempted to deal with the problem by requiring middle-school students with low scores on reading and math tests to stay after school for ninety minutes each day for tutoring and help with their homework. An additional voluntary session was scheduled for each Saturday morning.

It is noteworthy that one reason given for the high scholastic achievement rates of recent immigrants from Asian countries is their diligence in doing homework. Some observers, seeing how well Asian-Americans are doing in school, raise the possibility that genetics explains all. Others say that there are additional factors to be considered. A survey in San Francisco found that Asian-Americans spent an average of 11.7 hours a week doing homework, compared with 8 hours for whites and 6.3 hours for blacks. Asian-Americans also had the best attendance and paid greater attention to the teacher. What mainly seemed to be occurring was that Asian-Americans were working harder than other students, both in and out of school.

A study of homework habits by the U.S. Census Bureau, which did not examine Asian-Americans separately, disclosed that whites, blacks, and Hispanics all spent about 5.5 hours a week on homework, according to *The New York Times*. This was the average for students in all grades. At the elementary level, students each week spent an average of 4.9 hours on homework if they attended public school, and 5.5 hours if they went to nonpublic schools. Generally, in all grades and in all schools girls reported doing more homework than boys. More than 1 out of 10 students in all grades across the country, 12.8 percent, said they never did any homework at all.

Researchers at the University of Michigan found that American students spent considerably less time on homework than did students in Taiwan and Japan. First-graders spent 77 minutes on homework on weekdays in Taiwan, 37 minutes in Japan, and 14 minutes in the United States, according to estimates by their mothers. For fifth-graders, the estimates were 114 minutes for Taiwanese, 57 minutes for Japanese, and 47 minutes for Americans. The differences might be attributable not simply to less willingness by American children to do homework, but also to their being assigned less homework.

One has to wonder, though, whether it is desirable for American students to be put under pressure as great as that applied to some Japanese students, who attend tutoring schools to get into the best tutoring schools. They start attending tutoring school, known as *juku*, while they are still in elementary school, in order to qualify for the best of the one-year, post-college cram schools that prepare them for the tests to get into the most prestigious universities. Fortunately, this kind of tradition has not embedded itself in the United States.

There is a role for parents to play as far as homework

is concerned, but it should not include doing homework for their children, no matter how much they may think it will make the child look better in the eyes of the teacher. Parents should, however, review homework and be aware of it because that is one of the best ways to gain insights into the nature of the work being performed in school. By no means does homework reflect exactly what is being done in class, but it is a close enough approximation that parents can get a sense of the classwork.

Some better schools have ways of keeping parents informed about homework assignments and even of giving parents some grounding in the work being assigned so that they will be able to lend guidance to their children in doing homework. "Guidance," in fact, is the key word, because there is a large difference between guiding a child and doing the work for him or her. These are tips for parents to bear in mind when considering how involved to get in the child's homework:

- Ordinarily, do not do the work for the child.

- If there is a textbook or some other material on which the homework is based, read it before turning to the assignment so that you will have a proper background and be better able to keep your remarks in the context of the assignment.

- Ask questions of the child that will help steer the child toward the results that the teacher seems to be seeking.

- Admit that you do not know something rather than give a child wrong guidance.

- Be discreet about criticizing a faulty assignment, so that the child does not develop a negative attitude toward the teacher.

- For the most part, keep away while the child is doing homework and leave the child to work alone. The best parental involvement might come at the outset with an explanation by the child of what the assignment consists of, and then sitting down afterward with the child to review the work, raise questions, and offer observations.

- Be patient and do not criticize the child. Use this as a chance to spend constructive, loving time with the child. If you find yourself regularly getting into squabbles with your child, then being involved with homework is simply not a good idea. It is better to have no role than to make a mess of it.

- Be supportive and encouraging even when the child does not know the answer, building on what the child does know and bolstering confidence.

If a child regularly does not understand homework assignments and is unable to do them there is a problem that the parent should take up with the teacher. While a teacher may now and then deliberately give students homework that they are unable to do, intending it as a device to introduce them to a topic and to whet their appetite for an explanation the following day, this is not a good practice on a regular basis. Frustrating and exasperating students is not the best way to teach them. However, the repeated inability of a youngster to handle assignments that are appropriate may be indicative of a difficulty that parent, teacher, and child should work together to overcome.

Parents are no longer the only source for help with homework. In an increasing number of locales around the country, local teachers' unions and other groups are establishing "hot lines" that a student can telephone for assistance with homework.

Such aid can be of particular value when a student is stymied by a procedure in math or science or cannot locate a crucial fact around which an assignment revolves, say, in social studies or English. Where there are homework hot lines, teachers—sometimes paid by grants from outside groups—stand by on telephones, waiting to respond to questions. The responses may take the form of questions that the teachers ask to help direct the youngsters to the answers. In New York City, the United Federation of Teachers provides teachers to handle questions in seven different languages and also to respond to questions from parents who want to know how to help their children with homework.

There is another, more formal, outlet for students who need extra help on a regular basis. That is tutoring. Individual tutoring has been around for generations, usually involving a teacher who picks up extra money after school by providing the additional assistance either at the student's home or at his or her home. While some families have been reluctant to use such services out of fear that it would stigmatize the child, other families have felt no particular embarrassment over having to get additional academic help for their children.

The traditional ambivalence toward after-school tutoring was captured in this vignette from a charming short story in *The New Yorker* by H. L. Mountzoures in which a father describes the feelings he and his young son had over their sojourns to the tutor: "Each day that we had to go to the tutor's I felt depressed, humiliated, and angry. And what about Phillip? He chafed and swore and said he didn't want to go. Of course he'd much rather have been out in the afternoon—making swords from branches, collecting leaves and rocks, riding his bike to friends' houses, exploring a nearby creek."

In the last few years, a new form of tutoring has spread across the country in the form of profit-making businesses that operate tutoring centers out of suites in small office buildings or in storefronts at suburban shopping malls, not unlike McDonald's franchises. Some of the bigger companies in the field are Sylvan Learning Corporation, the Reading Game, Huntington Learning Centers, and Humanex Systems International. Tutoring of this sort has come to be seen by some families as a service not just for students who are lagging behind, but also for high-achieving students who want a boost to reach even higher.

Unlike individuals who tutor on the side, the companies tend to precede the process with a battery of tests that supposedly analyze the student's needs and prescribe methods and materials likely to yield the best results. Furthermore, the companies are more apt to tie their tutoring to computers that provide a programmed approach to the tutoring. Sometimes the battery of tests and the computers may be of benefit, but parents should not automatically conclude that such features are superior to a lone teacher who comes to the student's home in the afternoon without fancy appurtenances and offers lessons at the kitchen table.

Tutoring tends to be less expensive when it is done by someone working privately on the side. A survey by

Time magazine in 1986 found that fees for the tutoring companies ran in the range of $20 to $25 an hour.

Tutoring itself, whether through a company or a sole practitioner, can be of great benefit to some students and should definitely be considered by some families. While it is true that tutoring requires added expense, parents using public schools should view the extra cost in perspective. The amount spent on tutoring is but a fraction of what it would cost to send a student to a nonpublic school. Looked at this way, the expense of tutoring can be seen as a small part of what is being saved by using public schools. Many families have no reluctance about spending money for sending children to private classes that help prepare students for the Scholastic Aptitude Test. Surely if this exercise—which is a form of tutoring—is acceptable, then tutoring for regular schoolwork is no less legitimate.

A problem is that it may not be easy to tell whether your child is a good candidate for tutoring. And, once tutoring begins, sometimes it is not readily apparent whether it is being done well. Buying a tutoring service is something like dealing with automobile mechanics: you are at the mercy of the practitioner in terms of the diagnosis, and it is not easy to evaluate the quality or extensiveness of the work. These are some of the indicators that tutoring may be needed by your elementary school child:

- Lagging behind the class in the work, particularly in one subject.

- Lacking a good grasp of the fundamentals that were previously taught and without which it is very difficult to keep up with the work.

- Extremely slow in completing tasks.

- Unorganized and not able to work efficiently, seriously needing help in developing good study habits.

- Repeated failure to do homework and to work on one's own.

- Poor confidence in one's academic ability.

- Fright over tests.

It is perhaps easier to spot the signs indicating that tutoring would be helpful than it is to know whether the tutor is the right one. Certainly, if the student makes progress in dealing with the problems cited above, then something beneficial is probably resulting from the intervention. If the chemistry between student and tutor appears faulty or there is good reason to doubt the tutor's effectiveness, it might be a good idea to try another tutor rather than give up altogether on tutoring. *Instructor* magazine ran a series of suggestions to teachers to guide them in recommending a tutor to parents. According to the article, parents ought to ask themselves these same questions about a potential tutor:

- Is the tutor a certified teacher? Are credentials current? What other qualifications does the tutor have?

- What is the tutor's theoretical or philosophical approach?

- Does the tutor or tutoring center specialize or use any special techniques?

- With what age range does the tutor normally work?

- Does the tutor work out of a center or the child's home?

- What is the length and number of sessions per week? What hours is the tutor available?

- Will the tutoring program run indefinitely, or will a time frame be estimated?

- What are the fees? Are there any charges besides the basic fee—for testing, for example? Is there a sliding scale for tuition?

- How will the child's progress be determined?

- How will the program coordinate efforts with your school?

- Will written and verbal reports be made to the child's parents and teacher? How often?

- What materials will be used?

- Is the tutor's work supervised?

- If the tutor or center can no longer help, will they make a referral to someone who can?

- Can the child meet with the tutor before signing up to find out if their personalities mesh?

- Can the tutor or center provide two current references?

26

WEEKENDS, SUMMERS, AND AFTER SCHOOL

Learning occurs in a multitude of settings. We think first and foremost of school buildings in connection with learning, but many other places are equally productive in this connection. You can maximize your child's learning opportunities by seeing to it that some of the child's out-of-class time after school and on weekends, as well as during the summer, is spent in settings that augment and expand upon the learning that takes place in the classroom.

There are several advantages to these out-of-school settings, the most notable being that the instruction is often more informal than in school and the experience is more fun. The sad part is that learning in school, too, could be more informal and more fun than it is. One can only hope that in the long run more elementary schools will emulate some of the out-of-school programs and incorporate into the classroom some of the informality, joyfulness, and spontaneity that too often is missing in school.

Interestingly, higher education has shown more recognition of this kind of learning than elementary education has. College students can gain academic credits for part-time jobs, travel, independent study, and life experience. There has been growing recognition on campuses that students do not have to sit at desks surrounded by four walls to learn.

Parents can take steps on their own to put more freedom and flexibility into the education of their children by finding the right opportunities outside the school. Because children in elementary school spend long periods of time sitting still in school, it is wise to let them pursue out-of-school activities that are not so restrictive. Such experiences, more than anything else, should provide enjoyment to children. Ideally, the learning is a side benefit.

Programs of this sort operate in many settings, including libraries, museums, zoos, camps, gymnasiums, and even church basements. Parents should recognize the educational possibilities inherent in the programs and choose with care. Obviously, just giving children something wholesome and constructive to do during their free time is one of the goals in sending them off to a program. It is understandable that the programs to some extent fulfill a baby-sitting responsibility. But parents should strive for something more because—besides providing an enjoyable experience for the child—the activity can be an important part of the child's intellectual, physical, social, and emotional development. These are some of the features to seek in such programs:

• *A program that is not operating on a shoestring and so short of money that the quality is compromised.* The program need not be lavish, but if it seems limited by funds your child may not be getting sufficient returns for the time invested. On the other hand, for a program to have the resources it needs you may be called upon to pay tuition or a fee.

• *Adequately trained personnel are usually as important to these programs as they are to regular classrooms in elementary schools.* High school and college students may be on the staff, but the operation should have a thoroughly professional character.

• *Facilities should be first-rate, no less adequate than the classroom in which your child attends school.* It should be clean and safe and there should be toilets available. Space should be adequate to the activity.

• *Materials should be in ample supply if they are needed for the activity.* In an art program, for instance, supplies should be plentiful, so that the child's ability to participate is not limited by shortages of paper or paints. In a computer program there should be enough consoles, so that children do not have to wait long periods to participate.

• *Snacks and physical activity should ordinarily be features of these programs, because young children need both to keep their interest from flagging.*

MUSEUMS

Many museums around the country have programs throughout the year for children. In addition, a growing number of cities such as Portland, Oregon, and Saint Paul, Minnesota, have children's museums. Most such children's museums are concerned primarily with art, but there are others that have such specialties as natural history or science. A key to a successful out-of-school museum program is that students do not settle into the role of passive participants that is so familiar to adults who visit museums.

What often distinguishes children's museums and programs for children in regular museums is the interactive nature of the experience. Children are invited to touch, feel, and operate many of the displays and exhibits. Some are accompanied by activities that let children draw and construct their own projects. A telephone call to a local museum's education department will provide information on the programs available for children.

Remember that many museums, even ones that are not expressly for children, offer drawing, painting, and sculpting classes for children. Such classes afford a marvelous opportunity for students to get artistic instruction of a sort seldom given in school.

In addition to sending their younsters to formal programs at museums, parents can take advantage of museums by making them places to visit regularly with their children. You don't have to be an art expert to do this. The shared experience can be valuable whether or not the parent knows anything more about art than the child does. If you wish, however, it is possible to do a little advance reading about a particular exhibit or artist and add your own perspectives to the visit. These are some tips for taking your child to a museum:

• *Don't make the visit too long and don't try to see too much.* You might limit each visit to a possible theme, a certain gallery in the museum, or a particular exhibit. Don't make the visit so drawn out that it bores your child and makes the prospect of future visits unappealing.

• *Don't hurry a child who wants to take an extended look at one particular object.* Take the cue from the child as to what interests him or her. I am reminded of the teacher who took her class to the museum and then hurried the children who wanted to take time to look at the exhibits they liked, telling them they wouldn't see everything if they poked along. A museum is a place to poke.

• *Go when the museum is least crowded, avoiding weekends, if possible.* The pushing and shoving crowds will make the experience less pleasurable for a child. Also, those large adult bodies make it more difficult for little people to see the exhibits.

• *Telephone in advance and ask someone in the education department if there are any special exhibits that might be of particular interest to someone of your child's age.*

• *Find out about tours in the museum that are designed for children, but make sure the age group is appropriate for your child.*

• *If permitted by the museum, encourage your child to take a sketch pad or a camera.* This is another way of raising the child's interest level.

• *Young children should be supervised by adults in a museum.* However, there are ways of keeping an eye on them without making them feel that they are under criminal surveillance.

• *Discuss the visit afterward with your child, talking about what the child liked and disliked.* Don't be judgmental about your child's artistic tastes. Just be happy he or she enjoys going to the museum. If the child shows interest in the works of a certain artist, try to get an illustrated book of those works. Many such books are available in paperback editions that are less expensive than the hardbound copies. Also, many libraries are well supplied with art books.

LIBRARIES

On of the most convenient of all ways to extend your child's education in out-of-school hours is through trips to the library, an institution that can serve the needs of children throughout their years of schooling. And, of course, the habit of using the library carries over to a lifetime of pleasure for adults. If there is any one single weapon for countering the impact of television in a way that scores points for schooling, it is by helping your child get used to going to the library.

When the Farmington Library Council in Connecticut asked people in town to forego television viewing for a month, the campaign was launched with discussions by teachers and librarians about the effects of television viewing. Then libraries played a major role in the program by providing reading lists and special programs to engage the leisure time of people during the weeks that they kept the set turned off.

The library is a place to browse. There is usually a room in the library filled with books just for children. If the library is too small to have a separate room for children's books, it at least has shelves devoted to children's books, often organized by the age-appropriateness of the books.

An adult accompanying a kindergartener or first-grader to the library should give the child guidance in selecting books with lots of pictures that are suitable for a beginning reader. Older children can be allowed to make more of their own selections after they have been directed toward the shelves with books suitable for their age.

As noted earlier in this book, the example that parents set as far as books are concerned will have much to do with the role that the library plays in the lives of their children. Parents who accompany children to the library and return home empty-handed are communicating a message to their youngsters. If books are not good enough for adults, then what self-respecting child is going to be interested in them?

Some of the best guidance at the library can come from a trained librarian. Preferably, seek out a children's librarian, a professional trained in children's literature.

Good libraries are set up with places where children can read. Let your child do some reading at the library. This is a very special experience, and if it motivates the child to be more eager to read then there is a real bonus in going to the library. Surely, there is much that an adult can do at the library to keep busy while a child is reading.

But, of course, books should be brought home, too. Learn from experience how many books your child is likely to read in between trips to the library, and discourage the child from taking home extra books that are not likely to be read. First of all, that is a disservice to other children who might want to read the books. Furthermore, the child should get in the habit of reading the books that are brought home, not letting them sit around until they are returned unread.

On the other hand, it is not a crime to start a book and not finish it if it is uninteresting. Children should have the right to put aside books that do not satisfy them. Adults should not criticize them for this and should limit their comments to asking what the child did not like about the book. Moreover, children should be able to exercise a wide range of choice at the library, selecting books that appeal to them whether or not the books are favored by their parents. Certainly a parent can subtly try to influence a choice, but ultimately the selection is up to the child. What counts is that the child read the book. Even if the book seems too easy, too difficult, or not on a desirable topic, the fact that the child wants to read it is important.

Sometimes the library is a good place to take a child to do homework or to pursue research for a special project. It is desirable that students get accustomed to using research materials. They should be encouraged to use the resources of the library for this purpose. A visit to the library can also be a prelude to a family vacation trip, allowing a child to look up information about the place to be visited and to take note of sites of tourist interest.

Many libraries have storytelling hours and these sessions often appeal to children of various ages. It is good to find out about the services available at your local library and to encourage your child to participate in some of the activities. Libraries also schedule films and lend videocassettes.

If you are looking for ideas for books that your child can borrow from the library, here are some suggestions, drawn selectively from a list compiled by Reading Is Fundamental, a nonprofit group that distributes free books to schoolchildren to encourage them to read. The list comprises the favorites of children who have participated in the RIF program. You can get your own copy of the complete list for $1.50 from Reading Is Fundamental, Smithsonian Institution, 600 Maryland Ave. S.W., Suite 500, Washington, D.C. 20560. Some of these books are not newly published and can be found only at the library:

For First Through Third Grade

Alexander and the Terrible, Horrible, No Good, Very Bad Day by Judith Viorst. Atheneum and Aladdin, 1972.

Bedtime for Francis by Russell Hoban. Harper, 1960.

The Cat in the Hat by Dr. Seuss. Beginner Books, 1957.

Charlie and the Chocolate Factory by Roald Dahl. Knopf, Bantam, and Viking Penguin, 1964.

Charlotte's Web by E. B. White. Harper, 1952.

Curious George by H. A. Rey. Houghton Mifflin, 1941.

Freckle Juice by Judy Blume. Dell, 1978.

Make Way for Ducklings by Robert McCloskey. Viking and Puffin, 1941.

Miss Nelson is Missing! by Harry Allard. Houghton Mifflin, 1977.

Ramona Quimby, Age 8 by Beverly Cleary. Morrow and Dell, 1981.

Where the Sidewalk Ends: Poems and Drawings by Shel Silverstein. Harper, 1974.

Where the Wild Things Are by Maurice Sendak. Harper, 1962.

For Fourth Through Sixth Grade

The Adventures of Tom Sawyer by Mark Twain. Several editions.

Black Beauty by Anna Sewell. Several editions.

The Black Stallion by Walter Farley. Random House, 1941.

Garfield Counts to Ten by Jim Davis. Random House, 1983.

The Lion, the Witch and the Wardrobe by C. S. Lewis. Macmillan and Collier, 1968.

The Little House on the Prairie by Laura I. Wilder. Harper, 1935.

Nothing's Fair in Fifth Grade by Barthe DeClements. Viking and Scholastic, 1981.

Old Yeller by Fred Gipson. Harper, 1956.

Tales of a Fourth Grade Nothing by Judy Blume. Dutton and Dell, 1972.

The Wonderful Wizard of Oz by Frank L. Baum. Morrow and Dover, 1900, reissued 1987.

ZOOS

Most zoos, like most museums, have special educational programs for children. And, just as is the case with museums, there are children's zoos. The zoo is not likely to be a place that is visited as frequently as the library, but going to the zoo every now and then can be a way to ignite a child's interest in animal life, environmental issues, and world cultures.

Trips to the zoo can sometimes be scheduled to coincide with what is being studied at the moment in school —a trip to the polar bear and the moose for Alaska; the tiger for India; the elephant, the giraffe, the lion, and the zebra for the countries in Africa; the llama for Peru. The occasion can be preceded or followed by a trip to the library to gain further information about the zoo animals.

Try to add an off-beat feature to the zoo trip when possible. Find out about feeding schedules so that your child can watch the animals eat. Find out about guided tours that may include areas of the zoo that are usually off limits and not open to the public. Tours and lectures designed for children can be especially exciting.

Some zoos, like museums, have ongoing programs and classes on Saturday for children. Such an opportunity can be a wonderful experience for a child who has an interest in animals. The zoo is also a locale that can be combined with an introduction to another activity that might fascinate a child: photography. The gift of an inexpensive camera to a child still in elementary school can take on special meaning with the chance to photograph animals at the zoo.

Some of the same advice applies for a trip to the zoo as for a visit to the museum. Perhaps the advice has added application because a zoo is so much larger than a museum. The point to remember is that such a trip is not supposed to be a survival course for a child. Save some of the animals for another visit instead of trying to fit everything in at once. Then, the child won't be tired and there will be reason for returning.

PERFORMING ARTS

Concerts, operas, plays, and dance performances should be a vital part of the out-of-school development of any child. Handled well, the experiences can provide a foundation for the child's interest in the performing arts, both as an audience member and a participant.

Parents should keep alert for announcements of children's concerts and special performances for children. Large cities with major performing ensembles have such events regularly. They are more difficult to find in smaller towns. This is not to say that children should attend only special "children's" concerts. There is no reason why parents cannot carefully choose among regular performances and find ones of potential enjoyment for children. These are some ideas to keep in mind in selecting and attending the performing arts with a child:

- An adult should always accompany a child to a performance if it is not a special children's concert (and some of those, too, expect adults to attend with children), because a child who is bored or uninterested should never be permitted to become disruptive.

- Choose performances that tend to be short, because of the shorter attention span of children.

- Exercise common sense and recognize that performances that are particularly challenging for many adults are not the best ones for children.

- When possible, try to coordinate your choices of performances with what is being studied in school.

- If it is a musical event, try to get the album and play the music for your child in advance, so that he or she has some familiarity and appreciation for it before actually attending.

- If you have reason to suspect that sitting through a performance might be a problem for your child, try to get aisle seats in a row near the back so that if it is necessary to leave during the performance (which you normally should strive not to do) you will cause a minimum of disruption.

- Consider attending only the first half of a concert and leave at the intermission if that seems to be enough culture that particular day for your child.

- If it is a stage performance that you are selecting, you might want to lean toward a musical instead of a drama because a musical is more likely to hold your child's interest.

- During the days following the performance, discuss the experience with your child. If the child liked the music, get albums of other music by the same composer so that the child can listen to them.

Another approach to the performing arts is to encourage your child to take music, dance, or drama lessons. These lessons are not meant only for children whose parents think they have a budding virtuoso in the household. In fact, if at all possible, every child should take regular lessons out of school in some area of the performing arts or the studio arts.

Where lessons are available in the school as part of the regular curriculum, parents should encourage participation by their children. It is a good idea to consider augmenting the in-school lessons with out-of-school lessons. If a musical instrument is involved, it is generally possible to rent one rather than incur the expense at the outset by buying the instrument. If your child takes lessons of some kind these are some ideas to keep in mind:

- Don't lean too hard on the child or make extreme demands, because that is a surefire way to make the experience a sour one.

- Remember that most out-of-school lessons are tied to an expectation that the student will practice at home between lessons. Try to set up a reasonable practice schedule, following an approach similar to that taken in connection with homework.

- If getting the child to practice becomes a terrible struggle it may mean that the studies should be dropped or at least suspended. You might want to explore with the teacher whether there are sufficient benefits for the student if practice is only sporadic.

- Be supportive and encouraging of the activity. Discuss the experience with the child and, if invited, listen to practice. Don't be critical.

- Attend any performances, recitals, and exhibits that are open to parents of the students. Show that you believe in what the child is doing.

- If the child enjoys the experience during the elementary years, encourage a continuation during junior high school and high school.

SPORTS

One of the areas best organized for out-of-school involvement is that of sports. Children can enjoy themselves and derive many developmental benefits from regular participation in sports. There are not varsity teams in elementary school, so the only outlet for formal sports participation at this age is in out-of-school activities.

There are virtues in both individual sports and team sports, and parents might want to encourage their children to explore both. Organized leagues for baseball, soccer, and ice hockey are prevalent for children under twelve. There are also some organized teams for children this age to play tackle football, but parents might want to consider very carefully whether this is a safe activity for their children. In addition, elementary-aged children frequently get involved in gymnastics, swimming, tennis, and ice skating. Whether it is a team or individual sport in which your child participates, these can be some of the advantages:

- Hours of pleasure.

- A way to keep healthy and fit.

- The chance to learn the lessons of competition and sportsmanship.

- An outlet for making friends.

- The instilling of confidence that comes from success in physical activity.

- Experience that will enable a child to join a varsity team in junior high school.

In individual sports, in particular, parents might want to offer their children the chance to take lessons, just as is done in, say, music or art. An individual sport like tennis, golf, swimming, or skiing can be very much advanced by private coaching. Many of the international stars began their careers this way.

But there are possible problems in private coaching for your children, and parents should be aware of the pressures that might be placed on a child. The sport can become the focus of the child's existence to the detriment of a full, well-rounded life. Individual coaching is a way to build a champion, but there can be a heavy price exacted. Even in team sports, elementary-school-age children might feel more pressure than is healthy, and the problem can be exacerbated in individual sports with the intense early competition to which children are subjected.

Most children will be best served by out-of-school sports that are pleasurable and give them athletic experiences that can be a basis for continued sports participation and enjoyment as an adult.

CLUBS AND ORGANIZATIONS

It is during their years in elementary school that most children get their first extended exposure to being a member of something. A sports team might suffice for some, but for those who are less athletic—and for the many children who pursue activities in addition to sports—there are Brownies, Cub Scouts, Girl Scouts, Boy Scouts, and a host of other organizations operated through YMCAs, churches, synagogues, and other agencies.

Participation should be encouraged and parents should lend their support by being advisers and helpers to groups when they are asked. The group experience can be a satisfying and valuable part of development. It helps prepare youngsters for many of the roles that will be open to them in secondary school and as adults. Children who learn to be leaders and followers, who learn to cooperate in achieving group goals, and who develop loyalties to comrades have experiences with wide application.

These groups give children access to role models besides their parents and teachers. The need to belong is powerful in people of all ages, and youth associations can be a place to meet this need. Children gain a feeling of connectedness to the larger community and some of the activities help nurture a burgeoning sense of citizenship and responsibility. Building character is an important function of these organizations and it should not be taken lightly. Youngsters who are less willing to get involved or to take on challenges at home or in school might more readily do so in a Boys Club, Girls Club, 4-H Club, or some other youth association that is more neutral ground.

OUT-OF-SCHOOL EDUCATIONAL PROGRAMS

A smaller number of children supplement school with academically oriented enrichment programs that ordinarily meet in the afternoon or on Saturdays. Among the most popular activities of this sort are those that let students delve more deeply into computers or science. Some such extracurricular programs are offered by the school system, but often the sponsorship is private, tuition is charged, and the activity is not under school auspices.

These programs tend to draw especially able students whose academic curiosity and interest overflow the classroom. For them, learning about computers or science on a Saturday morning is as much fun as playing in a Little League baseball game might be for another child. This is not to say that the same child may not pursue sports as well as intellectual activities.

In any event, parents should be cognizant of out-of-school educational programs and seek direction from the child's regular classroom teacher, or perhaps the principal, in finding the right programs for their child.

Increasingly, there are also after-school and weekend academic programs for another kind of child—the underachiever. These are not as demanding as the high-powered programs for strong students, but they can help children who have not done well in school improve their performance and their attitude.

SPECIALIZED SUMMER CAMP

Finally, there is summer camp, once known only for its recreational aspects, but increasingly taking on an educational tone in recent years. There are math camps and science camps, computer camps and literary camps, music camps and art camps. There are even camps to teach children about finance and the stock market. Almost all these summer camps, whatever the special focus, include recreational activities, but the central theme is an activity that is educational in nature.

This sort of camp may be just right for a student who already has a strong interest in the featured academic specialty. Parents of children who have shown little interest in the camp's specialization should be chary of such camps, however, because a summer of suffering might be inflicted on a youngster who really does not want to be in such a camp. In other words, a camp for children who like math is probably not a good choice for a student who detests math but whose parents want him or her to like math.

Some ideas of summer camps and programs may be gleaned by reading the guides published by Peterson's, a company in Princeton, New Jersey, that specializes in guides of all sorts for students. The two most appropriate are *Peterson's Summer Opportunities for Kids and Teenagers* and *Peterson's Learning Vacations: The All-Season Guide to Educational Travel.*

It should be clear by now that parents can find as much learning for their children outside school as they wish. The difficulty is determining the proper balance for each child and keeping childhood in perspective. The years in elementary school are a time of wonderful development when a great deal of intellectual and emotional growth occurs in the natural course of life. It is worthwhile to supplement these events with a deliberate approach that includes a broader exposure. But childhood should not be subverted and stolen by parents who try to turn their offspring into miniature adults.

On the other hand, children are going to participate in a certain number of organized activities and they are going to attend a certain number of entertainment events. There is no reason why parents should not try to make these experiences educationally wholesome at the same time that they provide pleasure to children.

27

NEXT STEP,
JUNIOR HIGH SCHOOL

A book examining the life of students in elementary school would be incomplete if it did not conclude with a look ahead, anticipating the years that await youngsters after elementary school. For most, the next step will be junior high school; a smaller number will enter what is called middle school, and for some others there is simply a continuation of elementary school until the end of the eighth grade, when they go directly to high school.

What is distinctive about the period that begins at about the age of eleven or twelve and continues until the early teens, whatever kind of school a student attends, are the changes occurring inside the child. It is a time like no other, when the turbulence of adolescence is seething within a young person, waiting to erupt. These are children about to inhabit adult bodies. Almost everything that happens in these years, in and out of school, must be weighed in terms of the enormous physical and emotional cataclysm about to occur. It is probably only in infancy that so much development occurs in so brief a period.

Starting from about the time their children turn eleven or twelve and for three or four years thereafter, parents will perhaps find it most difficult to help them in school. When youngsters are still in elementary school, they are largely dependent on their parents and more readily willing to accept direction. By the time they reach high school they have some measure of maturity and can take on substantial responsibility.

But the period in between, pre- and early adolescence, is something else. Children's bodies are ruled at this time by their hormones and many can think of nothing but the opposite sex. They behave in ways that are positively bizarre. According to Jack Bloomfield, a former junior high school principal, students in junior high school conduct themselves in a manner in which, if they acted that way any other time in life, they would be considered insane.

What makes the situation less than humorous, however, is that junior high school comes at a time when students are particularly vulnerable. The academic work gets more demanding and the individual attention of teachers diminishes. Peer relations are problematic. Egos are delicate. Confidence is shaky. Children are on their own and more and more susceptible to drugs. Venereal diseases and pregnancy are potential problems. Even AIDS is a possibility. And some youngsters are already taking steps that seem almost irrevocable toward becoming dropouts.

In the midst of this developmental anguish, young people are inserted into an institution called junior high school or middle school, where many of the support structures of elementary school are not to be found. After having spent almost the entire school day with one teacher, they now see a half-dozen different teachers a day.

Familiarity is exchanged for anonymity. At the very time that it is so important for students to be known as individuals in order to shore up their confidence and gain a sense of identity, they find themselves floating in a sea of strangers, barely known to anyone. It feels as if everyone is bigger and older during that first year in junior high. There is not even a classroom closet anymore in which to hang up a coat. Now coats are parked in a locker or, as many students do, worn all day as if the whole situation in junior high school is temporary and could end at any moment.

Edwards Junior High School in Central, South Carolina, has an orientation program aimed at smoothing the transition into junior high school. It is an approach worth adopting elsewhere, and parents ought to expect similar features in their school systems. Here are the elements of the program, as described by John Wade, the principal:

• *Principal's visit.* The principal presents a slide show at each of the feeder elementary schools during the spring, when the students are nearing the end of sixth grade. He talks to them about what their schedule of classes might be and discusses the electives available to them. He even takes along some combination locks—an item some have never before used—to allay their concerns about using a locker.

• *Band concert.* The band from Edwards Junior High School gives a spring concert at each of the elementary schools, creating enthusiasm for the school among the sixth-graders and also helping to recruit prospects for the band.

• *School visits.* On three days in May, sixth-graders visit the junior high school for tours and lunch. They receive a booklet of letters from seventh-graders telling what it is like to attend the school.

• *Calendar.* During the last week of school, sixth-graders get calendars listing events for the coming year in junior high school.

• *Orientation day.* Held in August for incoming seventh-graders and their parents. Students pick up their schedules, get their locker assignments, buy physical education uniforms, and buy tickets for sports events and school dances. Parents meet with counselors.

• *First day of school.* The principal meets with seventh-graders in an assembly to explain school rules and distribute student handbooks.

• *Media center.* Two English-class periods during the first week of school are devoted to visiting the school library and learning about the services.

• *Counselors.* School counselors talk to seventh-graders in some social studies classes during the first week. Students fill out confidential guidance forms and indicate whether they want private conferences with counselors.

• *Assembly.* At an assembly for seventh-graders sometime during the first six weeks of the term, information is presented on the merit point system, the program for junior academic scholars, and academic awards for which students are eligible.

• *Open house.* An open house is held for all three grades —seventh, eighth, and ninth—early in the semester for students and their parents to meet with teachers.

Part of the difficulty that students have in adjusting to junior high school comes from their experience in sixth grade. Not enough is done during that crucial year to prepare students for what lies ahead. Most sixth-graders do not get the blend of individual attention and independence that they need to get them ready for the transition. Teachers should take advantage of the time to pump a large dose of self-confidence into students and to do all possible to ensure that they have the academic background they will need to cope in situations where they will be on their own more of the time. At the same time—and, admittedly, it is not easy—the sixth grade must be structured so that students are given more leeway to grow accustomed to operating independently.

A study of the sixth grade by John H. Lounsbury et al. was issued in 1988 by the National Association of Secondary School Principals. It found that the organizational structure that holds the best potential for helping students is an interdisciplinary team approach. This is a middle ground in between the self-contained classroom in which students spend the whole day with one teacher and the same group of youngsters and the departmental approach in which they change classes and see different teachers for each subject, just as in high school.

At its best, an interdisciplinary team approach involves at least two teachers and what would normally be at least two classes of children. The teachers divide up the subjects, perhaps one presenting a blend of math and science and the other presenting a blend of language arts and social studies. Students can be grouped and regrouped in various configurations. Flexible blocks of time are available as needed. Sometimes the teachers might even pull all the students together and lead a lesson jointly. About a quarter of the time is spent with specialist teachers in art, music, physical education, industrial arts, and other elective subjects. There is a taste of the departmentalization characteristic of junior high, while at the same time offering the security of a support system in which students are better known to their teachers than in the usual junior high.

The study made clear that the year called sixth grade should be used to greater advantage, that students already are embarking upon the difficult period when their bodies and minds are ruled by the onset of adolescence. The greatest percentage of students begin adolescence while they are in the sixth grade, according to the study.

Educators in a good junior high school recognize that almost every aspect of the program must take cognizance of the influence of adolescence on students. The presumptions that are made in elementary school or high school are not valid in junior high, and the school should not proceed as if no special provisions are needed for students at this age. Programs must be considered in terms of impact on peer-group relations, interaction with the opposite sex, the formation of confidence, and the paradoxical simultaneous need for freedom and limits. Guidance counselors are desperately needed by students in junior high school, and parents ought to object if the ratio of counselors to students is not sufficient to let students get the individual attention they need.

An important study, published as a book with the title *Successful Schools for Young Adolescents,* underscored the importance at the junior high school level of serving the special developmental needs of students. Commenting on the four schools that were profiled, it stated: "The most striking features of the four schools is their willingness and ability to adapt all school practices to the individual differences in intellectual, biological, and social maturation of their students."

Ultimately, though, junior high is an educational institution and its final measure must depend on how effectively it educates its students. Junior high is the last time for students to gear up for the demands of high school. If they enter junior high school lagging in achievement, the gap must be closed at this time or they will not be able to cope with a more demanding academic curriculum in high school.

Parents must do all they can to make sure that weaknesses are addressed in junior high and that students learn to capitalize on their strengths. Don't hesitate to get a tutor for a student who is trailing the class in academic work. It is not simply that the tutor can help the student with the classwork, but an able tutor will endeavor to teach the study skills that the youngster so desperately needs.

Junior high is not a time to despair in the face of academic trouble. It is a time to catch up. The courses, after all, do not yet get officially recorded for the student's college application; that begins in the ninth grade. The only course that is sequential is mathematics, and a considerable portion of the material in the seventh and eighth grades is a review and elaboration on what was taught in elementary school. A student who works hard can still close the gap.

Essentially, there is nothing specific taught in science or social studies that the student must master for success in high school. It is just that if the student does poorly in these subjects in the seventh and eighth grades, he or she will probably not fare well in these subjects in high school—not because of what was not learned, but because there are clearly deficiencies in the student's reading, writing, and/or study skills.

So for students in trouble it is not so much that it is necessary to learn to master the content of science and social studies in junior high school, as it is essential to become a proficient reader and an able writer, and a student who knows how to study.

A few school systems continue, as in elementary school, to teach reading as a separate subject in junior high school. Most others have a course in English and presume students have mastered what is required for success in reading. In any event, students tend not to get the kind of attention devoted to reading in elementary school. A student who finds reading difficult in junior high is a student at risk. Parents of such children must get help for their youngsters.

Junior high school is a time for many students to study a foreign language. Those who started foreign language study in elementary school have the choice of continuing with the same language or switching to another. Those who like the language they began in elementary school and took well to it might be best off pursuing that language in greater depth with the goal of gaining fluency.

Certainly it is possible to delay foreign language study until high school, but this may not be desirable—especially if a student wants to attain fluency. This goal requires extended study, and if such study begins in junior high school there are more years available to pursue the language than there would be if study commenced in high school.

Usually there are not many electives available in junior high and all students take the same range of mainline courses, not being able to insert electives for the regular courses in English, math, science, and social studies. If there are courses that can be substituted for the mainline courses, parents should tend to have their children resist doing so. Students who begin opting out of the main curriculum in junior high school run the risk of dooming their chance for an academic future and enrollment in college. A student, for example, who takes a watered-down elective instead of the regular precollege mathematics course in ninth grade is, in effect, stepping off the academic track.

In junior high, for the first time, students will be able to get extensively involved in extracurricular activities. There are varsity teams for both boys and girls, clubs, service organizations that perform volunteer work, and student government. The experience of participating in such activities is valuable and rewarding and adds to the fullness of a student's education.

Parents should usually be supportive of such participation, even if a student is doing poorly and seems to need extra time for his or her studies. Extracurricular activities can motivate students and give them reason for wanting to go to school. In most cases, participation is desirable, though if students are superactive parents might want to watch to see if a youngster is being too ambitious.

Junior high, for better or for worse, is generally—as its name implies—a smaller version of high school. What this means is that students must grow capable of handling independence and responsibility. Learning these lessons is one of the most important outcomes of junior high school.

Parents would do well to look for opportunities around home to reinforce these lessons in independence and responsibility for their children. Youngsters are going to have to handle more of their work without anyone to guide them through it; homework assignments will be more arduous, and they will get fewer pats on the backs from teachers. This is the time for students to learn to get along more on their own so that they will more readily be able to handle the demands of high school.

SELECTED READINGS

1. WHY YOU MUST BE AN ADVOCATE IN YOUR CHILD'S SCHOOLING

The American Teacher 1986. New York: Metropolitan Life, 1986.

Greenhouse, Steven. "The Average Guy Takes It on the Chin." *The New York Times,* July 13, 1986.

The National Assessment of Educational Progress. *The Writing Report Card: Writing Achievement in American Schools.* Princeton, N.J.: 1986.

———. *Writing Trends Across the Decade, 1974–84.* Princeton, N.J.: 1986.

U.S. Department of Education. *What Works: Research About Teaching and Learning.* Washington, D.C.: U.S. Government Printing Office, 1986.

2. CHOOSING A SCHOOL

National Education Association. *Rankings of the States, 1987.* Washington, D.C.: 1987.

Sinclair, Molly. "School Capacity Scuttles Subdivision." *The Washington Post,* October 16, 1986.

3. GETTING READY FOR PRESCHOOL

Bettelheim, Bruno. "The Importance of Play." *The Atlantic Monthly,* March 1987.

Bloom, Benjamin S. *All Our Children Learning: A Primer for Parents, Teachers and Other Educators.* New York: McGraw-Hill, 1982.

Cartwright, Sally. "Play Can Be the Building Block of Learning." *Young Children,* July 1988.

Fallows, James. "The Case Against Credentialism." *The Atlantic Monthly,* December 1985.

Missouri Department of Elementary and Secondary Education. *How Does Your Child Grow and Learn? A Guide for Parents of Young Children.* Jefferson City, Mo., 1982.

National Association for the Education of Young Children. *Toys: Tools for Learning.* Washington, D.C.

Sacks, Oliver. "Mysteries of the Deaf." *New York Review of Books,* March 27, 1986.

Snow, Catherine E., and C. Ferguson. *Talking to Children.* Cambridge: Cambridge University Press, 1983.

Sutton-Smith, Brian. "Ambivalence in Toyland." *Natural History,* December 1985.

U.S. Department of Education. *What Works: Research About Teaching and Learning.* Washington, D.C.: U.S. Government Printing Office, 1986.

White, Burton L. *The First Three Years of Life.* Englewood Cliffs, N.J.: Prentice-Hall, 1975.

4. BUILDING A READING FOUNDATION

American Library Association. *Caldecott Medal Books.* Chicago: 1988.

Heath, Shirley Brice. *Ways With Words: Language, Life and Work in Communities and Classrooms.* Cambridge: Cambridge University Press, 1983.

Rothstein, Mervyn. "Bernard Malamud, Author, Dies at 71." *The New York Times,* March 20, 1986.

Schickedanz, Judith A. "Helping Children Learn About Reading." National Association for the Education of Young Children, 1983.

Sloan, Glenna Davis. *Good Books Make Reading Fun for Your Child.* Newark, Del.: International Reading Association.

Trelease, Jim. *The Read-Aloud Handbook,* rev. ed. New York: Penguin, 1985.

5. FINDING THE BEST CHILD CARE

Cummings, Judith. "Child Care and Business, Side by Side." *The New York Times,* May 4, 1986.

IBM. *Child Care Handbook.* Boston: Work/Family Directions, 1984.

Olenick, Michael. "What Is Quality Child Care?" Unpublished speech to Los Angeles County League of Women Voters, June 7, 1986.

Seabrook, Charles. "Health Officials Caution Against 'Day-Care Diseases.'" *Atlanta Constitution-Journal,* March 23, 1986.

6. MAKING THE MOST OF THE YEAR BEFORE KINDERGARTEN

Ambach, Gordon M. "Should 4- and 5-Year-Olds Be in School? Yes, Optional Preschool Is Essential." *The Christian Science Monitor,* March 28, 1986.

Berrueta-Clement, John R., et al. *Changed Lives.* Ypsilanti, Mich.: The High/Scope Press, 1984.

Brandt, Ronald S. "On Long-Term Effects of Early Education: A Conversation with Lawrence Schweinhart." *Educational Leadership,* November 1986.

The Consortium for Longitudinal Studies. *As the Twig Is*

Bent: Lasting Effects of Preschool Programs. New York: Lawrence Erlbaum Associates, 1983.

Featherstone, Helen. "Preschool: It Does Make a Difference." *Harvard Education Letter,* June 1985.

Elkind, David. "Formal Education and Early Childhood Education: An Essential Difference." *Phi Delta Kappan,* May 1986.

Getting Ready for School. Chicago: World Book, 1987.

Goodlad, John. *A Place Called School.* New York: McGraw-Hill, 1984.

"Here Come the Four-Year-Olds." Editorial. *Principal,* May 1986.

"School at 4: A Model for the Nation." Editorial. *The New York Times,* February 20, 1986.

Soderman, Anne K. "Schooling All 4-Year-Olds: An Idea Full of Promise, Fraught with Pitfalls." *Education Week,* March 14, 1984.

Zigler, Edward F. "Should Four-Year-Olds Be in School?" *Principal,* May 1986.

7. THE KINDERGARTEN CONNECTION

"Full-Day Kindergarteners Outperform Half-Day Pupils for Years, Study Says." *Education Daily,* June 17, 1988.

Herman, Barry E. *The Case for the All-Day Kindergarten.* Bloomington, Ind.: Phi Delta Kappa Education Foundation, 1984.

Humphrey, Jack. *A Longitudinal Study of the Consequences of Full-Day Kindergarten: Kindergarten Through Grade Eight.* Evansville, Ind.: Evansville-Vanderbrugh School Corporation, 1988.

Ilg, Francis L., et al. *School Readiness—Behavior Tests Used at the Gesell Institute,* rev. ed. New York: Harper & Row, 1978.

Meisels, Samuel J. "Uses and Abuses of Developmental

Screening and School Readiness Testing." *Young Children*, January 1987.

Nebraska State Board of Education. *The Position Statement on Kindergarten*. Lincoln, Neb.: 1984.

Puleo, Vincent T. "A Review and Critique of Research and Full-Day Kindergarten." *The Elementary School Journal*, March 1988.

Solem, M. R. "Junior First Grade." *Phi Delta Kappan*, Vol. 63, No. 4.

8. THE IMPACT OF TELEVISION

Lesser, Gerald S. *Children and Television: Lessons from Sesame Street*. New York: Random House, 1974.

National Assessment of Educational Progress. *Television 1988*. Princeton, N.J.: Educational Testing Service, 1988.

Stein, Benjamin. "This Is Not Your Life: Television as the Third Parent." *Public Opinion*, November/December 1986.

Wilkins, Joan Anderson. *Breaking the TV Habit*. New York: Scribners, 1982.

9. READING: THE GREAT BEGINNING

American Library Association. *Notable Children's Books 1987*. Chicago: 1988.

Anderson, Richard C., et al. *Becoming a Nation of Readers: The Report of the Commission on Reading*. Washington, D.C.: National Institute of Education, 1985.

California Achievement Tests, Forms E and F—Class Management Guide: Using Test Results. Monterey, Calif.: CTB/McGraw-Hill, 1986.

Criscuolo, Nicholas P. "Ten Essentials for Reading Programs." *The Executive Educator*, March 1986.

Touchstone Applied Science Associates. *Degrees of Reading*

Power—Test Booklet Form PX-1. New York: The College Board, 1984.

10. GETTING STARTED IN MATHEMATICS

Kennedy, Leonard M. "A Rationale." *Arithmetic Teacher,* February 1986.

Kenschaft, Patricia Clark. "Making Math 'Add Up' for Kids." *Gifted Children Monthly,* November 1985.

National Council of Teachers of Mathematics."Curriculum and Evaluation Standards for School Mathematics: A Working Draft." Reston, Va.: 1987.

Stevenson, Harold W. "America's Math Problems." *Educational Leadership,* 1988.

U.S. Department of Education. *What Works: Research About Teaching and Learning.* Washington, D.C.: U.S. Government Printing Office, 1986.

11. WORKING WITH THE STAFF

The American Teacher 1986. New York: Metropolitan Life, 1986.

Making Parent-Teacher Conferences WORK for Your Child. National PTA, Chicago, and National Education Association, Washington, D.C.

Shedlin, Allan, Jr. "New Lenses for Viewing Elementary Schools." *Phi Delta Kappan,* October 1986.

Your School: How Well Is It Working? Columbia, Md.: National Committee for Citizens in Education, 1982.

13. THE GIFTED AND TALENTED

Gardner, Howard. *Frames of Mind: The Theory of Multiple Intelligences.* New York: Basic Books, 1985.

Torrance, E. Paul. *Handbook of Research on Teaching, 3rd ed.* American Educational Research Association, New York: Macmillan, 1986.

14. THE HANDICAPPED

Coles, Gerald S. "The Learning Disabilities Test Battery: Empirical and Social Issues." *Harvard Education Review*, August 1978.

A Parent's Guide to Special Education. Albany: New York State Education Department, 1984.

"Ways to Recognize an LD Child." *Today's Education*, November/December 1977.

15. SCIENCE

The American Chemical Society. *Building Bridges*. Washington, D.C.: American Chemical Society, 1986.

National Assessment of Educational Progress. *Science Achievement in the Schools*. Princeton, N.J.: Educational Testing Service, December 1987.

National Science Resources Center. *NSRC Newsletter*. Washington, D.C.: Smithsonian Institution, Spring 1988.

"Outdated Textbooks Are Cited in Survey." *The New York Times*, January 10, 1987.

"Science: It Really Should Be Elementary." *NEA Today*, May 1987.

"What Is Hands-On Science?" *Instructor* (special issue), Spring 1987.

16. SOCIAL STUDIES

Bradley Commission on History in Schools. *Building a History Curriculum: Guidelines for Teaching History in Schools*. Washington, D.C.: Educational Excellence Network, 1988.

Elementary School Social Studies: Research as a Guide to Practice. Virginia Atwood, ed. Washington D.C.: National Council for the Social Studies, 1986.

Elliott, David L. Kathleen Carter Nagel, and Arthur Woodward. "Do Textbooks Belong in Elementary Social Studies?" *Educational Leadership,* April 1985.

Guidelines for Geographic Education: Elementary and Secondary Schools. Prepared by Joint Committee on Geographic Education, Association of American Geographers and National Council for Geographic Education. Washington, D.C., 1984.

National Assessment of Educational Progress. *Changes in Social Studies Performance, 1972–76.* Denver: Education Commission of the States, 1978.

———. *Changes in Political Knowledge and Attitudes, 1969–76.* Denver: Education Commission of the States, 1979.

17. THE ARTS

National Assessment of Educational Progress. *Art and Young Americans, 1974–79.* Denver: Education Commission of the States, 1981.

———. *Music, 1971–79.* Denver: Education Commission of the States, 1981.

18. FOREIGN LANGUAGES

Met, Myriam. "Elementary School Foreign Languages: Key Link in the Chain of Learning." Unpublished paper.

U.S. Department of Education. *What Works: Research About Teaching and Learning.* Washington, D.C.: U.S. Government Printing Office, 1986.

20. THE ROLE OF COMPUTERS

Bork, Alfred. "Computers in Education Today—And Some Possible Futures." *Phi Delta Kappan,* December 1984.

Caissy, Gail A. "Evaluating Educational Software: A Practitioner's Guide." *Phi Delta Kappan,* December 1984.

Family Software Catalogue. Evanston, Ill.: Evanston Educators, Inc.

National Assessment of Educational Progress. *Computer Competence: The First National Assessment.* Princeton, N.J.: Educational Testing Service, 1988.

Norris, William C. "Computer-Based Education: A 'Key' to Reform." *Education Week,* November 18, 1987.

"What a Computer Means to Me." *Principal,* November 1985.

21. LEARNING HOW TO THINK

Bloom, Benjamin. *Human Characteristics and School Learning.* New York: McGraw-Hill, 1982.

Chaffee, John. *Thinking Critically.* Boston: Houghton Mifflin, 1985.

College Board. *Academic Preparation for College: What Students Need to Know and Be Able to Do.* New York, 1983.

Perkins, D. N. "Thinking Frames." *Educational Leadership,* May 1986.

Skowron, Cathy. "The 4th R: Reasoning." *NEA Today,* November 1986.

"Teaching Thinking." *Curriculum Report.* Reston, Va.: National Association of Secondary School Principals, May 1986.

Wasserman, Selma. "Teaching Thinking: Louis E. Raths Revisited." *Phi Delta Kappan,* February 1987.

22. BUILDING CHARACTER

Coles, Robert. "The Moral Life of Children." *Educational Leadership.* December 1985/January 1986.

Doyle, Robert P. "Censorship and the Challenge to Intellectual Freedom." *Principal,* January 1982.

"Education for Democracy: A Statement of Principles." American Federation of Teachers, 1987.

Gordon, Sol. "What Kids Need to Know." *Psychology Today,* October 1986.

London, Perry. "Character Education and Clinical Intervention: A Paradigm Shift for U.S. Schools." *Phi Delta Kappan*, May 1987.

McNamara, Debbie. "How to Teach Pride." *Instructor*, February 1986.

"Preaching, Practicing and Prodding: What Works in Character Education?" *Harvard Education Letter*. Cambridge, Mass.: Harvard Graduate School of Education, January 1987.

Religion in the Curriculum. Alexandria, Va.: Association for Supervision and Curriculum Development, 1988.

Ryan, Kevin. "The New Moral Education." *Phi Delta Kappan*, October 1986.

23. READING IN THE UPPER GRADES

American Library Association. *Notable Children's Books 1987*. Chicago, 1988.

National Assessment of Educational Progress. *The Writing Report Card: Writing Achievement in American Schools*. Princeton, N.J.: Educational Testing Service, 1986.

Ravitch, Diane. "Where Have All the Classics Gone? You Won't Find Them in Primers." *The New York Times Book Review*, May 17, 1987.

U.S. Department of Education. *What Works: Research About Teaching and Learning*. Washington, D.C.: U.S. Government Printing Office, 1986.

24. MATHEMATICS IN THE UPPER GRADES

National Assessment of Educational Progress. *Math Objectives: 1985–86 Assessment*. Princeton, N.J.: Education Commission of the States, 1987.

National Assessment of Educational Progress. *The Third National Mathematics Assessment: Results, Trends and Issues*. Denver: Education Commission of the States, 1983.

National Council of Teachers of Mathematics. "Curriculum

and Evaluation Standards for School Mathematics, A Working Draft." Reston, Va., 1988.

25. REINFORCING SCHOOLING IN THE HOME

Austin, Joe Dan. "Homework Research in Mathematics." *School Science and Mathematics.* Vol. 79 (1979).

"Helping Parents Choose Wisely." *Instructor,* February 1986.

Mountzoures, H. L. "At the Tutor's." *The New Yorker,* June 16, 1986.

"Survey Finds Homework Average Is Over an Hour for Each School Day." *The New York Times,* November 24, 1984.

26. WEEKENDS, SUMMERS, AND AFTER SCHOOL

When We Were Young. Washington, D.C.: Reading Is Fundamental, 1987.

27. NEXT STEP, JUNIOR HIGH SCHOOL

Lipsitz, Joan. *Successful Schools for Young Adolescents.* New Brunswick, N.J.: Transaction Books, 1984.

Lounsbury, John H., et al. *Life in the Three 6th Grades.* Reston, Va.: National Association of Secondary School Principals, 1988.

Wade, John. "Ease Kids into Junior High School." *The Executive Educator,* June 1986.

INDEX